The Ancient Nordic VIKING Kitchen:

More than 120 Authentic Mythical Recipes from the Cuisine of Jarls, Karls and Skalds - NORDMATUR FORNU, the Culinary Art of the Sons of Odin from the Age of Sagas, immerse yourself in the art of ancient SCANDINAVIAN cuisine.

Thank you for reading! If you enjoyed this book, please leave a little note and a rating.

★★★★★

That makes all the difference !

𝕾ummary

AXIS 3: BRAUÐ OK KORN - The Sacred Cereals of the Aesir - *The sacred cereals of the Aesir*..55

AXIS 4: KJÖT OK VEIÐIDÝR - *The meats of Odin's feasts*...71

AXIS 5: FISKR OK HAFDJÚP - *Treasures of the Nordic Seas* 92

AXIS 6: GRÆNMETI OK VILLIGRAS *Wild vegetables and herbs from Midgard* 111

AXIS 7: SÆLGÆTI OK BLÓT - *The sweets of Valhalla*......127

AXIS 8: DRYKKJUR OK VÍN *The nectars of Asgard*......136

History, Philosophy and Culinary Practices of the Peoples of the North

I. History and philosophy of Nordic cuisine

The legacy of the EDDAS and SAGAS in culinary tradition

Norse cuisine has its deepest roots in the literary and mythological heritage of the Eddas and Sagas, the fundamental texts of Scandinavian culture that reveal not only the beliefs and values of the Viking peoples, but also their dietary practices and sacred relationship with food. The Poetic Edda, a 13th-century collection of Icelandic mythological poems, makes numerous references to the banquets of the gods in Valhalla, where mead flows freely and the boar Sæhrímnir is replenished daily to feed the Einherjar, the warriors who died in battle. This cyclical vision of food, constantly renewed, profoundly influences the Norse conception of food as a source of spiritual and physical regeneration.

Family sagas, historical and legendary tales passed down orally and written down between the 12th and 14th centuries, are full of detailed descriptions of feasts and culinary practices. Egill Skallagrímsson's Saga describes grand banquets that blend politics, diplomacy, and gastronomy, while Njáll the Burnt Saga meticulously describes the preparations for festive meals and the importance placed on hospitality. These texts reveal that Norse cuisine was not just a matter of subsistence, but also a veritable social language, a means of asserting status, forging alliances, and honoring gods and ancestors.

Germanic, Celtic and Slavic influences

The evolution of Nordic cuisine cannot be understood without considering the multiple cultural influences that have shaped it over centuries of migration, trade, and conquest. The earliest and most profound of these influences is the Germanic influence, evident in the predominant use of grains such as barley and rye, in beer-

brewing techniques, and in the emphasis on fermented dairy products. Germanic tribes developed sophisticated methods of preserving meat through smoking and salting, techniques that were adopted and perfected by the Nordic peoples.

Celtic influence, particularly visible in the western regions of Scandinavia and Iceland, brings a crucial maritime dimension to Norse cuisine. The Celts, skilled navigators, passed on to the Vikings their knowledge of marine resources, the art of deep-sea fishing, and seafood preparation techniques. This influence explains the central place of fish in the Norse diet, as well as the use of seaweed as a nutritional supplement and condiment. Celtic traditions also introduced certain ritual practices related to the consumption of mead and libations to sea and fertility deities.

The Slavic influence, later but nonetheless significant, developed mainly through the trade routes that linked Scandinavia to the great plains of Eastern Europe and the Russian territories. The Varangians, those Vikings who sailed up the Russian rivers to Constantinople, brought back from their expeditions new fermentation techniques, the use of certain spices from the East, and methods of preparing root vegetables that considerably enriched the Nordic culinary repertoire. This Slavic influence explains in particular the importance of fermented cabbage (sauerkraut) in the winter diet and the use of certain herbs such as dill and coriander.

Historical manuscripts: Nordic GEOPONIKA and runic texts

Handwritten sources concerning Nordic cuisine, although fragmentary, provide valuable evidence of the dietary and agricultural practices of northern peoples. The most important corpus consists of the Nordic adaptations of the Byzantine Geoponics, treatises on agriculture and domestic economy that were translated and adapted to Scandinavian climatic and cultural conditions between the 11th and 13th centuries. These texts, preserved in several Icelandic and Danish monasteries, contain detailed instructions on growing cereals in Nordic conditions, food preservation techniques, and methods for preparing fermented beverages.

Runic inscriptions, carved on stone, wood, or metal, are another valuable, though more sparse, source of information. Several Swedish and Danish runestones contain references to food offerings, memorial banquets, and ritual practices related to food. The Rök stone in Sweden describes animal sacrifices and feasts in honor of the dead, while several Norwegian inscriptions describe the provisions needed for Viking expeditions and techniques for preserving food during long sea voyages.

Monastic manuscripts, preserved primarily in Iceland, offer a unique perspective on the evolution of Nordic cuisine under the influence of Christianity. These texts, written by monks often of Nordic origin, blend pagan culinary traditions with Christian dietary prescriptions, creating a unique synthesis that has had a lasting influence on Scandinavian dietary practices. Icelandic monastic rules from the 12th century meticulously describe fasting periods and permitted and prohibited foods according to liturgical seasons, while retaining references to ancient Nordic practices.

Norway's fjords as trade crossroads between Europe and the Arctic

The exceptional geography of the Norwegian fjords played a decisive role in the development of Nordic cuisine, transforming these deep glacial valleys into true commercial and cultural crossroads between continental Europe and the Arctic regions. The fjords provided ideal natural shelters for ships, allowing the development of trading ports that quickly became centers of exchange for products from the sea, land, and distant regions. Bergen, Trondheim, and other fjord port cities thus became hubs of the food trade, combining herring from the North Sea, furs and whale oil from the Far North, grains from the European plains, and spices from the East via trade routes.

This strategic position of the fjords explains the richness and diversity of Nordic cuisine, which is not limited to local resources alone but incorporates culinary influences from all over Europe and beyond. Hanseatic merchants, established in the fjord ports from the 12th century onwards, introduced new fish preservation techniques, spices previously unknown in the North, and preparation methods that enriched the local culinary repertoire. In return, they exported Nordic specialties such as dried fish (tørrfisk), aged cheeses, and whale oil to continental Europe.

Fjords also constitute unique ecosystems that directly influence available food resources. Their deep, cold waters are home to an exceptionally rich marine fauna, from small surface fish to large marine mammals, while their steep slopes offer high-altitude pastures where herds graze and forests rich in game and wild foods. This

ecological diversity is reflected in fjord cuisine, which develops unique specialties adapted to each season and specific environment.

The five major regions: Norway, Sweden, Denmark, Iceland, Greenland

Nordic cuisine is not a homogeneous whole, but is shaped by the geographical, climatic, and cultural specificities of five major regions, each of which, while sharing a common heritage, has developed its own culinary traditions. This regional diversity is explained by differences in climate, available natural resources, external cultural influences, and historical development, creating a gastronomic patchwork of exceptional richness.

Norway , with its deep fjords and rugged coastlines, has developed a cuisine that is essentially maritime , dominated by seafood. Salmon, herring, cod, and shellfish are the staple foods, prepared using preservation techniques inherited from the Vikings: smoking, drying, and fermentation. The mountainous geography also favors sheep and goat farming, whose cheeses are a recognized specialty. The influence of the Gulf Stream allows the cultivation of certain vegetables and cereals in the south of the country, but the bulk of the diet remains based on marine and pastoral resources.

Sweden , more continental, developed a more diverse cuisine that blended the maritime influences of its Baltic and Atlantic coasts with the resources of its vast forests and agricultural plains. Cereals, mainly oats, rye , and barley, occupied a central place, accompanied by the products of hunting (elk, reindeer, wild boar) and freshwater fishing (pike, perch, grayling). Fermentation preservation techniques reached a particular sophistication in Sweden, giving rise to specialties such as surströmming (fermented herring), which illustrate the Nordic mastery of these processes.

Denmark , as a bridge **between** Scandinavia and continental Europe, has developed a cuisine that synthesizes Nordic and Germanic influences. Its fertile agricultural lands allow for significant grain production, complemented by prosperous livestock farming (pigs, cattle, poultry) and active fishing in the North Sea and the Baltic. Danish cuisine is characterized by its refinement and diversity, integrating external culinary influences more easily than its Nordic neighbors while retaining its traditional specificities.

Iceland , isolated in the middle of the North Atlantic, developed a survival cuisine remarkably adapted to extreme climatic conditions. The almost total absence of trees and the short growing season drastically limited plant resources, concentrating the diet on products from the sea, hunting, and livestock. Icelanders perfected the most advanced preservation techniques, creating unique specialties such as hákarl (fermented shark) or harðfiskur (dried fish). The use of geothermal energy for cooking is an Icelandic peculiarity that directly influences culinary techniques.

Greenland , the northernmost territory, develops an Arctic subsistence cuisine based almost exclusively **on** hunting and fishing. Resources are limited to marine mammals (seal, whale, walrus), Arctic fish, and terrestrial game (caribou, musk ox). Preservation techniques reach their most extreme here, with fermentation and drying methods perfectly adapted to the polar climate. This Greenlandic cuisine influences other Nordic traditions through its seafood preparation techniques and its methods of preservation in harsh climatic conditions.

II. Essential ingredients and Viking techniques

Guide to Nordic condiments (SURSTRÖMMING, RAKFISK, GRAVLAKS)

Condiments and fermented preparations are the soul of Nordic cuisine, reflecting a millennia-old mastery of fermentation processes developed out of necessity in regions where food preservation is a vital survival issue. These preparations, far from being simple gastronomic curiosities, reveal a profound understanding of biochemical processes and a remarkable adaptation to the climatic constraints of the North.

SURSTRÖMMING represents the pinnacle of the Nordic art of controlled fermentation. This fermented herring, whose production follows a precise calendar inherited from Viking traditions, requires a complex process **lasting** several months. The herring, caught in the spring in the Baltic waters, are headed and gutted, then placed in a weak brine where a controlled lactic fermentation takes place. This fermentation, initiated by bacteria naturally present on the fish, gradually transforms the proteins and develops aromas of exceptional intensity. Traditional surströmming was eaten with boiled potatoes, red onion, and aquavit, a combination that balances the aromatic power of the fermented fish while revealing its subtle flavors.

Norwegian RAKFISK illustrates another approach to fish fermentation, this time applied to freshwater species. Trout or grayling, caught in autumn in mountain lakes and rivers, are prepared using a technique dating back to the Viking era. The fish, simply scaled and gutted, is buried in rock salt for several weeks, allowing anaerobic fermentation that develops complex flavors while preserving the flesh. This technique, perfected in the mountainous regions of Norway where natural refrigeration makes the process easier to control, produces a delicate condiment with tangy notes that traditionally accompanies potato pancakes (lefse) and juniper aquavit.

Gravlaks represents a more recent but no less traditional evolution of these fish preparation techniques. The salmon, marinated in a mixture of salt, sugar , and dill, undergoes a cure that combines controlled dehydration and flavoring. This preparation, whose name literally means "buried salmon" in reference to the ancient technique of burying the fish in beach sand, reveals the adaptability of Nordic techniques. Modern gravlaks

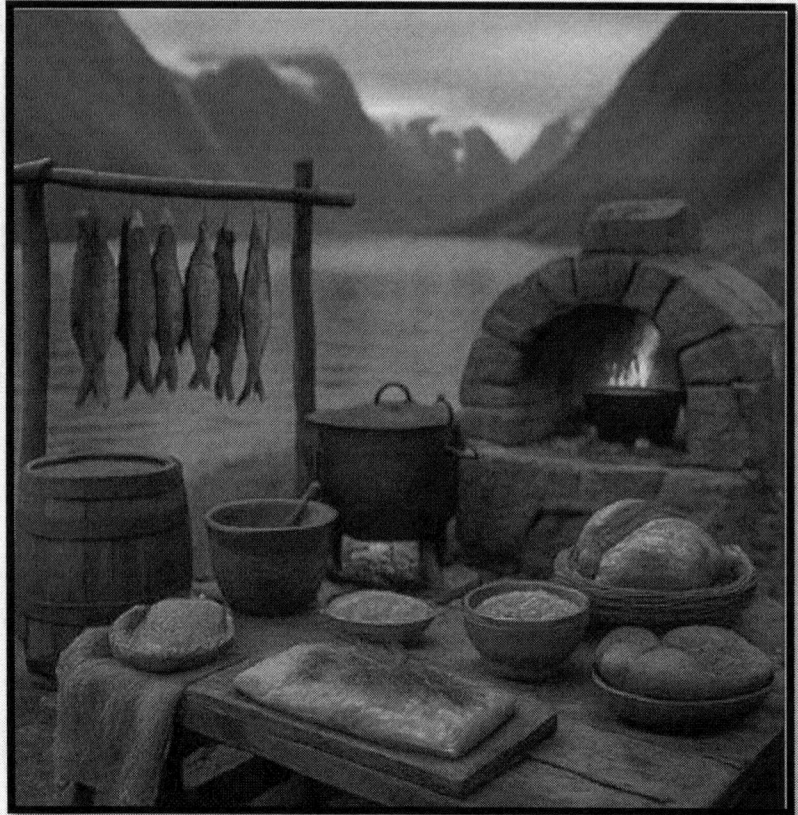

preserves the spirit of tradition while adapting to contemporary tastes, demonstrating the vitality and sustainability of the Nordic culinary heritage.

Sacred cereals: HAFRI (oats), BYGG (barley), RÚG (rye)

In Nordic cosmogony, cereals occupy a sacred place that goes beyond their simple nutritional function to become part of a spiritual and mythological relationship with the nourishing earth. The three main cereals—HAFRI (oats), BYGG (barley), and RÚG (rye)—constitute the pillars of the Nordic diet, each contributing its own nutritional and cultural specificities to a food system perfectly adapted to the climatic constraints of the North.

HAFRI (oats) holds a special place in the Nordic diet due to its remarkable adaptation to cold and humid climates. This hardy cereal, capable of growing in poor soils and withstanding late frosts, is often the last available grain resource in the northernmost regions. Nordic oats, generally eaten in the form of porridge (grøt) or cakes (havrekake), provide a substantial energy intake thanks to their high fat and soluble fiber content. Viking traditions associated oats with Freyja, goddess of fertility and abundance, and the first ears were ritually offered to the gods during harvest festivals. The preparation of oat porridge followed precise rules, with slow cooking in milk or broth allowing the full flavor of the cereal to be revealed while optimizing its digestibility.

BYGG (barley) is the fundamental cereal of Norse culture, not only for its nutritional importance but also for its central role in the production of beer, the sacred beverage of the Vikings. Nordic barley, selected over the centuries for its resistance to cold and its ability to germinate quickly, comes in several varieties adapted to different uses. Hulled barley, stripped of its husks, forms the basis of many traditional dishes such as byggotto (barley risotto) or is used in the thick soups that are a staple of winter meals. But it is above all in its transformation into malt for brewing that barley reveals its full cultural importance. Barley beer (øl) accompanies all the important moments of Norse social life, from ritual banquets to diplomatic negotiations, and its quality often determines the prestige of the producer.

RÚG (rye) represents the grain of endurance and survival, the one that allows Nordic populations to survive the long winters thanks to its exceptional storage capacity and high nutritional value. Nordic rye, adapted to acidic soils and short seasons, produces a dark flour, rich in fiber and minerals, which forms the basis of traditional bread (rugbrød). This dense and compact bread can be stored for several weeks without losing its nutritional qualities, an essential characteristic in a civilization where winter provisions determine survival. Rye breadmaking techniques, passed down from generation to generation, often incorporate natural ferments (levains) that enrich the flavors while improving preservation. Rye bread traditionally accompanies meals of dried fish and cheese, this combination forming the basis of the daily diet of Nordic populations.

Documented utensils: stone mortars, iron cauldrons, BAKSTEINN

Archaeology and written sources reveal the existence of sophisticated Nordic cooking tools, perfectly adapted to the climatic conditions and available resources. These utensils, far from being simple utilitarian tools, bear witness to a developed culinary culture and elaborate food processing techniques that characterized the Viking civilization.

stone mortars, carved from local rocks such as granite or schist, are key pieces of traditional culinary equipment. These mortars, some of which have been found during archaeological excavations, reach impressive dimensions, and were primarily used for grinding cereals and preparing spices and herbs. The knapping technique, inherited from Neolithic traditions but perfected by Viking craftsmen, produces perfectly rough work surfaces that optimize grinding efficiency. The largest mortars, used communally, were used to prepare the large quantities of flour needed for winter provisions, while individual mortars were used for the daily preparation of spices and herb mixtures. The use of the stone mortar was accompanied by specific rituals, with the first grinding of the season often being dedicated to the household gods who protect the home and ensure abundance.

Iron cauldrons represent the pinnacle of Nordic culinary metallurgy and demonstrate the technical mastery achieved by Viking blacksmiths. These cauldrons, forged from a single piece or assembled by riveting, could hold several dozen liters and were used for the preparation of community meals and ritual banquets. The characteristic shape of these cauldrons, with their rounded belly and flared opening, optimized heat distribution and facilitated the stirring of preparations. The most prestigious of them, adorned with decorative motifs and runic inscriptions, were prestigious pieces passed down from generation to generation and used during important ceremonies. The maintenance of these cauldrons followed precise rules, their internal surface being regularly treated with animal fats to prevent corrosion and improve their culinary qualities.

The **BAKSTEINN** (cooking stone) illustrates Nordic ingenuity in adapting to environmental constraints. These flat stones, carefully selected for their heat retention capacity and resistance to thermal shock, were used as cooking plates for preparing flatbreads, flatbreads, and grilled meats. The baksteinn was heated directly in contact with the fire and then used as a cooking surface, a technique that allows for even heat distribution and produces particularly flavorful dishes. This technique, still used in some rural regions of Scandinavia, illustrates the continuity of Nordic culinary traditions and their perfect adaptation to local resources. The most prized baksteinn, carved from special soapstone or schist, developed a natural seasoning over time that improved their cooking performance.

The art of birch fire and cooking at the communal STEINOFN

Fire control is a fundamental art in Nordic civilization, where long winter nights and limited fuel resources require optimal management of thermal energy. The use of birch as a standard fuel and the development of communal ovens (STEINOFN) illustrate this technical and social mastery of culinary fire.

Birch fires represent much more than a simple technical choice; they constitute a true Nordic culinary philosophy based on a detailed understanding of the combustible properties of wood. Nordic birch, an emblematic tree of the boreal forests, offers exceptional combustion qualities: its high calorific value, its regular combustion, and the aromatic quality of its smoke make it the ideal fuel for traditional cooking. Birch bark, rich in essential oils, produces a bright, hot flame perfect for lighting, while the wood itself burns with a clear, stable flame ideal for cooking. The Vikings perfectly mastered the different species of birch and their specific uses: white birch for delicate cooking requiring gentle heat, black birch for grilling requiring high temperatures, and dwarf birch from the Arctic regions for long-term cooking.

The art of birch fires is accompanied by particularly sophisticated smoking techniques that reveal Nordic mastery of food processing. Birch smoke, with its delicate, slightly resinous aroma, gives smoked foods subtle aromas while ensuring their preservation. This technique, applied primarily to fish and meat, requires precise control of temperature and humidity, acquired only through extensive experience. Traditional smokehouses, built of stone and wood, use complex smoke circuits that allow for finely regulated smoking intensity depending on the products being processed.

The **communal STEINOFN** (stone oven) represents the culmination of Nordic culinary technology and perfectly illustrates the social organization of these civilizations. These ovens, built collectively in the center of villages or hamlets, represent considerable community investments that require the cooperation of the entire community. The construction of a steinofn calls upon the skills of specialists: masons for the assembly of stones, blacksmiths for the metal elements, carpenters for the ancillary structures. These ovens, with a capacity of several dozen loaves, operate according to a principle of thermal restitution that optimizes the use of fuel: once heated by an intense fire, they retain their heat for long hours and allow successive cooking of different types of food.

The use of the communal steinofn is organized according to precise social rules that reflect the organization of Nordic society. The order of passage, the types of permitted foods, and the contribution to maintenance costs are all subject to community conventions that strengthen social ties. The day of baking at the communal oven thus becomes a major social event where practical concerns and interpersonal relationships blend. This communal dimension of baking perfectly illustrates the Nordic spirit, which favors cooperation and mutual aid in addressing environmental challenges.

Preservation techniques: smoking, fermentation, TØRRFISK

Survival in the extreme climatic conditions of the North requires a perfect mastery of food preservation techniques, an area in which Nordic peoples have developed unparalleled expertise. These techniques, perfected over the centuries, not only preserve food but also transform it, creating new flavors and textures that considerably enrich the Nordic culinary palette.

smoking is a preservation and flavoring technique that has reached an exceptional level of sophistication in this region. This technique relies on the **combined** action of dehydration, moderate heat, and the chemical compounds contained in smoke, mainly aldehydes and phenols, which have antiseptic and antioxidant properties. Traditional Nordic smokehouses, built of stone or dug into hillsides, allow precise control of temperature and humidity thanks to elaborate air circulation systems. Cold smoking, carried out at temperatures below 30°C, allows for long-term preservation while preserving the original texture of the food, a technique particularly suited to oily fish such as salmon or herring. Hot smoking, carried out between 60 and 90°C, produces directly edible food with more pronounced flavors, a method preferred for meats and certain fish.

Fermentation is arguably the preservation technique most characteristic of Nordic culinary culture, giving rise to unique specialties that often challenge uninitiated palates but reveal a profound understanding of biochemical processes. This technique harnesses the action of beneficial microorganisms (lactic acid bacteria, yeasts) that transform sugars and proteins while creating an acidic environment hostile to pathogenic germs. Lactic fermentation, applied to vegetables (cabbage, turnips, radishes), produces preserves rich in vitamins and probiotics that compensate for the nutritional deficiencies of winter diets. Protein fermentation, more complex to master, is applied to fish and meat to create condiments with a powerful flavor but exceptional nutritional qualities .

TØRRFISK (dried fish) is a perfect example of Nordic adaptation to **local** resources and climatic conditions. This technique, which exploits the cold, dry winds of the Arctic, allows fish to be preserved for years while concentrating its nutritional qualities. The traditional process begins with the careful selection of fish, generally caught in winter when the flesh is firmest and least fatty. Cod, pollock, and haddock are the preferred species for this preparation. The fish, carefully cleaned and headed, are hung in pairs on wooden drying racks (hjell) exposed to the prevailing winds. The dehydration process, which can last several months depending on climatic conditions, gradually transforms the fresh flesh into a product as hard as wood but retaining all its nutritional qualities intact. Traditional tørrfisk can be stored for decades and constitutes an absolutely reliable food reserve, an essential characteristic in a civilization subject to the vagaries of the climate.

These conservation techniques are accompanied by rituals and know-how passed down from generation to generation, creating a true culture of conservation that goes beyond mere technical aspects. Social organization is partially structured around these seasonal activities: periods of intensive fishing, times of collective smoking, community monitoring of drying sheds. This social dimension of conservation techniques strengthens community cohesion and ensures the transmission of traditional knowledge.

III. Nutritional principles according to VÖLUR (midwives)

The Nine Worlds Theory Applied to Nutrition

Nordic cosmology, structured around the concept of the nine worlds (Níu Heimar) connected by the cosmic tree Yggdrasil, finds its application in a holistic approach to nutrition that goes far beyond simple food concerns to become part of a global vision of the balance between body, mind, and the cosmos. The VÖLUR, these wise women who hold traditional Nordic knowledge, developed a complex nutritional system that associates each type of food with one of the nine cosmic worlds, thus creating a sacred diet where each meal becomes an act of universal harmonization. **Ásgard**, the world of the Æsir (chief gods), corresponds to the noblest and rarest foods, reserved for exceptional occasions and high-ranking figures. This category includes fermented mead, roasted wild boar, premium smoked salmon, and aged cheeses. These foods, considered to carry the divine essence, may only be consumed with the appropriate rituals and in accordance with sacred rules. The preparation of these dishes requires particularly refined techniques and ingredients of absolute purity, characteristics that reserve them for ritual banquets and religious ceremonies.

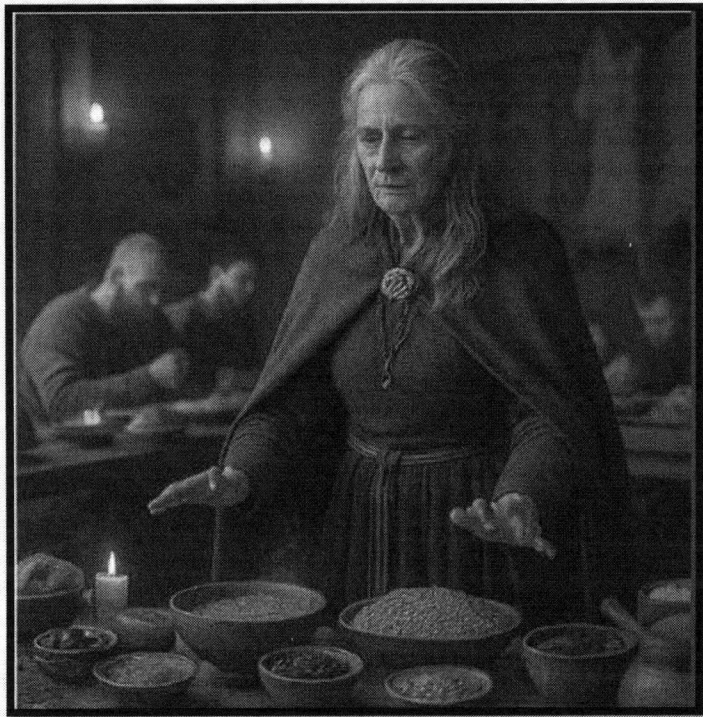

Vanaheim, the domain of the Vanir (gods of fertility and prosperity), governs foods linked to the fertility of the earth and abundant harvests. This category includes new grains, the first fruits of the season, root vegetables, and fresh dairy products. These foods, best eaten at their peak of ripeness, are believed to promote reproductive health and ensure household prosperity. The VÖLUR prescribe their consumption according to precise lunar cycles and in specific combinations that respect the cosmic laws of fertility.

Ljósálfgard (Alfheim), the world of the light elves, corresponds to delicate and refined foods that nourish the mind as much as the body. This category includes aromatic herbs, wild berries, unfermented honey, and certain fine-fleshed freshwater fish. These foods, renowned for their purifying properties and their ability to enlighten the mind, are particularly recommended for healers, poets, and all those whose work requires particular intellectual acuity.

Midgard, the world of humans, encompasses the everyday foods that form the basis of ordinary diets. Rye bread, oatmeal, dried fish, and preserved vegetables comprise this category of earthly foods that anchor humans in their mortal condition while providing the energy necessary for their activities. This balanced and substantial Midgard diet reflects the human condition, neither divine nor bestial, and must be consumed with gratitude to the forces that provide sustenance.

Jötunheim , the world of giants, corresponds to powerful and wild foods that provide strength and endurance but require caution in their use. This category includes big game meats, large sea fish, mushrooms with special properties, and certain very strong fermented preparations. These foods, carrying a raw and primitive energy, are particularly suitable for warriors and hard workers, but their excessive consumption can unbalance inner harmony.

Svartálfheim (Nidavellir), the world of dwarven blacksmiths, governs foods transformed by art and technology, those whose qualities are revealed through human action. This category includes leavened breads, matured cheeses, brewed beers, and all preparations resulting from artisanal know-how. These foods, fruits of the alliance between the gifts of nature and human ingenuity, symbolize the capacity for transformation and improvement that characterizes civilization.

Muspelheim , the world of primordial fire, corresponds to grilled, roasted, and smoked foods that carry within them fiery energy. This category includes all preparations that involve the direct action of fire: grilled meats, smoked fish, stone-baked breads. These foods, marked by the element of fire, bring warmth and vitality, particularly recommended during the winter months and for cold and damp temperaments.

Niflheim , a world of mist and primordial cold, encompasses cold and moist foods that refresh and soothe. This category includes fresh dairy products, raw or undercooked fish, aquatic vegetables, and all preparations served cold. These foods are particularly suited to hot and dry temperaments and are recommended during periods of extreme heat or fever.

Helheim , the world of the dead, corresponds to the foods of rebirth and regeneration, those that allow one to overcome difficult periods and regain vitality. This category includes concentrated broths, organ preparations, food remedies, and all dishes that restore strength after illness or exhaustion. These foods, linked to the cycles of death and rebirth, are prescribed sparingly and according to precise ritual rules.

This cosmic classification of foods is accompanied by detailed prescriptions concerning the favorable or harmful associations between the different categories, creating a complex dietary system that governs not only the choice of foods but also their preparation, presentation, and consumption. The VÖLUR, custodians of this ancestral knowledge, adapt these general prescriptions to the specific needs of each individual according to their temperament, activity, and social position.

Social hierarchy of food: jarls, karls, thralls

JARLS   KARLS   THRALLS

Nordic society, rigorously stratified according to a tripartite system inherited from Indo-European traditions, developed a food hierarchy that reflected and reinforced the established social order. This classification, far from being arbitrary, was based on precise criteria: rarity of ingredients, complexity of preparation, symbolic value, and supposed nutritional qualities. The VÖLUR, guardians of traditions and health advisors, codified this food hierarchy by associating it with the cosmological prescriptions and practical needs of each social class.

The diet of the JARLS (aristocracy) is characterized by its refinement, diversity, and abundance, reflecting the high social status and political responsibilities of this ruling class. Jarls have access to the most prestigious foods: choice meats (wild boar, venison, top-quality beef), noble fish (salmon, trout, sturgeon), imported products (spices, wines, exceptional honey), and complex preparations requiring advanced artisanal know-how. Their table is also distinguished by the variety of dishes served simultaneously, a practice that testifies not only to their wealth but also to their generosity, a cardinal virtue of the Nordic aristocracy.

Aristocratic banquets follow a complex protocol in which each element—choice of dishes, order of service, arrangement of guests—observes precise rules that reinforce the hierarchical order while creating bonds of loyalty and mutual obligation. Mead, the royal beverage par excellence, flows abundantly during these feasts, and its quality—determined by the age of the honey, the purity of the water, and the mastery of fermentation— constitutes an indisputable social marker. The jarls also consume particularly elaborate processed products:

cheeses aged for several years, charcuterie matured using secret techniques, breads enriched with eggs and butter.

This aristocratic diet was not only a response to the pursuit of pleasure or ostentation; it was part of a specific political and social logic. Through their food generosity, the jarls created and maintained alliance networks essential to their power. Their kitchens, veritable centers of artisanal production, employed numerous specialists (bakers, brewers, butchers, cooks) whose expertise contributed to the prestige of the master. This economic dimension of aristocratic diet made it a determining factor in Nordic social and political organization.

The diet of the Karls (free men) constitutes the foundation of Nordic nutrition, balanced between economic constraints and the nutritional needs of an active and productive social class. The Karls, ordinary farmers, artisans, merchants, and warriors, developed a pragmatic cuisine that optimized available resources while maintaining the nutritional quality necessary for their activities. Their diet was based on local produce: cereals grown on their land (oats, barley, rye), products of family livestock (pork, sheep, poultry), resources from fishing and hunting, vegetables and fruits from their gardens.

This social class particularly developed the art of food preservation and processing, essential skills for surviving the long northern winters and coping with the vagaries of the climate. The Karls' smoking, drying, fermentation, and salting techniques reached a remarkable level of sophistication, creating a range of preserved products that considerably enriched their culinary palette. Their expertise in home brewing produced beers of variable but generally satisfactory quality, a daily drink that accompanied most meals.

The social organization of the Karls directly influenced their eating habits: meals eaten as a family, sharing of cooking tasks according to gender and age, and adapting the menu to the seasons and agricultural activities. This family diet, less spectacular than that of the aristocracy but more diverse than that of the servile classes, created a culinary identity specific to this Nordic middle class. The Karls also developed regional specialties linked to their professional activities: fishermen perfected fish preparation techniques, livestock breeders created specific cheeses, and farmers developed recipes using their particular products.

The diet of the THRALLS (slaves and servants) is characterized by its simplicity, frugality, and adaptation to the strictest economic constraints. This social class, deprived of land and means of production, depends entirely on the generosity of its masters for its subsistence. Their diet consists mainly of inexpensive staple foods: coarse grain porridge, common vegetables, inferior fish, less noble meats or offal, and simple dairy products.

Despite these severe economic constraints, the thralls' diet is not necessarily unbalanced. Nordic masters, aware that the productivity of their workforce depends on its health, generally ensure that sufficient food is provided in quantity and quality. This servile diet develops its own culinary specificities, often linked to the optimization of limited resources: preparations using the entire animal (including offal and bones), preparation techniques that maximize the nutritional value of basic ingredients, and economical recipes that create flavor with few resources.

The thralls, often responsible for culinary tasks in large houses, paradoxically developed considerable technical expertise that influenced the entire Nordic cuisine. Their innovations, born of necessity, enriched the culinary repertoire and demonstrated that gastronomic creativity did not necessarily depend on abundant resources. This contribution of the servile classes to culinary evolution illustrates the complexity of cultural exchange in the stratified Nordic society.

Nordic Seasonal Calendar and Fasting Periods

The temporal organization of Nordic food follows a complex calendar that combines climatic constraints, agricultural cycles, religious prescriptions, and social traditions. This calendar, codified by the VÖLUR and transmitted orally from generation to generation, structures not only food practices but also the entirety of Nordic social life around natural and cosmic rhythms.

The winter cycle (October-March) is the most critical period of the Nordic year, when survival depends entirely on the quality of provisions built up during the preceding months and the ability to rationally manage these reserves. Winter diets are based mainly on preserved products: smoked and salted meats, dried fish, aged cheeses, fermented vegetables, stored cereals. This period sees the development of a warming cuisine favoring hot and substantial preparations: thick soups, long-simmered stews, porridges enriched with fat.

The winter solstice (Jól) marks the culmination of this season with festivities that traditionally last twelve days and are accompanied by an exceptional consumption of the finest reserves. These solstice banquets, far from being simple feasts, take on a fundamental ritual dimension: through this ostentatious consumption, the community affirms its confidence in the future and honors the gods who will ensure the return of light. The traditional foods of Jól—roasted wild boar, aged mead, enriched breads—are consumed according to precise rituals that strengthen social cohesion and reaffirm community values.

This winter period is also accompanied by fasts prescribed by the VÖLUR according to both health and spiritual criteria. These fasts, generally short (one to three days), aim to purify the body and conserve reserves while maintaining the collective discipline necessary for winter survival. Winter fasts favor the exclusive consumption of clear broths and herbal infusions, preparations that maintain hydration and provide essential nutrients without depleting food reserves.

The spring cycle (April-June) marks the rebirth of nature and the gradual resumption of productive activities. This transitional period sees the Nordic diet gradually evolve from a reliance on winter reserves to the use of the first fresh resources of the year. Young nettle shoots, the first wild grasses, and eggs from spring spawning gradually enrich a diet often depleted by the harshness of winter.

The spring equinox (Ostara) celebrates this renewal with specific food rituals that honor the resurgent fertility. The first fresh produce of the season—decorated eggs, new herbs, the first white cheeses—is consumed in ceremonies that combine gratitude for natural forces with hope for future harvests. This period also sees the practice of purifying fasts intended to eliminate toxins accumulated during the winter and prepare the body for the intense activities of the summer season.

The summer cycle (July-September) represents the peak of northern abundance, a period when nature offers its most diverse resources and human activity reaches its peak. Summer diets favor the immediate consumption of fresh produce—new vegetables, wild fruits, seasonal fish, fresh meat—while actively preparing winter reserves through conservation activities.

The summer solstice (Midsommar) marks the culmination of this abundance with festivities celebrating the plenitude of nature and the creative power of the sun. Midsommar banquets, held outdoors, showcase all the season's produce in an orgy of colors, flavors, and scents that contrast dramatically with the austerity of winter. This celebration is accompanied by rituals of gathering magical herbs and preparing special brews believed to capture and concentrate the sun's energy.

Summer fasts, less frequent and less rigorous than those of other seasons, are primarily aimed at maintaining spiritual discipline during a time of abundance that could lead to excess. These fasts, often associated with the lunar phases, favor the exclusive consumption of fresh plant products and pure water, a practice that lightens the body and maintains the mental clarity necessary for the intense activities of the season.

The Viking VEIZLA (banquet) and feast protocol

The VEIZLA represents the most refined social institution of Nordic civilization, a perfect synthesis of culinary art, social organization, and pagan spirituality. These banquets, far from being simple collective meals, constitute true political and religious ceremonies where alliances are negotiated, hierarchies are reaffirmed, and gods and ancestors are honored. The organization of a VEIZLA obeys complex rules codified by tradition and transmitted by the VÖLUR, these wise women who master all Nordic social and religious protocols.

Preparation for the VEIZLA begins several weeks before the event and mobilizes all the resources of the organizing community. The choice of date is based on both practical considerations (availability of ingredients, climatic conditions) and symbolic considerations (lunar phases, religious calendar, significant birthdays). Developing the menu requires in-depth knowledge of the guests' tastes and dietary restrictions, their social status, and their mutual relationships. This planning phase reveals the diplomatic importance of the VEIZLA as an instrument of inter-community politics.

The selection of ingredients is a crucial aspect that largely determines the success and prestige of the banquet. The organizers mobilize their best reserves: meats aged under optimal conditions, mead fermented for several years, cheeses matured to perfection, breads prepared with the finest flours. This rigorous selection is often accompanied by special acquisitions: game hunted especially for the occasion, fish caught in the best areas, imported products obtained through commercial exchange. The quality of the ingredients testifies not only to the wealth of the organizer but also to their network of contacts and their ability to mobilize community resources.

The service protocol follows immutable rules that reflect the Norse cosmic and social order. The layout of the banquet hall symbolically reproduces the structure of the Norse universe: the place of honor, reserved for the chief guest, corresponds to Odin's throne in Valhalla, while the arrangement of the other guests scrupulously respects social hierarchies and alliance relationships. This social geography of the banquet does not tolerate any improvisation, and failure to respect it would constitute a serious offense likely to provoke lasting conflicts.

The order of service also obeys precise rules that combine practical considerations with religious symbolism. The initial libations, poured in honor of the gods and ancestors, solemnly open the banquet and place the entire ceremony under divine protection. These libations, made with the most precious mead, are accompanied by specific invocations depending on the occasion: prayers to Odin for political banquets, to Thor for war celebrations, to Freyja for fertility festivities.

The serving of food follows a skillfully orchestrated progression that maintains the interest of the guests while respecting social precedence. The most prestigious dishes are presented first to distinguished guests, this priority constituting an honor that reinforces their social status. The carving of meat itself follows a rigorous protocol: the choice cuts go to the most important people according to a hierarchical order that all participants know perfectly. This codified distribution of food transforms each course into a reaffirmation of the social order and a public recognition of the merits of each individual.

The social functions of VEIZLA extend far beyond mere gastronomic pleasure to become part of the political and religious functioning of Nordic society. These banquets provide privileged opportunities for negotiating matrimonial, commercial, or military alliances, with diplomatic discussions taking place in a relaxed setting that fosters compromise and agreement. The generosity displayed by the organizer creates moral obligations among his guests, obligations that can later be activated to obtain support and services.

The VEIZLA also fulfilled an important economic function by stimulating artisanal production and promoting the circulation of wealth. Preparing a large banquet mobilized numerous specialists—cooks, brewers, bakers, and goldsmiths for ceremonial tableware—and generated significant economic activity. This economic dimension partly explains why banquets were strategic investments for Nordic elites keen to maintain their social position and political influence.

Sacred hospitality according to the laws of GÍSLI

Norse hospitality, codified in the sagas and particularly in the laws attributed to GÍSLI, constitutes one of the moral and legal foundations of Viking civilization. This institution, which goes far beyond simple social courtesy, is rooted in a sacred concept of hospitality that combines religious prescriptions, practical necessities, and moral obligations. The VÖLUR, guardians of ancestral traditions, transmit and interpret these laws of hospitality, which govern not only social relations but also culinary and dietary practices.

The mythological foundations of Norse hospitality date back to the cosmogonic tales that describe Odin's wanderings across the nine worlds. The supreme god, often traveling in disguise, regularly tests the hospitality of mortals and rewards or punishes according to the quality of the welcome received. This divine dimension of hospitality transforms every arrival of a stranger into a potential test in which the moral worth of the host is revealed. Failure to respect the laws of hospitality can attract divine wrath and jeopardize the prosperity of the home, while their scrupulous observance ensures protection and blessings.

The laws of GÍSLI establish specific obligations regarding the reception of travelers, obligations that vary according to the social status of the host and the guest but that are universally imposed as soon as a request for hospitality is made. These laws distinguish several categories of hospitality according to the length of the stay, the season, and the circumstances of arrival. Emergency hospitality, granted to travelers surprised by bad weather or at night, requires immediate reception without regard for social rank. Planned hospitality, for official visits or extended stays, allows for preparation adapted to the status of the visitors.

Alimony is the most concrete and binding aspect of Norse hospitality. The host must offer the best of his reserves in proportion to his means, this proportionality being assessed according to precise social criteria that everyone knows. A jarl who received his guests with the frugality of a karl would immediately lose his social prestige, while a karl who exhausted his reserves to honor a distinguished guest would gain in reputation and honorability. This adaptation of hospitality to the host's means avoids economic ruin while maintaining the requirement of relative excellence.

Hospitality menus follow specific rules that reflect Nordic values and practical constraints. The first meal offered to the guest must include, at a minimum, fresh bread, quality meat or fish, an alcoholic beverage, and a dairy product. This basic composition ensures a balanced nutritional intake while demonstrating respect for the guest. Subsequent meals may be simpler but must maintain a consistent level of quality that avoids any impression of neglect or weariness.

The welcoming ritual begins with the offering of a drink that symbolically seals the guest's acceptance into the household's protection. This initial libation, usually consisting of mead or fine beer, is accompanied by ritual formulas that place the guest under the protection of the household gods and guarantee their safety during

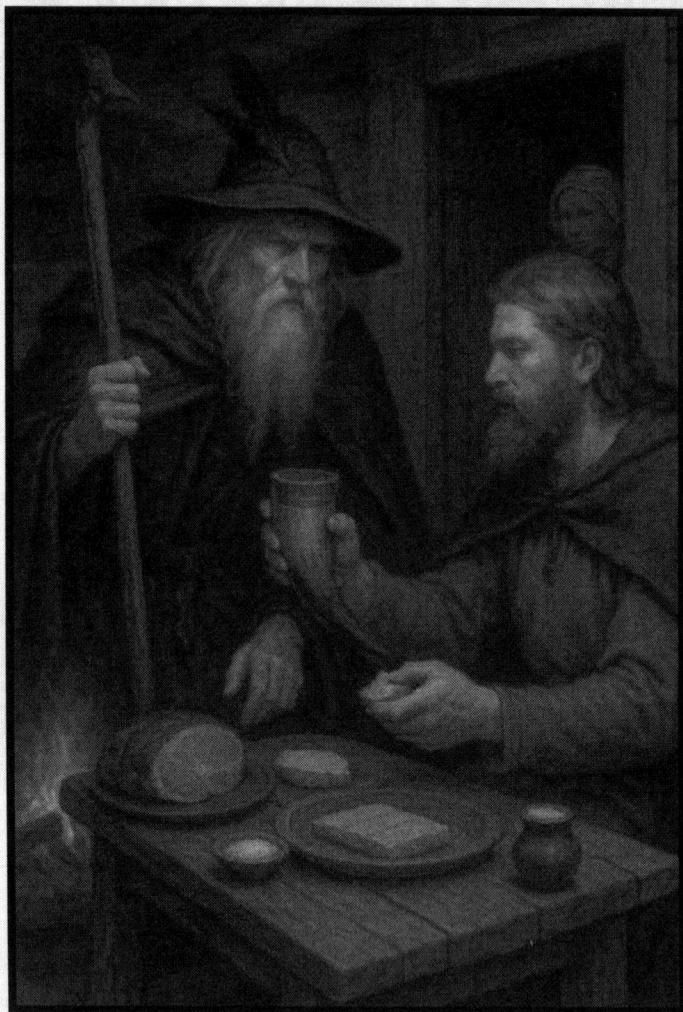

their stay. Refusal of this welcoming drink would constitute a serious offense likely to sever relations between the families concerned.

The sharing of salt, another ritual element of Nordic hospitality, creates a sacred bond between host and guest. This precious substance, often imported at great expense, symbolizes purity and preservation. By sharing salt with their guest, the host commits to their safety and maintaining friendly relations. This salt covenant can later be invoked for help and protection, creating networks of mutual obligation that structure inter-community relations.

The prohibitions and sanctions associated with non-compliance with the laws of hospitality are clearly defined and rigorously enforced by the community. Refusal of hospitality without serious grounds (insufficient resources, declared enmity, religious prohibition) exposes the defaulting host to social opprobrium and community exclusion. This social sanction, particularly formidable in a society where cooperation determines survival, constitutes a powerful incentive to respect the obligations of hospitality.

Nordic hospitality also creates obligations for the guest, who must respect certain rules of behavior: discretion regarding the private affairs of their hosts, participation in common tasks according to their abilities, and public recognition of the quality of the welcome received. These reciprocal obligations balance hospitality relationships and prevent abuses that could compromise the institution as a whole.

ANNEXES AND SUPPLEMENTS

Old Norse-present-day glossary

Old Norse term	French translation	Detailed definition
ÁLFABLÓT	Sacrifice to the Elves	Autumn food ritual honoring the elves and asking for their protection for the crops
BAKSTEINN	Baking stone	Flat stone used as a baking tray, heated over a fire and then used to cook pancakes and flatbreads
BLÓT	Sacrifice	Religious ceremony involving food offerings to the gods
BYGGOTTO	Barley risotto	Creamy preparation made from hulled barley, the Nordic ancestor of Italian risotto
BYGG	Barley	A fundamental cereal in the Nordic diet, the basis of bread and beer
DÍSABLÓT	Sacrifice to the dice	Women's Winter Ritual Honoring the Protective Goddesses of Family and Home
DRÁPA	Poem of praise	Epic recitation accompanying banquets, often rewarded with choice dishes
EINHERJAR	Dead Warriors	Odin's chosen ones feasting eternally in Valhalla, a model of earthly banquets
F Q RUNEYTI	Travel supplies	Food specially prepared for sea and land expeditions
GJALLARHORN	Heimdall's Horn	Instrument used to summon ritual banquets and assemblies
GRAVLAKS	Marinated salmon	Raw salmon marinated in salt, sugar and dill, a Nordic preservation technique
GRØT	Porridge	Basic preparation based on cereals cooked in water or milk, fundamental daily food
HAFRI	Oats	Cold-resistant cereal, mainly eaten as porridge or cakes
HARÐFISKUR	Hard fish	Dried fish until completely cured, can be stored for several years
HÁKARL	Fermented shark	Icelandic specialty of fermented shark underground, a ritual dish of great strength

HEIMBRYGÐ	Home brewing	Family art of beer production, essential skill of the housewife
HJALLR	Dryer	Wooden construction for drying fish and meat in the open air
HORN	Drinking horn	Ritual vessel carved from bovine horn, used for mead and beer
HÚSFREYJA	Mistress of the house	Woman responsible for food management in the household, holder of the keys to the pantry
JÓL	Winter Solstice	Major 12-day festival with ritual banquets and consumption of the best reserves
KARL	Free man	Middle class, develops a balanced and practical family cuisine
KJÖT	Meat	Generic term designating all animal flesh, a food of social prestige
LEFSE	Thin pancake	Traditional Norwegian flatbread, baked on a hot stone, accompanies dried fish
MJÖÐR	Mead	Fermented honey-based drink, beverage of the gods and the aristocracy
MUSPELL	Destructive fire	Primordial igneous element, associated with grilling and smoking techniques
NIFLHEIM	World of Mist	Kingdom of damp cold, associated with fresh and refreshing foods
ØL	Beer	Fermented barley drink, daily consumption by all social classes
RAKFISK	Fermented fish	Trout or grayling fermented in salt, a Norwegian mountain specialty
RÚG	Rye	Hardy cereal that produces black bread, the basis of winter food
SEIÐR	Magic	Magical practices including the preparation of potions and food remedies
STEINOFN	Stone oven	Communal oven built of stone, used collectively for baking bread
SURSTRÖMMING	Fermented herring	Swedish fermented herring specialty, the pinnacle of the Nordic art of fermentation
THRALL	Slave	Servile class developing an economical and creative cuisine out of necessity
TØRRFISK	Dried fish	Arctic air-dried cod, a staple food that can be stored indefinitely

VEIZLA	Banquet	Great ritual feast, major social and political event in Nordic society
VÖLUR	Wise women	Priestesses who hold traditional knowledge in nutrition and medicine
YGGDRASIL	Cosmic Tree	Sacred ash tree connecting the nine worlds, model of universal nutritional harmony

Guide to Nordic Spices and Substitutes

Nordic spice	Latin name	Geographical origin	Modern substitute	Traditional use
Enebær	Juniperus communis	Scandinavian boreal forests	Juniper berries	Flavoring of game meats, distillation of aquavit
Dill	Anethum graveolens	Nordic cultures	Fresh dill	Marinating salmon (gravlaks), preserving vegetables
Kvan	Angelica archangelica	Arctic regions	Angelic	Confectionery, digestive liqueurs, traditional medicine
Bjørneklo	Heracleum sphondylium	Wet meadows	Common Hogweed	Young edible shoots, aromatic seeds
Myrhol	Myrrhis odorata	Scandinavian Mountains	Musky chervil	Seasoning soups, digestive infusions
Geitrams	Allium ursinum	Deciduous forests	Wild garlic	Spring condiment, purifying properties
Tyrihjelm	Aconitum napellus	Mountainous regions	Monkshood	Medical use only (TOXIC)
Revebjelle	Campanula rotundifolia	Nordic moors	Bellflower	Young leaves in salad, decorative flowers
Mjødurt	Filipendula ulmaria	Wetlands	Meadowsweet	Flavoring mead, infusions
Strandrødder	Rhodiola rosea	Arctic coasts	Rhodiola	Stimulant, adaptation to climatic stress
Islandsmose	Cetraria islandica	Icelandic tundra	Iceland moss	Thickener, survival food

| Finngull | Antennaria dioica | Alpine lawns | Cat's foot | Soothing infusions, feminine medicine |

AXIS 1: FYRIRRÉTTIR OK SÁÐMATR -
Midgard's appetizers and starters

Jarls' Starters (8 recipes), Sauces and Condiments (4 recipes)

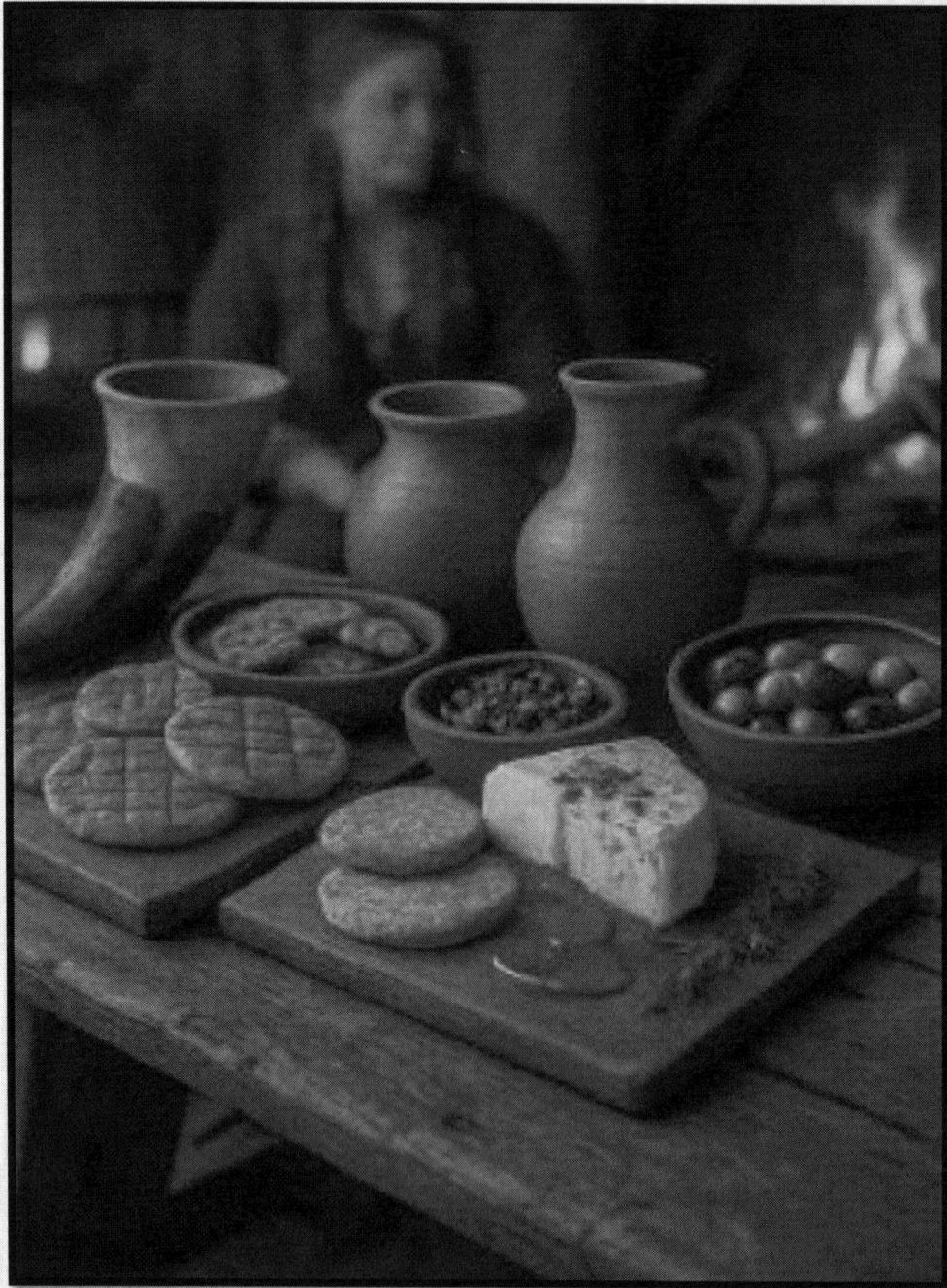

1. OSTAKAKA HELGI ~ Odin's Sacred Cheesecake

PRACTICAL INFORMATION: 🖼 **Historical period:** 9th-10th century | 🏛 **Source:** HEIMSKRINGLA/Archaeology Birka | 🕐 **Preparation time:** 25 min | **Cooking time:** 45 min | 🔥 **Calories:** 320 kcal per portion | 👥 **Servings:** 8 people | 📋 **Nutritional value:** Protein: 18g / Carbohydrates: 22g / Fat: 19g | 💡 **Ancient advice:** Bake on a flat stone heated over a birch fire according to the VÖLUR | 🔄 **Modern method:** Oven at 180°C with a buttered mold | 💰 **Estimated cost:** €12.50 / £11.20 / $14.80 | 🍴 **Nordic utensils:** BAKSTEINN (cooking stone), iron cauldron, stone mortar | ⚙ **Difficulty:** Initiated ★★☆

🏛 **OSTAKAKA HELGI:** Ritual cake offered to Odin during the autumn blót, mentioned in the sagas as a dish of the jarls during the assemblies of the thing. Traditionally served with mead during ceremonies dedicated to the All-Father, a symbol of prosperity and fertility in Norse mythology.

INGREDIENTS :

- 400g of MJÓLKOSTR (white goat cheese) | • 180g of HAFRAKORN (fine oat flour)
- 3 EGG GÆSIR (goose eggs) or 4 chicken eggs | • 120g of HUNANG (heather honey)
- 50ml of MJÓLK (fresh goat's milk) | • 1 tsp of STEINSTEINN (crushed rock salt)
- 2 tbsp SMJÖR (sour milk butter) | • Pinch of KANEL (merchant cinnamon)

METHOD

1. **Initial preparation:** Crush the MJÓLKOSTR in a stone mortar until smooth, then add the EGG GÆSIR, beaten vigorously by hand according to VÖLUR tradition. Gently melt the SMJÖR in the cauldron.
2. **First firing:** Heat the BAKSTEINN over a birch fire for 30 minutes, maintain a gentle, constant heat by regularly adding chips, test the temperature by pouring in a drop of water which should sizzle.
3. **Main assembly:** Mix the cheese with the eggs, gradually incorporate the sifted HAFRAKORN, add the warmed HUNANG, the MJÓLK and the STEINSTEINN. Beat vigorously to obtain a smooth paste without lumps, let stand for 10 minutes.
4. **Final cooking:** Pour the mixture onto the oiled BAKSTEINN, cover with an iron lid, cook for 45 minutes, making sure the edges brown without burning.
5. **Finishing:** Sprinkle with KANEL, gently unmold with a wooden spatula, leave to cool on oak boards.
6. **Service:** Serve warm with liquid HUNANG and MJÖÐUR, cut into triangular pieces according to the tradition of the nine worlds.

🔄 **Modern Substitutes:** MJÓLKOSTR → fresh ricotta, HAFRAKORN → ground oat flour, EGG GÆSIR → organic eggs, HUNANG → acacia honey, MJÓLK → whole goat's milk, STEINSTEINN → fleur de sel.

ANCIENT METHOD: Direct cooking on a BAKSTEINN heated in the embers, turning halfway through cooking with a reindeer horn spatula.

Secrets of the MATSTJÓRAR: The jarls' cooks incorporated filtered birch ash to alkalize the dough and obtain a more airy texture, a method passed down by the skalds in their tales of royal feasts, sacred proportion of 3 eggs to honor the Norns.

Nutritional values: 320 kcal | Protein: 18g | Carbohydrates: 22g | Fat: 19g

2. EGGJAVAFLA MJÓLK ~ Egg and reindeer milk waffles

PRACTICAL INFORMATION: 📺 **Historical period:** 8th-9th century | 🏛 **Source:** EGILS SAGA/Hedeby excavations | 🕐 **Preparation time:** 20 min | **Cooking time:** 30 min | 🜂 **Calories:** 280 kcal per portion | 👥 **Servings:** 6 people | 📗 **Nutritional value:** Protein: 14g / Carbohydrates: 28g / Fat: 16g | 💡 **Ancient advice:** Cook between two irons engraved with runes according to Lappish tradition | 🔲 **Modern method:** Electric waffle iron or ridged pan | 🪙 **Estimated cost:** €8.90 / £7.80 / $10.60 | 🎛 **Nordic utensils:** VAFLUBERG (waffle iron), cauldron, birch whisk | ⚙️ **Difficulty:** Novice ★☆☆

🏛 **EGGJAVAFLA MJÓLK:** A specialty of the northern regions mentioned in EGILS SAGA during winter feasts. Wrought iron VAFLUBERG often bore runic motifs and were used during winter solstice celebrations to honor the goddess Sunna and ensure the return of light.

INGREDIENTS :

- 250g BYGGMJÖL (barley flour) | • 200ml HREINDÝRMJÓLK (reindeer milk) or whole milk
- 4 EGG ANDAR (wild duck eggs) | • 80g of HUNANG LYNGS (heather honey)
- 60g of SMJÖR SÚRT (sour butter) | • 1 tsp of STEINSTEINN (rock salt)
- 2 tbsp BJÖRGRAS (dried mountain herbs) | • Pinch of FJALLAPIPAR (wild pepper)

METHOD

1. **Initial preparation:** Sift the BYGGMJÖL into a wooden bowl, make a well in the center, beat the EGG ANDAR with the HUNANG LYNGS until whitened using the traditional VÖLUR method.
2. **First firing:** Heat the VAFLUBERG over a birch fire, maintain a constant temperature by moving the embers, brush the surfaces with melted SMJÖR SÚRT to prevent sticking.
3. **Main assembly:** Gradually incorporate the lukewarm HREINDÝRMJÓLK into the beaten eggs, pour this mixture into the flour well, mix vigorously with a birch whisk to avoid lumps. Add the STEINSTEINN and the finely crushed BJÖRGRAS.
4. **Final cooking:** Pour a ladleful of batter onto the hot VAFLUBERG, close and cook for 3-4 minutes, turning once, ensuring the surface is golden and crispy.
5. **Finishing:** Sprinkle lightly with ground FJALLAPIPAR, stack the waffles, separating them with birch leaves to prevent them from sticking.
6. **Service:** Serve immediately with liquid HUNANG and chilled SMJÖR, accompanied by candied cranberries in their own juice.

🔲 **Modern Substitutes:** BYGGMJÖL → organic barley flour, HREINDÝRMJÓLK → whole milk, EGG ANDAR → free-range eggs, HUNANG LYNGS → mountain honey, SMJÖR SÚRT → semi-salted butter, BJÖRGRAS → thyme-rosemary mixture, FJALLAPIPAR → long pepper.

ANCIENT METHOD: Direct cooking between two wrought iron plates held over the fire, turning with a horn spatula.

Secrets of the MATSTJÓRAR: Master chefs incorporated fresh snow into the dough to make it lighter, a technique learned from the Sami during trade, the runic patterns engraved on the VAFLUBERG conveyed blessings to the food according to Nordic beliefs.

Nutritional values: 280 kcal | Protein: 14g | Carbohydrates: 28g | Fat: 16g

3. MJÖÐUR KRYDDAÐR ~ Spiced rosehip mead

PRACTICAL INFORMATION: 🖼 Historical period: 8th-11th century | 🏛 Source: PROSE EDDA/BEOWULF | 🕐 Preparation time: 30 min | Cooking time: 60 min | 🜄 Calories: 180 kcal per serving | 👥 Servings: 10 people | 📓 Nutritional value: Protein: 1g / Carbohydrates: 42g / Fat: 0g | 💡 Ancient advice: Ferment in ox horns according to Odin's rites | 🔄 Modern method: Stainless steel saucepan and sterilized bottles | 💰 Estimated cost: €15.80 / £14.20 / $18.90 | 🍯 Nordic utensils: KETILL (bronze cauldron), HORN (drinking horns), linen filter | ⚙ Difficulty: Master ★★★

🏛 **MJÖÐUR KRYDDAÐR:** Odin's sacred brew mentioned in SNORRI'S EDDA, a symbol of wisdom and poetic inspiration. Consumed during blót and thing assemblies, this fermented drink was offered to honored guests in carved horns, an essential ritual of Norse hospitality and warrior oaths.

INGREDIENTS :

- 800g of HUNANG SKÓGAR (raw forest honey) | • 3 liters of UPPSPRETTA VATN (pure spring water)
- 100g SHIPAKJARNA (dried rosehip berries) | • 6 KANEL STENGUR (cinnamon sticks)
- 12 NELLIKOR (whole cloves) | • 2 MUSKATHNETUR (nutmeg)
- 1 piece of INGIFER (fresh ginger root) | • 8 EINIBER (juniper berries)
- Peel of 1 APPELSÍNA (bitter orange) | • 1 sachet of GJAR VILLT (wild yeast)

METHOD

1. **Initial preparation:** Boil the UPPSPRETTA VATN in the bronze KETILL, slowly add the HUNANG SKÓGAR, skimming regularly, maintain a gentle boil for 15 minutes to remove impurities according to the teachings of the ancient brewmasters.
2. **First cooking:** Add the crushed SHIPAKJARNA, the broken KANEL STENGUR, the NELLIKOR and the grated MUSKATHNETUR, let it infuse over low heat for 30 minutes, stirring with a consecrated ash wood spoon.
3. **Main blend:** Incorporate the peeled and sliced INGIFER, the lightly crushed EINIBER, and the APPELSÍNA bark. Maintain a temperature of 70°C for 15 minutes to extract the aromatic essences. Filter the mixture through a fine linen cloth, gently pressing the residue to recover all the juices.
4. **Final cooking:** Let the must cool to 25°C, add the GJAR VILLT diluted in a little warm must, mix gently to activate fermentation.
5. **Finishing:** Transfer to airtight fermentation containers, place in a cool (15-18°C) and dark place, leave to ferment for 4-6 weeks according to tradition.
6. **Service:** Filter one last time, serve in the sculpted HORNs at cellar temperature, accompany the toasts and ritual oaths.

🔄 **Modern Substitutes:** HUNANG SKÓGAR → untreated acacia honey, UPPSPRETTA VATN → filtered water, SHIPAKJARNA → organic rose hips, GJAR VILLT → fresh baker's yeast, EINIBER → edible juniper berries.

ANCIENT METHOD: Direct fermentation in ox horns sealed with beeswax, buried in cold earth.

Secrets of the MATSTJÓRAR: The master brewers added charred oak shavings to naturally filter and flavor the mead, a secret method passed down by the skalds, fermentation was initiated during the full moon to respect the sacred cycles of the Aesir, divine proportion of 1 volume of honey for 4 volumes of water according to the laws of Odin.

Nutritional values: 180 kcal | Protein: 1g | Carbohydrates: 42g | Fat: 0g

4. SMJÖRKRAUT ~ Butter with crushed wild herbs

PRACTICAL INFORMATION: 🖼 **Historical period:** 9th-10th century | 🏛 **Source:** LAXDÆLA SAGA/Jorvik Archaeology | 🕐 **Preparation time:** 45 min | **Cooking time:** 0 min | 🍶 **Calories:** 95 kcal per serving | 👥 **Servings:** 12 people | 🧾 **Nutritional value:** Protein: 0.5g / Carbohydrates: 1g / Fat: 10g | 💡 **Ancient advice:** Churn by hand in wooden churns according to the VÖLUR | 🔄 **Modern method:** Electric mixer and refrigerator | 💲 **Estimated cost:** €6.70 / £5.90 / $7.80 | 🍯 **Nordic utensils:** SMJÖRKERFI (wooden churn), stone mortar, flint knife | ⚙ **Difficulty:** Novice ★☆☆

🏛 **SMJÖRKRAUT:** An essential preparation of Nordic farms mentioned in LAXDÆLA SAGA, preserved in buried clay pots. Wild herbs were gathered by women according to a precise lunar calendar, each region having its specific varieties passed down from mother to daughter in the secrecy of family traditions.

INGREDIENTS :

- 400g SMJÖR FERSKUR (fresh unsalted butter) | • 30g GRÄSLAUKUR (wild chives)
- 20g of STEINSELERA (rock parsley) | • 15g of VILLIMINTA (wild mint)
- 10g BERGJÚRT (mountain oregano) | • 8g ÞÝMIÁN (moorland thyme)
- 1 tbsp. teaspoon of STEINSTEINN FÍNUR (fine rock salt) | • 1/2 tsp. teaspoon of HVÍTLAUKUR VILLT (wild garlic)
- A few drops of REGNVATN (pure rainwater) | • Pinch of PIPAR LANGUR (ground long pepper)

METHOD

1. **Initial preparation:** Remove the SMJÖR FERSKUR from the refrigerator 2 hours before use, let it soften naturally at fjord temperature. Gently wash the herbs in spring water, drain them on a linen cloth and chop them finely with a flint knife according to ancestral tradition.
2. **First cooking:** No cooking necessary, this preparation follows the cold preservation methods of Nordic farmers who thus preserved summer flavors for the long winters.
3. **Main blend:** Pound the chopped herbs in the stone mortar with the STEINSTEINN FÍNUR until you get a smooth green paste. Stir in the finely chopped HVÍTLAUKUR VILLT, add a few drops of REGNVATN to facilitate mixing and release the aromatic essences of the wild plants.
4. **Final cooking:** Vigorously mix the softened butter with the herb paste using a beechwood spatula, working until a uniform green color and creamy texture are obtained.
5. **Finishing:** Season with a pinch of PIPAR LANGUR, taste and adjust the seasoning according to your tastes, form into a roll in a damp cloth.
6. **Serving:** Refrigerate for at least 2 hours, serve sliced on warm BRAUÐ BYGGUR, accompany dishes of smoked fish and root vegetables.

🔄 **Modern Substitutes:** SMJÖR FERSKUR → unsalted farm butter, GRÄSLAUKUR → fresh chives, STEINSELERA → flat-leaf parsley, VILLIMINTA → fresh mint, BERGJÚRT → fresh oregano, HVÍTLAUKUR VILLT → fresh garlic, REGNVATN → water filtered.

ANCIENT METHOD: Hand-threshing in the wooden SMJÖRKERFI, preservation in airtight clay pots.

Secrets of the MATSTJÓRAR: The housewives added fermented milk to facilitate preservation and develop flavors, they harvested the herbs at dawn when the dew concentrated the essential oils, a method passed on by midwives during seasonal gatherings, a magical proportion of 7 different herbs to invoke the protection of the spirits of nature.

Nutritional values: 95 kcal | Protein: 0.5g | Carbohydrates: 1g | Fat: 10g

5. BRAUÐ HVÍTR KONUNGR – White bread of the Nordic kings

PRACTICAL INFORMATION: 📖 **Historical period:** 10th-11th century | 🏛 **Source:** HEIMSKRINGLA/Royal Chronicles | 🕐 **Preparation time:** 180 min | **Cooking time:** 50 min | 🔥 **Calories:** 245 kcal per serving | 👥 **Servings:** 8 people | 📋 **Nutritional value:** Protein: 8g / Carbohydrates: 48g / Fat: 4g | 💡 **Ancient advice:** Knead 1000 times according to the royal rites of the jarls | 🔄 **Modern method:** Bread machine or mechanical kneading | 🪙 **Estimated cost:** €4.20 / £3.70 / $5.10 | 🏺 **Nordic utensils:** DEIGÁLL (oak kneading trough), STEINOFN (stone oven), birch shovel | 🎛 **Difficulty:** Master ★★★

🏛 **BRAUÐ HVÍTR KONUNGR:** Prestigious bread reserved for kings and jarls mentioned in HEIMSKRINGLA during royal banquets. Its white color symbolized purity and high social rank, the flour being sifted several times by maids. Served only on special occasions: coronations, princely weddings and peace treaties between Nordic kingdoms.

INGREDIENTS :

- 600g HVEITIMJÖL FÍNUR (fine wheat flour) | • 350ml of MJÓLK HLÝR (warm milk)
- 80g SMJÖR (fresh butter) | • 60g of HUNANG (clear honey)
- 2 tsp STEINSTEINN (fine rock salt) | • 1 tbsp GJAR (fresh yeast)
- 2 EGG HÆNS (chicken eggs) | • 1 tbsp. OLÍA VALNÖT (walnut oil)
- 1 tbsp. teaspoon of KÚMEN MALAÐUR (ground cumin) | • VALMÚAFRÆ (poppy) seeds for decoration

METHOD

1. **Initial preparation:** Sift the HVEITIMJÖL FÍNUR three times through the oak DEIGÁLL according to royal tradition, creating a well in the center. Dissolve the GJAR in the MJÓLK HLÝR with a pinch of HUNANG, let it foam for 10 minutes to activate the wild ferments.
2. **First cooking:** Warm the SMJÖR without melting it, beat the EGG HÆNS with the remaining HUNANG until pale, using the techniques of royal cooks. Heat the STEINOFN with oak wood for 2 hours to obtain the ideal temperature.
3. **Main assembly:** Pour the yeast-milk mixture into the flour well, add the beaten eggs, the lukewarm SMJÖR and the OLÍA VALNÖT. Knead vigorously for 15 minutes until you obtain a smooth and elastic dough that no longer sticks to your hands. Add the STEINSTEINN and the KÚMEN MALAÐUR at the end of kneading.
4. **Final cooking:** Form a ball, place in an oiled container, cover with a damp cloth and let rise for 2 hours near the fire. Degas, shape into a round loaf, place on the baking peel, incise with runic crosses and bake in the hot STEINOFN for 50 minutes.
5. **Finishing:** Brush the surface with MJÓLK before baking, sprinkle with VALMÚAFRÆ, check for even golden browning without burning, according to the art of royal bakers.
6. **Service:** Leave to cool on a birch rack, slice at the table with an honor knife, accompany with SMJÖR and HUNANG during official feasts.

🔄 **Modern Substitutes:** HVEITIMJÖL FÍNUR → T45 flour, MJÓLK HLÝR → whole milk 37°C, GJAR → fresh baker's yeast, OLÍA VALNÖT › sunflower oil, KÚMEN MALAÐUR → cumin powder, VALMÚAFRÆ → blue poppy seeds.

ANCIENT METHOD: Kneading by hand for 1000 strokes according to the rites, directly cooked on a heated stone slab.

Secrets of the MATSTJÓRAR: The royal bakers added filtered beech ash to alkalize the dough and obtain a whiter crumb, they kneaded while reciting runic incantations to invoke the blessing of Freyja, goddess of abundance, the round shape symbolized the solar cycle and the protection of the Aesir gods against the forces of chaos.

Nutritional values: 245 kcal | Protein: 8g | Carbohydrates: 48g | Fat: 4g

6. VÍNKRYDD DULARFULLT - Mystical spiced wine with juniper

PRACTICAL INFORMATION: 📖 **Historical period:** 9th-10th century | 🏛 **Source:** VOLSUNGA SAGA/Rune codices | 🕐 **Preparation time:** 20 min | **Cooking time:** 30 min | 💧 **Calories:** 165 kcal per portion | 👥 **Servings:** 8 people | 📙 **Nutritional value:** Protein: 0.2g / Carbohydrates: 18g / Fat: 0g | 💡 **Ancient advice:** Infuse under a full moon according to the rites of the VÖLUR | 🔲 **Modern method:** Stainless steel saucepan and kitchen thermometer | ⏱ **Estimated cost:** €22.60 / £19.80 / $26.40 | 🍶 **Nordic utensils:** KETILL (bronze cauldron), HORN (drinking vessels), hemp filter | ⚙ **Difficulty:** Initiate ★★☆

🏛 **VÍNKRYDD DULARFULLT:** Ritual drink of the VÖLUR mentioned in VOLSUNGA SAGA, used during divinatory ceremonies and rites of passage. The sacred juniper trees of Yggdrasil conferred prophetic properties according to Norse beliefs, this drink was reserved for seiðr (magical practices) and consultations of the oracles in the temples dedicated to the Aesir.

INGREDIENTS :

- 750ml VÍN RAUÐR (red grape wine) | • 80g of HUNANG SKÓGAR (forest honey)
- 15 EINIBER (fresh juniper berries) | • 4 KANEL STENGUR (cinnamon sticks)
- 8 NELLIKOR (whole cloves) | • 2 STJÖRNUANÍS (star anise)
- 1 piece of INGIFER RÓT (ginger root) | • Peel of 1 SÍTRÓNA (Nordic lemon)
- 6 KORIANDERFRJÓ (coriander seeds) | • 1 LÁRVIÐR (wild bay) leaf
- Pinch of PIPAR SVARTAÐR (black pepper) | • 200ml of UPPSPRETTA VATN (pure water)

METHOD

1. **Initial preparation:** Lightly crush the EINIBER in a mortar to release their resinous essences, break the KANEL STENGUR into pieces, and gently crush the NELLIKOR. Peel and finely slice the INGIFER RÓT according to Nordic herbalist techniques.
2. **First cooking:** Heat the UPPSPRETTA VATN in the bronze KETILL, dissolve the HUNANG SKÓGAR in it while stirring with a consecrated wooden spoon, keep at a gentle simmer for 5 minutes to obtain an aromatic syrup.
3. **Main blend:** Add all the crushed spices to the hot syrup, cover, and let it infuse for 15 minutes off the heat to allow the active ingredients to be fully extracted. Then gradually add the VÍN RAUÐR, stirring gently to preserve the subtle aromas.
4. **Final cooking:** Reheat everything over very low heat without ever boiling to preserve the alcohol and delicate aromas, maintain at 70°C for 10 minutes, stirring occasionally.
5. **Finishing:** Carefully filter through a fine hemp cloth to remove all spice residue, taste and adjust the sweetness with a little HUNANG if necessary.
6. **Serving:** Serve hot in the HORNs carved during ritual ceremonies, accompanied by oatcakes and runic recitations according to the VÖLUR tradition.

🔲 **Modern Substitutes:** VÍN RAUÐR → full-bodied red wine such as Côtes du Rhône, HUNANG SKÓGAR → chestnut honey, EINIBER → edible juniper berries, INGIFER RÓT → fresh ginger, SÍTRÓNA → organic lemon, LÁRVIÐR → leaf of laurel.

ANCIENT METHOD: Direct infusion in a cauldron suspended above the embers, filtered by slow pouring.

Secrets of the MATSTJÓRAR: The VÖLUR incorporated Yggdrasil ash wood shavings to amplify the divinatory properties, the preparation was done exclusively on a clear night to capture the energy of the stars, sacred temperature maintained according to the practitioner's breathing, the proportions followed the mystical number of 9 different spices to honor the nine worlds of Nordic cosmogony.

Nutritional values: 165 kcal | Protein: 0.2g | Carbohydrates: 18g | Fat: 0g

7. ÓLÍFUR ILMANDI ~ Olives flavored with arctic herbs

PRACTICAL INFORMATION: 🖳 **Historical period:** 10th-11th century | 🏛 **Source:** Byzantine trade routes/Jorvik Codex | 🕐 **Preparation time:** 15 min | **Cooking time:** 0 min | 💧 **Calories:** 85 kcal per serving | 👥 **Servings:** 10 people | 🍴 **Nutritional value:** Protein: 1g / Carbohydrate: 2g / Fat: 8g | 💡 **Ancient advice:** Marinate in clay jars according to Byzantine traders | 🔲 **Modern method:** Sterilized jars and refrigeration | 💰 **Estimated cost:** €9.40 / £8.30 / $11.20 | 🍶 **Norse utensils:** LEIRKER (clay jars), flint knife, stone mortar | ⚙ **Difficulty:** Novice ★☆☆

🏛 **ÓLÍFUR ILMANDI:** A precious imported delicacy that arrived via Byzantine trade routes, mentioned in the accounts of Jorvik merchants. These olives, flavored with local herbs, represented luxury and an opening to the Mediterranean world, served at diplomatic receptions and trade agreements between jarls and foreign merchants.

INGREDIENTS :

- 400g ÓLÍFUR SVARTAR (black olives from Byzantium) | • 200g ÓLÍFUR GRÆNAR (imported green olives). 60ml of OLÍA ÓLÍFUR (pure olive oil) | • 2 tbsp. tablespoon of HVÍTLAUKUR (fresh garlic)
- 15g of ÞÝMIÁN FJALLA (mountain thyme) | • 10g of RÓSMARÍN VILLT (wild rosemary)
- 8 LÁRBLÖÐ (bay leaves) | • 1 tsp FENIKALFRJÓ (fennel seeds)
- Zest of 1 SÍTRÓNA (Nordic lemon) | • 1 tsp RAUÐPIPAR (crushed red pepper)
- 2 tbsp EDIKSÝRA (cider vinegar) | • 1 tsp STEINSTEINN (rock salt)

METHOD

1. **Initial preparation:** Carefully drain the ÓLÍFUR SVARTAR and GRÆNAR, rinse them with pure water to remove excess brine according to the advice of the Byzantine merchants. Finely chop the HVÍTLAUKUR with a flint knife, gently remove the zest of SÍTRÓNA without the bitter white part.
2. **First cooking:** No cooking required, this preparation follows Mediterranean preservation methods adapted to Nordic tastes by merchants established in the Baltic ports.
3. **Main assembly:** In a clay LEIRKER, gently mix the olives with the chopped HVÍTLAUKUR, add the previously dried and crumbled ÞÝMIÁN FJALLA and RÓSMARÍN VILLT. Stir in the broken LÁRBLÖÐ, the lightly crushed FENIKALFRJÓ and the finely grated SÍTRÓNA zest.
4. **Final cooking:** Drizzle with OLÍA ÓLÍFUR and EDIKSÝRA, sprinkle with STEINSTEINN and RAUÐPIPAR according to the guests' taste, mix gently with a wooden spatula to coat evenly.
5. **Finishing:** Leave to marinate in a cool place for at least 2 hours to allow the flavors to develop and the Nordic herbs to perfume the Mediterranean olives.
6. **Serving:** Serve at room temperature in clay bowls, accompanied by BRAUÐ DUR and SMJÖRKRAUT, and present at ambassador receptions.

🔲 **Modern Substitutes:** ÓLÍFUR SVARTAR → Kalamata olives, ÓLÍFUR GRÆNAR → Picholine olives, OLÍA ÓLÍFUR → extra-virgin olive oil, ÞÝMIÁN FJALLA → fresh thyme, RÓSMARÍN VILLT → fresh rosemary, EDIKSÝRA → white wine vinegar.

ANCIENT METHOD: Direct preservation in clay jars sealed with pine resin, partial burial. **Secrets of the MATSTJÓRAR:** Port cooks added dried seaweed to bring a typically Nordic salty flavor, they incorporated honey to soften the bitterness according to local tastes, a technique learned during trade with the merchants of Constantinople, the proportions respected Byzantine commercial codes while adapting to Scandinavian palates.

Nutritional values: 85 kcal | Protein: 1g | Carbohydrates: 2g | Fat: 8g

8. OSTR OK HUNANG BJALLA - Mountain Honey Cheese

PRACTICAL INFORMATION: 📰 **Historical period:** 8th-9th century | 🏛 **Source:** GRETTIS SAGA/Pastoral traditions | 🕐 **Preparation time:** 10 min | **Cooking time:** 0 min | 🔥 **Calories:** 190 kcal per portion | 👥 **Servings:** 6 people | 📖 **Nutritional value:** Protein: 12g / Carbohydrates: 8g / Fat: 13g | 💡 **Ancient advice:** Mature cheese in caves according to the FJALLMENN tradition | 🖳 **Modern method:** Cheese cellar or refrigerator | 💰 **Estimated cost:** €7.90 / £6.80 / $9.30 | 🍯 **Nordic utensils:** OSTSKÁL (cheese bowl), horn knife, beech boards | ⚙ **Difficulty:** Novice ★☆☆

🏛 **OSTR OK HUNANG BJALLA:** A specialty of mountain shepherds mentioned in GRETTIS SAGA, a symbol of hospitality in the isolated farms of the fjells. The cheese aged in natural caves developed unique flavors, the mountain honey was harvested by the FJALLMENN during the summer transhumance, this alliance represented the harmony between livestock farming and wild Nordic beekeeping.

INGREDIENTS :

- 300g of GAMALOSTR (aged hard cheese) | • 150g of HUNANG BJALLA (crystallized mountain honey)
- 60g of VALNETUR (fresh crushed walnuts) | • 30g ÞURRKAÐR RÚSÍNUR (raisins)
- 2 tbsp MJÓLK FERSKUR (fresh milk) | • 1 tsp KANELDUFT (ground cinnamon)
- A few leaves of MINTA FJALLA (mountain mint) | • Pinch of STEINSTEINN (fine salt)
- 1 tbsp SMJÖRSKINN (thick cream) | • RÚGBRAUÐ (rye bread) to accompany

METHOD

1. **Initial preparation:** Remove the GAMALOSTR from the refrigerator 1 hour before use to allow it to soften naturally, then grate it coarsely or cut it into small cubes depending on the desired texture. Lightly crush the VALNETUR to preserve their crunchiness, then finely chop the MINTA FJALLA using shepherds' techniques.

2. **First cooking:** No cooking necessary, this preparation respects the methods of natural preservation of dairy products in the northern mountain pastures where the natural cold preserved the food.

3. **Main assembly:** In the wooden OSTSKÁL, gently mix the grated cheese with the slightly softened HUNANG BJALLA, add a pinch of STEINSTEINN to enhance the flavors. Stir in the ÞURRKAÐR RÚSÍNUR previously soaked in the warm MJÓLK FERSKUR for 10 minutes.

4. **Final cooking:** Add the SMJÖRSKINN to obtain a creamy consistency, sprinkle with KANELDUFT and mix until perfectly homogeneous without crushing the pieces of cheese.

5. **Finishing:** Garnish with crushed VALNETUR and chopped MINTA FJALLA leaves, leave to stand for 30 minutes so that the flavors blend harmoniously.

6. **Service:** Serve in wooden bowls with sliced RÚGBRAUÐ, accompanied by MJÖÐUR or fermented milk according to pastoral tradition.

🖳 **Modern Substitutes:** GAMALOSTR → aged comté or gruyere, HUNANG BJALLA → mountain honey, VALNETUR → walnut kernels, ÞURRKAÐR RÚSÍNUR → currants, SMJÖRSKINN → thick crème fraîche, MINTA FJALLA → fresh mint.

ANCIENT METHOD: Direct mixing by hand in horn bowls, preservation in cool caves.

Secrets of the MATSTJÓRAR: The shepherds added fermented whey to develop the acidity and balance the sweetness of the honey, they incorporated different herbs depending on the altitude and the harvest season, a method passed down by the elders during transhumance gatherings, the proportion respected the sacred balance between the gifts of the earth (honey) and the cattle (cheese) according to the beliefs of the LANDVÆTTIR (earth spirits).

Nutritional values: 190 kcal | Protein: 12g | Carbohydrates: 8g | Fat: 13g

9. FISKISÓSA GÖMUL – Ancient fermented fish sauce

PRACTICAL INFORMATION: 📖 **Historical period:** 8th-11th century | 🏛 **Source:** ORKNEYINGA SAGA/Archaeology Lofoten | 🕐 **Preparation time:** 30 min | **Cooking time:** 0 min (fermentation 6 months) | 💧 **Calories:** 15 kcal per portion | 🍴 **Servings:** 50 guests | 📋 **Nutritional value:** Protein: 3g / Carbohydrates: 1g / Fat: 0g | 💡 **Ancient advice:** Ferment in airtight jars according to Lofoten fishermen | 🔁 **Modern method:** Sterilized jars and cool cellar | 💰 **Estimated cost:** €8.50 / £7.40 / $10.10 | 🏺 **Nordic utensils:** LEIRKER (clay jars), wooden press, hemp filter | ⚙️ **Difficulty:** Master ★★★

🏛 **FISKISÓSA GÖMUL:** Essential condiment for fishermen mentioned in ORKNEYINGA SAGA, the basis of the Nordic coastal diet. This fermented sauce concentrated the marine proteins necessary for the long winters, each fishing family jealously guarded its ancestral recipe passed down from generation to generation, the jars were marked with protective runes to ward off evil spirits.

INGREDIENTS :

- 2kg of SMÁFISKUR (small whole fish) | • 400g of STEINSTEINN GRÓFUR (coarse sea salt)
- 200g of RÆKJUR (whole shrimp) | • 100g of KRABBASKINN (crab shells)
- 50g of ÞANGAR (dried seaweed) | • 30g of HVÍTLAUKUR (wild garlic)
- 20g of INGIFER (fresh ginger) | • 15g of EINIBER (juniper berries)
- 10g LÁRBLÖÐ (bay leaves) | • 1 liter of UPPSPRETTA VATN (spring water)
- 5g of ÞÝMÍAN (wild thyme) | • Pinch of RAUÐPIPAR (red pepper)

METHOD

1. **Initial preparation:** Carefully clean the SMÁFISKUR without peeling them, retaining the heads and bones to maximize the flavors. Roughly crush the KRABBASKINN and RÆKJUR in a stone mortar, and finely chop the HVÍTLAUKUR and INGIFER using coastal canner techniques.
2. **First cooking:** No cooking, this ancestral process is based entirely on natural lactic fermentation which transforms proteins into concentrated amino acids, a method developed for the need for conservation in the Nordic regions.
3. **Main assembly:** In a clay LEIRKER, arrange the fish in alternating layers with the STEINSTEINN GRÓFUR, crushed shellfish, and aromatic herbs. Add the rehydrated ÞANGAR, HVÍTLAUKUR, and INGIFER, pressing each layer firmly to remove air and promote anaerobic fermentation.
4. **Final cooking:** Cover with salted UPPSPRETTA VATN, place a clean stone weight to maintain total immersion, close the jar tightly with a clay lid sealed with moist clay.
5. **Finishing:** Leave to ferment for 6 months in a cool, dark place, check regularly that the brine level remains constant, gently filter the amber liquid obtained.
6. **Serving:** Dilute with water to desired strength, use as a universal seasoning for meats, vegetables and grains, store in small sealed jars.

🔁 **Modern Substitutes:** SMÁFISKUR → fresh anchovies, STEINSTEINN GRÓFUR → coarse sea salt, ÞANGAR → kombu seaweed, replace with artisanal nuoc-mam for immediate use.

ANCIENT METHOD: Direct fermentation in rock pits lined with clay, pressing by stacked stones.

Secrets of the MATSTJÓRAR: Master preservers added whale blood to accelerate fermentation and enrich the umami taste, they buried the jars in the beach sand to maintain a constant temperature, secret formulas included precise proportions of salt according to the lunar phases, each family marked their jars with personal runes to identify their production and invoke the protection of Ægir, god of the oceans.

Nutritional values: 15 kcal | Protein: 3g | Carbohydrates: 1g | Fat: 0g

10. VÍNFISKISÓSA – Wine and fish sauce

PRACTICAL INFORMATION: 📖 **Historical period:** 10th-11th century | 🏛 **Source:** Trade routes/Codex Hedeby | ⏱ **Preparation time:** 15 min | **Cooking time:** 25 min | 💧 **Calories:** 25 kcal per serving | 👥 **Servings:** 20 people | 📋 **Nutritional value:** Protein: 2g / Carbohydrates: 3g / Fat: 0g | 💡 **Ancient advice:** Reduce over low heat according to Rhine merchants | 🖸 **Modern method:** Stainless steel saucepan and controlled reduction | 💰 **Estimated cost:** €11.20 / £9.90 / $13.40 | 🏺 **Nordic utensils:** KETILL (bronze cauldron), wooden ladle, linen filter | ⚙ **Difficulty:** Beginner ★★☆

🏛 **VÍNFISKISÓSA:** A sophisticated condiment developed by merchants on trade routes, a fusion of traditional FISKISÓSA and imported wines. Mentioned in the Hedeby codices as a symbol of the culinary refinement of the merchant classes, this sauce represented the Nordic adaptation of Mediterranean influences, served at trade banquets and diplomatic agreements.

INGREDIENTS :

- 300ml FISKISÓSA GÖMUL (fermented fish sauce) | • 400ml of VÍN RAUÐR (full-bodied red wine) / 60g of HUNANG (forest honey) | • 2 tbsp. tablespoon of EDIKSÝRA (cider vinegar)
- 30g HVÍTLAUKUR (chopped fresh garlic) | • 15g of RÓSMARÍN (fresh rosemary)
- 10g of ÞÝMIÁN (wild thyme) | • 6 LÁRBLÖÐ (bay leaves)
- 1 tsp PIPAR SVARTAÐR (crushed black pepper) | • 2 tbsp OLÍA (walnut oil)
- 1 LAUKUR (chopped sweet onion) | • Pinch of STEINSTEINN (fine salt)

METHOD

1. **Initial preparation:** Finely chop the HVÍTLAUKUR and LAUKUR with an iron knife, crumble the RÓSMARÍN and ÞÝMÍAN between your fingers to release their essential oils. Lightly crush the PIPAR SVARTAÐR in a mortar using Nordic grocers' techniques.
2. **First cooking:** Heat the OLÍA in the bronze KETILL, brown the HVÍTLAUKUR and LAUKUR over low heat until transparent without coloring, add the aromatic herbs and let infuse for 2 minutes to develop the aromas.
3. **Main blend:** Pour in the VÍN RAUÐR, bring to a boil, then reduce the heat and let it reduce by half to concentrate the flavors and eliminate the alcohol. Gradually add the FISKISÓSA GÖMUL, stirring constantly with a wooden ladle to prevent the liquids from separating.
4. **Final cooking:** Add the HUNANG and EDIKSÝRA, maintain a gentle simmer for 15 minutes, skimming regularly, taste and adjust the sweet and sour balance according to the table's tastes.
5. **Finishing:** Gently strain through a linen cloth to obtain a smooth and homogeneous sauce, correct the seasoning with a pinch of STEINSTEINN if necessary.
6. **Serving:** Serve warm in a clay gravy boat with roast meats and grilled vegetables, keep refrigerated for a maximum of 1 week in sealed jars.

🖸 **Modern Substitutes:** FISKISÓSA GÖMUL → quality nuoc-mam, VÍN RAUÐR → tannic red wine, EDIKSÝRA → red wine vinegar, OLÍA → light olive oil, substitute with Worcestershire sauce for a quick approximation.

ANCIENT METHOD: Direct reduction in a suspended cauldron, filtering by slow decantation in jars.

Secrets of the MATSTJÓRAR: The merchants' cooks added charred oak shavings to filter and flavor naturally, they incorporated wild grape verjuice to acidify without vinegar, a technique learned from Rhine merchants at trade fairs, the reduction followed the rhythm of the tides to respect natural cycles according to the beliefs of the sea peoples, secret proportion of 1/3 wine to 2/3 fish sauce to balance Nordic and Mediterranean flavors.

Nutritional values: 25 kcal | Protein: 2g | Carbohydrates: 3g | Fat: 0g

11. SALTLEGI SÝRÐ ~ Tangy Juniper Brine

PRACTICAL INFORMATION: 🎞 Historical period: 8th-10th century | 🏛 Source: Salting traditions/LANDNÁMABÓK | 🕐 Preparation time: 20 min | Cooking time: 15 min | 🌢 Calories: 5 kcal per portion | 🐾 Servings: 40 people | 📋 Nutritional value: Protein: 0g / Carbohydrates: 1g / Fat: 0g | 💡 Ancient advice: Store in clay jars according to LANDNÁMSMENN | 🔄 Modern method: Airtight jars and sterilization | 💰 Estimated cost: €3.80 / £3.30 / $4.50 | 🍶 Nordic utensils: KETILL (cauldron), LEIRKER (jars), wicker strainer | ⚙ Difficulty: Novice ★☆☆

🏛 **SALTLEGI SÝRÐ:** Preserving brine mentioned in LANDNÁMABÓK, essential for preserving vegetables and meat during the long Icelandic winters. The LANDNÁMSMENN (first settlers) developed this technique adapted to local resources, Icelandic junipers conferring natural antiseptic properties, this preparation was considered a family treasure kept preciously on isolated farms.

INGREDIENTS :

- 1.5 liters of UPPSPRETTA VATN (pure spring water) | • 300g of STEINSTEINN (pure rock salt)
- 100ml EDIKSÝRA EPLI (apple vinegar) | • 40g of EINIBER (juniper berries)
- 20g of DILL FRÆ (wild dill seeds) | • 15g of KORIANDERFRJÓ (coriander seeds)
- 10 LÁRBLÖÐ (bay leaves) | • 8g of HVÍTLAUKUR (wild garlic)
- 6g of RAUÐPIPAR (red pepper) | • 1 piece of INGIFER (fresh ginger)
- 4 NELLIKOR (cloves) | • 2 tbsp HUNANG (heather honey)

METHOD

1. **Initial preparation:** Lightly crush the EINIBER in a mortar to release their resinous oils without reducing them to powder, gently crush the DILL FRÆ and KORIANDERFRJÓ. Finely chop the HVÍTLAUKUR and mince the INGIFER according to Nordic preservation techniques.
2. **First cooking:** Bring the UPPSPRETTA VATN to a boil in the KETILL, gradually dissolve the STEINSTEINN in it, stirring with a wooden spoon until completely dissolved, carefully skim off any impurities that rise to the surface.
3. **Main blend:** Add all the crushed spices, HVÍTLAUKUR, INGIFER and LÁRBLÖÐ to the boiling brine, reduce the heat and let it infuse for 10 minutes to extract all the active and aromatic ingredients of the Nordic plants.
4. **Final cooking:** Stir in the EDIKSÝRA EPLI and HUNANG, maintain a gentle simmer for another 5 minutes, taste and adjust the salt-acid balance according to the intended use.
5. **Finishing:** Strain the hot brine through a wicker strainer lined with fine linen, let cool completely before use to allow the flavors to stabilize.
6. **Service:** Use for preserving root vegetables, cabbage and meat, pour cold into the LEIRKER with the food to be preserved, keep submerged under weight.

🔄 **Modern Substitutes:** STEINSTEINN → unrefined sea salt, EDIKSÝRA EPLI → organic apple cider vinegar, EINIBER → edible juniper berries, DILL FRÆ → dill seeds, HVÍTLAUKUR → fresh garlic, INGIFER → organic ginger.

ANCIENT METHOD: Direct cooking in a bronze cauldron, preservation in buried watertight jars.

Secrets of the MATSTJÓRAR: Experienced preservers added birch bark for its antiseptic tannins, they respected lunar proportions to optimize fermentation, a technique inherited from the VÖLUR who knew the magical properties of plants, the brine was blessed by runic incantations to ensure perfect preservation throughout the winter, sacred concentration of 20% salt to block the evil spirits of putrefaction according to Nordic beliefs.

Nutritional values: 5 kcal | Protein: 0g | Carbohydrates: 1g | Fat: 0g

12. VÍNSTRÚP ~ Nordic Concentrated Grape Syrup

PRACTICAL INFORMATION: 📖 **Historical period:** 8th-11th century | 🏛 **Source:** SAGAS/Archaeology of trading posts | 🕐 **Preparation time:** 45 min | **Cooking time:** 180 min | 💧 **Calories:** 285 kcal per serving | 👥 **Servings:** 8 people | 📋 **Nutritional value:** Protein: 0.8g / Carbohydrates: 71.2g / Fat: 0.1g | 💡 **Ancient advice:** Jarls stored this syrup in stone jars for long journeys | 🖵 **Modern method:** Cooking over a controlled low heat replaces birch fire | 🪙 **Estimated cost:** €12.50 / £11.00 / $14.00 | 🏺 **Nordic utensils:** iron KETILL, ash spoons, clay jars | ⚙️ **Difficulty:** Initiate ★★☆

🏛 **VÍNSTRÚP** : This sacred syrup was prepared by the jarls' MATSTJÓRAR (master chefs) during the great autumn festivals. Mentioned in SNORRI'S SAGA as "the golden nectar of the gods," it was used to sweeten mead and accompanied roast meats at seasonal blót. Viking traders traded it for oriental spices at the trading posts of Constantinople. Its preparation required grapes imported from Frankish lands, a marker of high social rank.

INGREDIENTS :

- 2 kg of VÍNBER SVARTAR (black Burgundy grapes)
- 500 ml of HUNANGVATN (pure honey water)
- 1 spoon of SALT HAFIÐ (fjord sea salt)
- 3 sprigs of TIMIAN VILLR (wild mountain thyme)
- 1 bark of EINIBER (dried arctic juniper)

METHOD

1. **Initial preparation:** Crush the VÍNBER in a stone mortar until smooth, keeping some skins for color. Coarsely strain through a linen cloth to separate the seeds.
2. **First cooking:** Pour the juice into an iron KETILL and bring to a gentle boil over birch embers. Continue cooking steadily for 90 minutes, regularly skimming the surface.
3. **Main assembly:** Stir in the warmed HUNANGVATN and SALT HAFIÐ. Add the TIMIAN VILLR and EINIBER bark tied in a cloth bag. Continue cooking for another 60 minutes, stirring with an ash spoon.
4. **Final cooking:** Reduce the heat and let it concentrate for 30 minutes until a drop poured onto a cold stone no longer runs.
5. **Finishing:** Remove the herbs and pour the boiling syrup into previously heated clay jars.
6. **Serving:** Serve warm as an accompaniment to grilled meats or to sweeten mead at feasts.

🖵 **Modern Substitutes:** VÍNBER SVARTAR → currants + black grapes, HUNANGVATN → water + acacia honey, TIMIAN VILLR → Provence thyme, EINIBER → dried juniper berries

ANCIENT METHOD: Cooking in cauldrons suspended above hollowed-out hearths, with hot stones to maintain a constant temperature.

Secrets of the MATSTJÓRAR: The perfect color is achieved by adding a handful of black grape skins during the last 30 minutes. Skalds recommend testing the consistency by pouring a drop onto a cooled sword blade.

Nutritional values: 285 kcal | Protein: 0.8g | Carbohydrates: 71.2g | Fat: 0.1g

AXIS 2: SÚPUR OK SOÐIR - *The Soups and Broths of Valhalla The Soups and Broths of Valhalla*

Hearty Soups (6 recipes), Medicinal Broths (4 recipes)

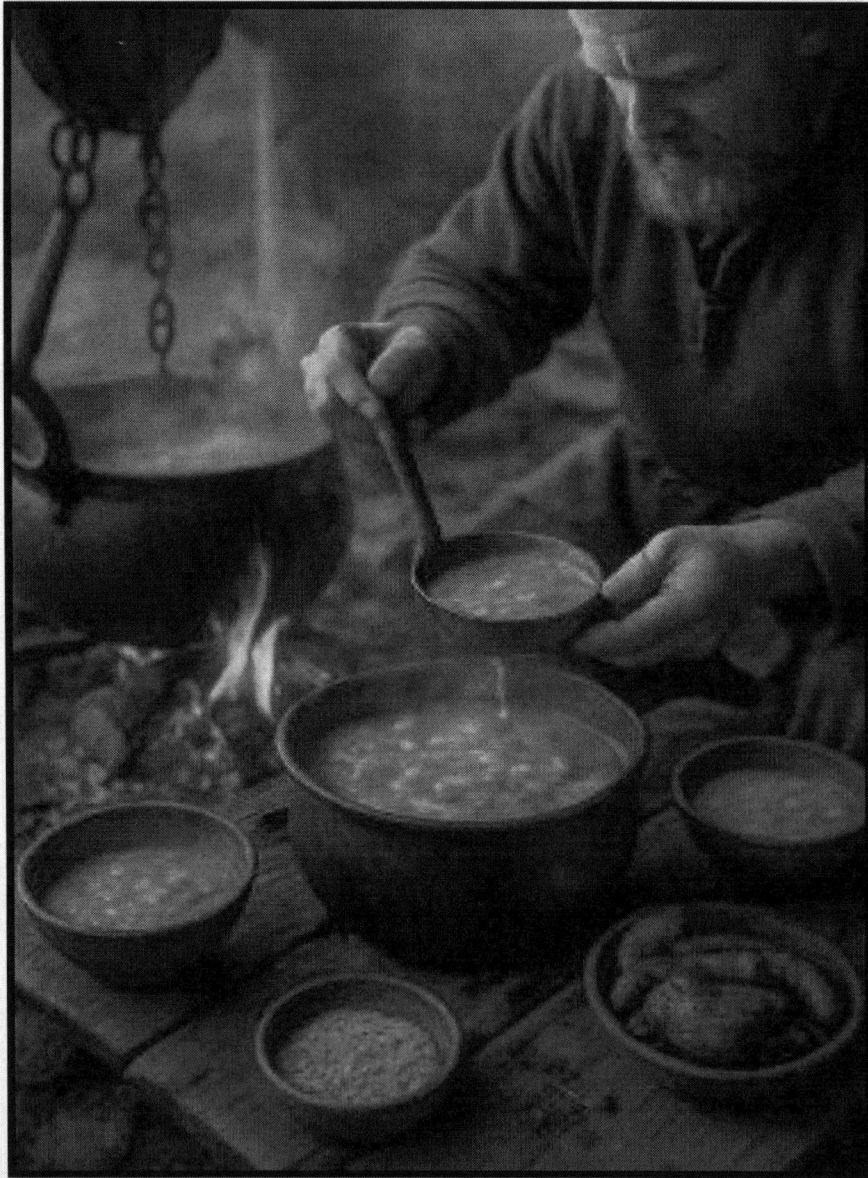

13. GRJÓNAGRAUTR STÓRKOSTLEGR ~ Noble Porridge with Root Vegetables

PRACTICAL INFORMATION: 📖 Historical period: 8th-11th century | 🏛 Source: EDDA/Birka excavations | 🕐 Preparation time: 25 min | **Cooking time:** 90 min | 🜄 Calories: 320 kcal per serving | 👭 Servings: 6 people | 🗒 Nutritional value: Protein: 8.5g / Carbohydrates: 58.2g / Fat: 7.8g | 💡 Ancient advice: Dish prepared before raids to feed warriors | 🔄 Modern method: Blender replaces stone pestle for roots | 🍶 Estimated cost: €8.75 / £7.50 / $9.25 | 🏺 Nordic utensils: Deep KETILL, carved spoons, mortar | ⚙ Difficulty: Novice ★☆☆

🏛 **GRJÓNAGRAUTR STÓRKOSTLEGR** : This porridge was the staple food of Viking warriors before expeditions. VÖLUR (midwives) added medicinal herbs according to the lunar phases. Documented in the Hedeby excavations, it was served in ash wood bowls at winter assemblies. Its nutritional richness sustained sailors during the long voyages to Iceland and Greenland.

INGREDIENTS :

- 300g of GRJÓN HAFRI (Nordic oat flakes)
- 1.2L of MJÓLK GEITA (fresh goat's milk)
- 2 RÓFUR STÓRAR (large fjord turnips)
- 3 GULRÓT (wild carrots)
- 1 LAUKR (marsh onion)
- 50g of SMJÖR (sour milk butter)
- SALT HAFIÐ to taste

METHOD

1. **Initial preparation:** Peel and cut the RÓFUR and GULRÓT into small cubes. Finely slice the LAUKR. Fry in the melted SMJÖR until golden brown.
2. **First cooking:** Bring the MJÓLK GEITA to a boil in an iron KETILL. Gradually add the GRJÓN HAFRI, stirring constantly with an ash spoon.
3. **Main assembly:** Add the sautéed vegetables to the oatmeal porridge. Season with salt and cook gently for 45 minutes. Stir regularly to prevent them from sticking to the bottom of the pot.
4. **Final Cooking:** Reduce heat and simmer for an additional 30 minutes until creamy and smooth.
5. **Finishing:** Adjust the seasoning and add a knob of fresh SMJÖR off the heat.
6. **Serving:** Serve steaming hot in wooden bowls with black bread and goat cheese.

🔄 **Modern Substitutes:** MJÓLK GEITA → whole milk + cream, RÓFUR → turnips + rutabaga, SMJÖR → farmhouse butter, GRJÓN HAFRI → organic oat flakes

ANCIENT METHOD: Slow cooking in hanging pots, stirring with birch wood spatulas engraved with protective runes.

Secrets of the MATSTJÓRAR: Adding a pinch of ash wood ash gave a sought-after umami flavor. Jarls requested that GRAVLAKS dice be incorporated to mark their rank.

Nutritional values: 320 kcal | Protein: 8.5g | Carbohydrates: 58.2g | Fat: 7.8g

14. KJÖTSÚPA KRYDDKJÖT ~ Meat Broth with Boreal Spices

PRACTICAL INFORMATION: 🎞 **Historical period:** 9th-11th century | 🏛 **Source:** SAGAS/Trondheim Archaeological Sites | ⏱ **Preparation time:** 40 min | **Cooking time:** 240 min | 🜂 **Calories:** 285 kcal per serving | 👥 **Servings:** 8 people | 🍽 **Nutritional value:** Protein: 28.5g / Carbohydrates: 12.8g / Fat: 15.2g | ♀ **Ancient advice:** Broth prepared during Odin's blót to purify the spirit | 🔲 **Modern method:** Pressure cooker cuts cooking time in half | 🜚 **Estimated cost:** €15.25 / £13.75 / $16.50 | 🜛 **Nordic utensils:** Large KETILL, horn skimmer, horsehair sieve | ⚙ **Difficulty:** Initiated ★★☆

🏛 **KJÖTSÚPA KRYDDKJÖT** : Ritual broth served during large assemblies (THING) and religious festivals. The bones were broken according to a precise protocol to release the animal's vital essence. Mentioned in the SAGA OF NJÁLL as a remedy for winter ailments, it was enriched with spices brought back from eastern expeditions via the Volga route.

INGREDIENTS :

- 1.5 kg of NAUT bones (beef with marrow)
- 800g KJÖT LAMB (lamb shoulder)
- 2 LAUKAR STÓRIR (large leeks)
- 1 STIKA SELLERI (wild celery stalk)
- 5 grains of PIPAR SVARTR (black pepper)
- 3 EINIBER berries (Arctic juniper)
- 1 leaf of LÁRVIÐR (fjord laurel)
- HAFIÐ SALT and fresh herbs

METHOD

1. **Initial preparation:** Grill the bones in a STEINOFN until brown. Cut the KJÖT LAMB into regular pieces and sear them in a KETILL with a little fat.
2. **First cooking:** Cover with cold water and slowly bring to a boil. Skim carefully for the first 30 minutes with a horn-shaped skimmer.
3. **Main assembly:** Add the sliced LAUKAR, SELLERI, PIPAR SVARTR and EINIBER spices, and LÁRVIÐR. Maintain a constant simmer for 3 hours, topping up the water if necessary.
4. **Final cooking:** Strain the broth through a horsehair sieve. Adjust the seasoning with SALT HAFIÐ.
5. **Finishing:** Skim off any grease on the surface and stir in the finely chopped fresh herbs.
6. **Serving:** Serve piping hot with shredded meat and toasted barley bread.

🔲 **Modern Substitutes:** NAUT → beef bone marrow, LÁRVIÐR → Mediterranean bay leaf, SELLERI → celery, EINIBER → dried juniper berries

ANCIENT METHOD: Cooking in pits lined with hot stones, with the gradual addition of red-hot stones to maintain the temperature.

Secrets of the MATSTJÓRAR: Adding a spoonful of FISKISÓSA in the last few minutes gave a delicious depth. Soothsayers read the bubbles on the surface to predict the outcome of battles.

Nutritional values: 285 kcal | Protein: 28.5g | Carbohydrates: 12.8g | Fat: 15.2g

15. BYGGGRAUTR LÆKNINGR ~ Therapeutic Barley Soup

PRACTICAL INFORMATION: 📅 **Historical period:** 8th-10th century | 🏛 **Source:** VÖLUR manuscripts/Medical archaeology | 🕐 **Preparation time:** 30 min | **Cooking time:** 120 min | 🍲 **Calories:** 245 kcal per serving | 👥 **Servings:** 4 people | 🍴 **Nutritional value:** Protein: 7.2g / Carbohydrates: 48.5g / Fat: 3.8g | 💡 **Ancient advice:** Prescribed by healers for convalescents after battle | 🔄 **Modern method:** Pre-soaking reduces cooking time | 💰 **Estimated cost:** €6.25 / £5.50 / $7.00 | 🍶 **Nordic Utensils:** Medium KETILL, Birch Ladle, Healing Bowl | ⚙️ **Difficulty:** Novice ★☆☆

🏛 **BYGGGRAUTR LÆKNINGR** : Medicinal soup of the VÖLUR (healers) prescribed to wounded warriors and women in childbirth. Barley was considered a sacred grain dedicated to Frigg, the protective goddess of the home. The herbs added varied according to the symptoms to be treated, forming a true Nordic pharmaco-alimentary documented in runic healing texts.

INGREDIENTS :

- 200g BYGG PERLAÐ (Nordic pearl barley)
- 1L of KJÚKLINGASÚPA (chicken broth)
- 2 GULRÓT (peat carrots)
- 1 LAUKR LILLR (small onion)
- 3 sprigs of DILL VILLR (wild dill)
- 2 leaves of SALVÍA (common sage)
- 1 spoon of HUNANG (heather honey)
- SALT HAFIÐ and PIPAR HVÍTR

METHOD

1. **Initial preparation:** Rinse the BYGG PERLAÐ in cold water until it runs clear. Finely slice the GULRÓT and mince the LAUKR LILLR.
2. **First cooking:** Sauté the vegetables in a little fat until tender. Add the barley and cook for a few minutes.
3. **Main assembly:** Pour in the boiling KJÚKLINGASÚPA and maintain a steady simmer for 90 minutes. The barley should become tender and the broth slightly thickened.
4. **Final cooking:** Stir in the Dill Villr and chopped Salvia leaves. Cook for another 15 minutes.
5. **Finishing:** Sweeten with HUNANG and season with SALT HAFIÐ and PIPAR HVÍTR to taste.
6. **Serving:** Serve warm in wooden bowls with an oatcake and cottage cheese.

🔄 **Modern Substitutes:** BYGG PERLAÐ → organic pearl barley, KJÚKLINGASÚPA → chicken broth, DILL VILLR → fresh dill, SALVÍA → fresh sage

ANCIENT METHOD: Slow cooking in terracotta pots buried near the hearths, with constant monitoring of the VÖLUR.

Secrets of the MATSTJÓRAR: Adding a pinch of ground bone powder gave it fortifying properties. The healers chanted galdr (incantations) during the cooking to enhance the therapeutic effect.

Nutritional values: 245 kcal | Protein: 7.2g | Carbohydrates: 48.5g | Fat: 3.8g

16. LINSUBAUNIR KORIANDER ~ Lentils with Wild Coriander

PRACTICAL INFORMATION: 📖 **Historical period:** 9th-11th century | 🏛 **Source:** SAGAS/Eastern Trade Routes | ⏱ **Preparation time:** 20 min | **Cooking time:** 75 min | 🜄 **Calories:** 298 kcal per serving | 👥 **Servings:** 6 people | 📋 **Nutritional value:** Protein: 18.5g / Carbohydrates: 42.8g / Fat: 4.2g | 💡 **Ancient advice:** Dish of merchants on the road to Byzantium | 🖳 **Modern method:** Pressure cooker allows rapid cooking without soaking | 🝙 **Estimated cost:** €7.50 / £6.75 / $8.25 | 🝙 **Nordic utensils:** Medium cauldron, wicker strainer, bowl | ⚙ **Difficulty:** Novice ★☆☆

🏛 **LINSUBAUNIR KORIANDER** : Imported by Viking traders via Constantinople and Kiev, lentils were a luxury appreciated by the jarls. Coriander arrived from the Black Sea trading posts, testifying to the extent of the Nordic trade network. This dish symbolized cultural openness and enrichment through trade, often served when welcoming foreign delegations.

INGREDIENTS :

- 300g LINSUBAUNIR RAUÐAR (red lentils)
- 1.2L of GRÆNMETISRÚPA (vegetable broth)
- 1 LAUKR MEÐAL (medium onion)
- 2 hvítlaukstennur (garlic cloves)
- 1 spoon of KORIANDER MALAÐR (ground coriander)
- 2 TÓMATAR (dried tomatoes)
- 3 spoons of ÓLÍFUOLÍA (olive oil)
- SALT HAFIÐ and PIPAR RAUÐR

METHOD

1. **Initial preparation:** Rinse the LINSUBAUNIR in cold water and drain. Finely slice the LAUKR and chop the garlic. Rehydrate the TÓMATAR in warm water.
2. **First cooking:** Heat the ÓLÍFUOLÍA in a pot and fry the LAUKR until transparent. Add the garlic and KORIANDER, cook for 2 minutes.
3. **Main assembly:** Stir in the drained and chopped lentils and tomato. Pour in the boiling GRÆNMETISRÚPA and bring to a boil. Reduce heat and simmer for 45 minutes, stirring occasionally.
4. **Final cooking:** Continue cooking for 15 minutes until the lentils break down slightly and the broth thickens.
5. **Finishing:** Season with SALT HAFIÐ and PIPAR RAUÐR. Adjust the consistency with stock if necessary.
6. **Serving:** Serve hot with rye pancakes and aged sheep's milk cheese.

🖳 **Modern Substitutes:** LINSUBAUNIR RAUÐAR → coral lentils, GRÆNMETISRÚPA → organic vegetable broth, TÓMATAR → sun-dried tomatoes, ÓLÍFUOLÍA → first-pressed olive oil

ANCIENT METHOD: Cooking in sealed earthenware jars, buried in hot ash for several hours.

Secrets of MATSTJÓRAR: Adding a spoonful of VÍNSTRÚP at the end of cooking brought a welcome sweet note. The spices were dry-roasted before use to reveal their aromas.

Nutritional values: 298 kcal | Protein: 18.5g | Carbohydrates: 42.8g | Fat: 4.2g

17. MJÓLKGRAUTR RÍKR - Noble Oatmeal with Goat's Milk

PRACTICAL INFORMATION: 🗓 **Historical period:** 8th-11th century | 🏛 **Source:** EDDA/Nordic pastoral traditions | 🕐 **Preparation time:** 15 min | **Cooking time:** 45 min | 🔥 **Calories:** 385 kcal per serving | 👥 **Servings:** 4 people | 📋 **Nutritional value:** Protein: 12.8g / Carbohydrates: 52.5g / Fat: 14.2g | 💡 **Ancient advice:** Dish of jarls' children to strengthen their growth | 🔄 **Modern method:** Cooking in a bain-marie avoids lumps | 🍶 **Estimated cost:** €9.75 / £8.50 / $10.25 | 🏺 **Nordic utensils:** KETILL with a thick base, whisk made of birch twigs | ⚙ **Difficulty:** Novice ★☆☆

🏛 **MJÓLKGRAUTR RÍKR** : Oatmeal reserved for the Nordic social elite, prepared with the milk of mountain goats. Jarls' children consumed it daily to ensure their physical and intellectual development. Enriched with rare honey and imported dried fruits, it demonstrated family status and prepared future leaders for the responsibilities of rank.

INGREDIENTS :

- 200g of HAFRI FÍNR (fine oat flakes)
- 800ml MJÓLK GEITA (fresh goat's milk)
- 200ml of RJÓMI (thick cream)
- 3 spoons of HUNANG LYNGS (heather honey)
- 1 handful of RÚSÍNUR (raisins)
- 6 HNETUNÓTUR (crushed walnuts)
- 1 pinch of SALT HAFIÐ
- Cinnamon and Vanilla if available

METHOD

1. **Initial preparation:** Soak the RÚSÍNUR in lukewarm water. Bring the MJÓLK GEITA to a simmer in a heavy-bottomed KETILL.
2. **First cooking:** Gradually incorporate the HAFRI FÍNR, whisking constantly with birch twigs to avoid the formation of lumps.
3. **Main assembly:** Add the RJÓMI and cook gently for 25 minutes, stirring frequently. Stir in the drained RÚSÍNUR and the HUNANG LYNGS.
4. **Final cooking:** Continue cooking for 10 minutes until creamy and smooth.
5. **Finishing:** Add the crushed HNETUNÓTUR and a pinch of SALT HAFIÐ to enhance the flavors.
6. **Serving:** Serve immediately in carved bowls, sprinkled with cinnamon if available.

🔄 **Modern Substitutes:** MJÓLK GEITA → whole milk + goat's milk, RJÓMI → thick crème fraîche, HUNANG LYNGS → mountain honey, HNETUNÓTUR → walnuts

ANCIENT METHOD: Cooking in hanging bronze cauldrons, stirring constantly with cherry wood spatulas engraved with prosperity runes.

Secrets of the MATSTJÓRAR: Adding a spoonful of salted SMJÖR at the end of cooking created a silky texture. Nobles sometimes incorporated oriental spices brought back from Byzantium.

Nutritional values: 385 kcal | Protein: 12.8g | Carbohydrates: 52.5g | Fat: 14.2g

18. BAUNASÚPA FISKISÓSA ~ Bean Soup with FISKISÓSA

PRACTICAL INFORMATION: 🎞 **Historical period:** 9th-11th century | 🏛 **Source:** SAGAS/Nordic monastic traditions | 🕐 **Preparation time:** 35 min | **Cooking time:** 150 min | 🝆 **Calories:** 265 kcal per serving | 👥 **Servings:** 6 people | 📋 **Nutritional value:** Protein: 16.8g / Carbohydrates: 38.5g / Fat: 5.2g | 💡 **Ancient advice:** Dish of Christian monks adapting pagan traditions | 🔄 **Modern method:** Overnight soaking speeds up the cooking of legumes | ⑤ **Estimated cost:** €8.25 / £7.25 / $9.00 | 🥄 **Nordic utensils:** Large KETILL, skimmer, monastic bowls | ⚙ **Difficulty:** Beginner ★★☆

🏛 **BAUNASÚPA FISKISÓSA** : A Christian adaptation of pagan culinary traditions, this soup was prepared in monasteries established in Nordic lands. FISKISÓSA replaced animal fat during periods of fasting, creating a bridge between ancestral practices and the new faith. Irish monks settled in Iceland developed this recipe to feed pilgrims and converts.

INGREDIENTS :
- 400g of BAUNIR HVÍTAR (dried white beans)
- 1.5L of GRÆNMETISRÚPA (vegetable broth)
- 2 LAUKAR (marsh leeks)
- 1 SELLERIROT (celery root)
- 3 spoons of FISKISÓSA (fermented fish sauce)
- 2 LÁRVIÐRBLÖÐ (bay leaves)
- 1 bunch of STEINSELJA (rock parsley)
- SALT HAFIÐ and PIPAR SVARTR

METHOD
1. **Initial preparation:** Soak the BAUNIR HVÍTAR in cold water for 12 hours. Drain and rinse thoroughly. Slice the LAUKAR and cut the SELLERIROT into small cubes.
2. **First cooking:** Bring the beans to a boil in fresh water, skimming carefully for the first 20 minutes. Cook for 90 minutes until tender.
3. **Main assembly:** In another KETILL, fry the LAUKAR and SELLERIROT with a little oil. Add the drained cooked beans, pour in the GRÆNMETISRÚPA and the LÁRVIÐRBLÖÐ. Simmer for 45 minutes.
4. **Final cooking:** Stir in the FISKISÓSA and cook for an additional 15 minutes so that the flavors blend harmoniously.
5. **Finishing:** Remove the bay leaves, add the chopped STEINSELJA and adjust the seasoning.
6. **Serving:** Serve warm with rye bread and fresh herbs, accompanied by salted butter.

🔄 **Modern Substitutes:** BAUNIR HVÍTAR → dried white beans, FISKISÓSA → Asian fish sauce, SELLERIROT → celeriac, STEINSELJA → flat-leaf parsley

ANCIENT METHOD: Cooking in large iron pots suspended in the hearth of the monastic kitchens, with constant supervision by the cooking brothers.

Secrets of the MATSTJÓRAR: Adding a crust of aged cheese at the end of cooking enriched the soup. The monks incorporated blessed herbs according to the liturgical calendar.

Nutritional values: 265 kcal | Protein: 16.8g | Carbohydrates: 38.5g | Fat: 5.2g

19. MELTINGARSÚPA GRAS ~ Digestive Broth with Nordic Herbs

PRACTICAL INFORMATION: 📖 **Historical period:** 8th-10th century | 🏛 **Source:** VÖLUR manuscripts/Nordic Pharmacopoeia | ⏱ **Preparation time:** 25 min | **Cooking time:** 60 min | 🜄 **Calories:** 45 kcal per portion | 👥 **Servings:** 4 people | 📋 **Nutritional value:** Protein: 2.1g / Carbohydrates: 8.5g / Fat: 0.8g | 💡 **Ancient advice:** Prescribed after feasts to aid digestion | 🔄 **Modern method:** Controlled infusion replaces decoction on embers | 💰 **Estimated cost:** €4.75 / £4.25 / $5.25 | 🏺 **Nordic utensils:** medicinal KETILL, fine sieve, glass bottles | ⚙ **Difficulty:** Novice ★☆☆

🏛 **MELTINGARSÚPA GRAS :** Therapeutic broth of the VÖLUR prescribed after the great drinking bouts and Nordic feasts. Each herb was harvested according to the lunar phases and seasons to maximize its healing properties. Warriors consumed it before long journeys to prevent digestive disorders due to the change in food and water.

INGREDIENTS :

- 1L of HREINVATN (pure spring water)
- 2 branches of MINTA VILLR (wild mint)
- 1 spoon of FENIKELFRJÓ (fennel seeds)
- 3 leaves of MELISSA (lemon balm)
- 1 sprig of ÞÍMÍAN (mountain thyme)
- 1 pinch of ENGIFER (dried ginger)
- HUNANG to taste to sweeten

METHOD

1. **Initial preparation:** Gently rinse all fresh herbs in cold water. Lightly crush the FENIKELFRJÓ in a mortar to release the essences.
2. **First cooking:** Bring the HREINVATN to a simmer in a KETILL reserved for medicinal preparations.
3. **Main assembly:** Add all herbs and spices. Maintain a very gentle simmer for 30 minutes, partially covered to retain the essential oils.
4. **Final cooking:** Remove from heat and let infuse for another 20 minutes, covered.
5. **Finishing:** Strain carefully through a fine-mesh strainer lined with linen. Sweeten with HUNANG if necessary.
6. **Serving:** Serve warm in small glasses, in slow sips after large meals.

🔄 **Modern Substitutes:** MINTA VILLR → peppermint, MELISSA → lemon balm, FENIKELFRJÓ → organic fennel seeds, ÞÍMÍAN → fresh thyme

ANCIENT METHOD: Decoction in small hanging copper cauldrons, with heated stones to maintain a constant temperature without violent boiling.

Secrets of the MATSTJÓRAR: Adding a drop of VÍNSTRÚP masked the bitterness of certain herbs. The VÖLUR recited healing galdr during the infusion to enhance the therapeutic efficacy.

Nutritional values: 45 kcal | Protein: 2.1g | Carbohydrates: 8.5g | Fat: 0.8g

20. HUNANGVATN ~ Therapeutic Honey Water

PRACTICAL INFORMATION: 🖳 **Historical period:** 8th-11th century | 🏛 **Source:** EDDA/Nordic Beekeeper Traditions | 🕐 **Preparation time:** 10 min | **Cooking time:** 30 min | 🜄 **Calories:** 125 kcal per serving | 👥 **Servings:** 6 people | 🍴 **Nutritional value:** Protein: 0.3g / Carbohydrates: 32.8g / Fat: 0g | 💡 **Ancient advice:** Sacred drink of the skalds to clear the voice | 🔄 **Modern method:** Cold dissolution preserves the honey's enzymes | 🝎 **Estimated cost:** €6.50 / £5.75 / $7.25 | 🝯 **Nordic utensils:** Copper cauldron, horn spoons, sealed jars | ⚙ **Difficulty:** Novice ★☆☆

🏛 **HUNANGVATN** : A fundamental medicinal drink in the Norse pharmacopoeia, considered a gift from the gods. Bees were venerated as messengers between Midgard and Asgard. This preparation served as both a universal remedy and a ritual drink during religious ceremonies. Skalds drank it to clear their voices before epic recitations.

INGREDIENTS :

- 1.5L of HREINVATN (iced spring water)
- 200g of HUNANG LYNGS (pure heather honey)
- 1 sprig of ROSMARÍN (wild rosemary)
- 3 EINIBER berries (Arctic juniper)
- 1 pinch of KANELL (oriental cinnamon)
- Zest of a SÍTRON (lemon if available)

METHOD

1. **Initial preparation:** Gently heat one-third of the HREINVATN until lukewarm. Dissolve the HUNANG LYNGS completely in it, stirring with a horn spoon.
2. **First cooking:** Add the ROSMARÍN, the lightly crushed EINIBER berries and the KANELL. Keep at a gentle simmer for 20 minutes.
3. **Main assembly:** Stir in the remaining cold water to cool the mixture and preserve the properties of the honey.
4. **Final cooking:** Reheat very gently without ever bringing to a boil to preserve the therapeutic enzymes.
5. **Finishing:** Strain through a fine cloth and add the zest of SÍTRON if available.
6. **Serving:** Serve warm in drinking horns or wooden cups, ideally at sunrise and sunset.

🔄 **Modern Substitutes:** HUNANG LYNGS → organic heather honey, ROSMARÍN → fresh rosemary, EINIBER → juniper berries, SÍTRON → organic lemon

ANCIENT METHOD: Preparation in red copper cauldrons suspended over birch embers, with constant temperature monitoring by the VÖLUR.

Secrets of the MATSTJÓRAR: Adding a drop of aged mead enhanced the taste. Norse beekeepers recited blessings to the bees during the honey harvest to increase its virtues tenfold.

Nutritional values: 125 kcal | Protein: 0.3g | Carbohydrates: 32.8g | Fat: 0g

21. BYGGKJARNA SÍAÐ ~ Filtered Barley Broth

PRACTICAL INFORMATION: 🖼 **Historical period:** 8th-10th century | 🏛 **Source:** Monastic manuscripts/Nordic medicine | 🕐 **Preparation time:** 20 min | **Cooking time:** 180 min | 🔥 **Calories:** 85 kcal per serving | 👥 **Servings:** 8 people | 📋 **Nutritional value:** Protein: 3.2g / Carbohydrates: 17.8g / Fat: 0.8g | 💡 **Ancient advice:** Fortifying agent prescribed for convalescents and newborns | 🔄 **Modern method:** Fine filtration replaces the horsehair sieve | 💰 **Estimated cost:** €3.25 / £2.75 / $3.75 | 🍯 **Nordic utensils:** Heavy-bottomed KETILL, ancestral sieve, flasks | ⚙ **Difficulty:** Novice ★☆☆

🏛 **BYGGKJARNA SÍAÐ** : Therapeutic broth obtained by prolonged decoction of barley, considered to be the nutritive essence of this sacred cereal. Prescribed to the sick, women in childbirth and weaned infants for its exceptional digestibility. Copyist monks drank it to maintain their concentration during long sessions of transcription of Nordic manuscripts.

INGREDIENTS :

- 150g of BYGG HEILL (world barley)
- 2L of HREINVATN (spring water)
- 1 pinch of SALT HAFIÐ (fine sea salt)
- 1 spoon of HUNANG (honey to sweeten)
- 1 sprig of ÞÍMÍAN (medicinal thyme)
- A few drops of SÍTRONJÚÍMI (lemon juice)

METHOD

1. **Initial preparation:** Rinse the BYGG HEILL thoroughly until the water runs clear. Soak it for 2 hours in cold water to soften the casing.
2. **First cooking:** Drain and bring to a boil with the HREINVATN in a heavy-bottomed KETILL. Continue cooking very gently for 2.5 hours.
3. **Main assembly:** Add the SALT HAFIÐ and the ÞÍMÍAN branch during the last hour of cooking. The barley should completely break down.
4. **Final cooking:** Continue to cook until the liquid takes on a slightly milky, gelatinous consistency.
5. **Finishing:** Carefully filter through several layers of linen to obtain a perfectly clear broth. Sweeten with HUNANG and acidify with SÍTRONJÚÍMI.
6. **Service:** Serve warm in small quantities, several times a day for convalescents.

🔄 **Modern Substitutes:** BYGG HEILL → organic pearl barley, HREINVATN → low-mineral spring water, ÞÍMÍAN → fresh thyme, SÍTRONJÚÍMI → organic lemon

ANCIENT METHOD: Slow cooking in pots buried in hot ash, with gradual addition of hot water to maintain the level.

Secrets of the MATSTJÓRAR: Adding a spoonful of sour whey at the end of cooking provided beneficial ferments. The VÖLUR stored this broth in animal bladders for travel.

Nutritional values: 85 kcal | Protein: 3.2g | Carbohydrates: 17.8g | Fat: 0.8g

22. JURTATE ILMANDI ~ Herbal Tea with Aromatics

PRACTICAL INFORMATION: 📖 **Historical period:** 8th-11th century | 🏛 **Source:** VÖLUR traditions/Rune herbariums | 🕐 **Preparation time:** 15 min | **Cooking time:** 25 min | 🜄 **Calories:** 15 kcal per serving | 👥 **Servings:** 4 people | 📑 **Nutritional value:** Protein: 0.5g / Carbohydrates: 3.8g / Fat: 0.2g | 💡 **Ancient advice:** VÖLUR herbal tea to purify the mind before divination | 🔄 **Modern method:** Short infusion preserves volatile essential oils | 💲 **Estimated cost:** €5.25 / £4.50 / $5.75 | 🝮 **Nordic Utensils:** Small Ritual Cauldron, Sacred Sieves, Rune Cups | ⚙ **Difficulty:** Novice ★☆☆

🏛 **JURTATE ILMANDI :** Ritual herbal tea of the VÖLUR prepared according to secret teachings passed down from mother to daughter. Each plant was harvested at specific times in the Nordic calendar to maximize its magico-medicinal properties. This infusion accompanied divination sessions and spiritual healing rituals, creating a link between the physical world and supernatural forces.

INGREDIENTS :

- 1L of HREINVATN (sacred spring water)
- 1 spoon of KAMILLUAUGU (chamomile flowers)
- 6 leaves of MELISSUBLÖÐ (lemon balm)
- 1 branch of HVANN VILLR (wild angelica)
- 1 pinch of LÁRVIÐR (dried bay leaves)
- 3 EINIBER berries (Arctic juniper)
- HUNANG according to spiritual taste

METHOD

1. **Initial Preparation:** Bless the water and herbs according to ancestral rites. Gently cleanse the plants while reciting the names of the protective goddesses.
2. **First cooking:** Heat the HREINVATN in a cauldron reserved for sacred preparations, without ever reaching a violent boil.
3. **Main blend:** Add the herbs in order of their spiritual strength: LÁRVIÐR, crushed EINIBER, HVANN VILLR, then the delicate flowers. Infuse for 15 minutes over very low heat.
4. **Final cooking:** Remove from heat and let stand for 10 minutes, covering with a clean white cloth.
5. **Finishing:** Strain with a ritual strainer and sweeten with HUNANG according to divine inspiration.
6. **Serving:** Serve in rune-engraved cups, reciting a protective spell before each sip.

🔄 **Modern Substitutes:** KAMILLUAUGU → German chamomile, MELISSUBLÖÐ → Lemon balm, HVANN VILLR → True angelica, EINIBER → Organic juniper berries

ANCIENT METHOD: Infusion in bronze cauldrons suspended in temples, with constant blessing of the VÖLUR and fumigation of sacred herbs.

Secrets of the MATSTJÓRAR: Adding a drop of morning dew collected on runestones increased the powers of the herbal tea tenfold. The proportions varied according to the visions received in dreams.

Nutritional values: 15 kcal | Protein: 0.5g | Carbohydrates: 3.8g | Fat: 0.2g

AXIS 3: BRAUÐ OK KORN - The Sacred Cereals of the Aesir - *The sacred cereals of the Aesir*

Jarls' Breads (5 recipes), Noble Grains (5 recipes); Sacred Legumes (5 recipes)

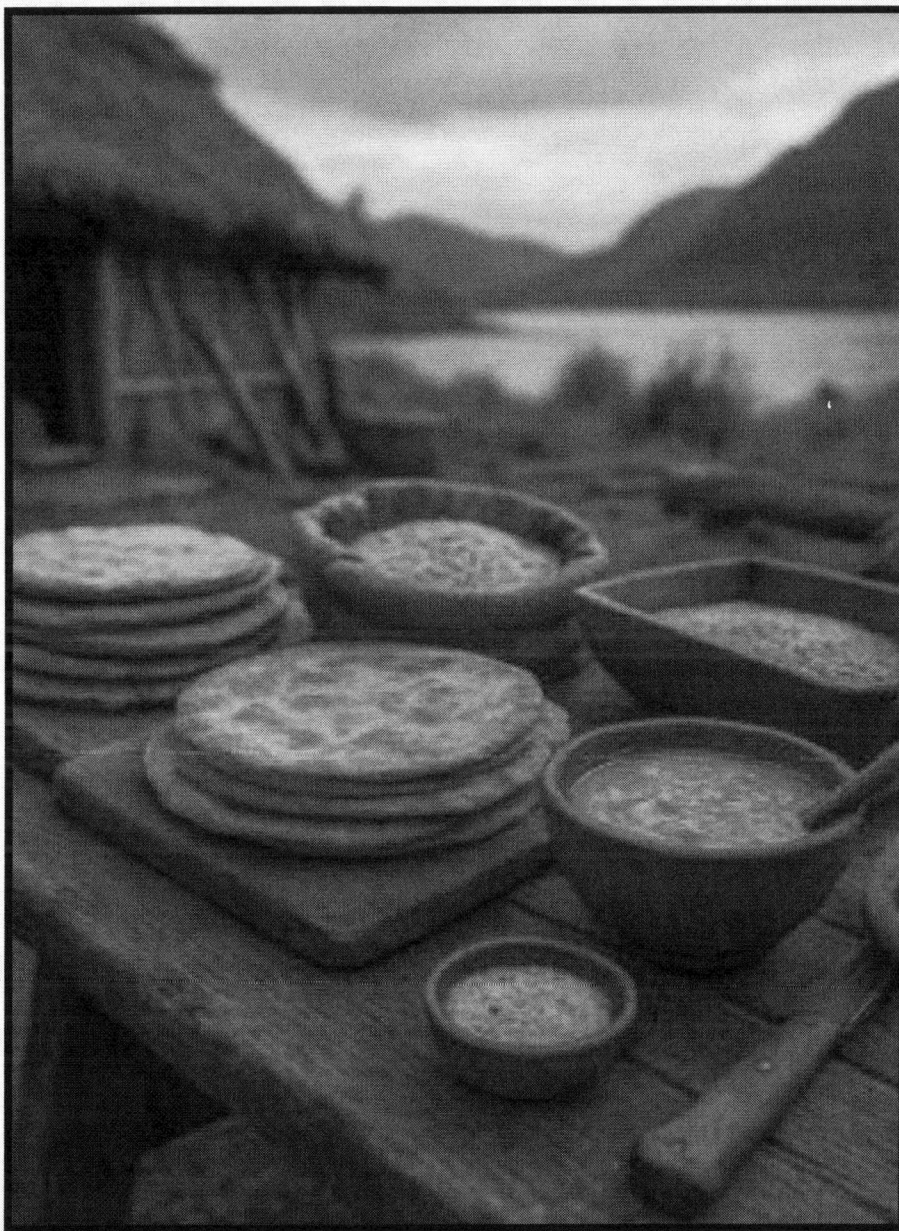

23. BRAUÐ FERKANTAÐ HERMAÐR ~ Warriors' Square Bread

PRACTICAL INFORMATION: 🖼 Historical period: 9th-11th century | 🏛 Source: SAGAS/Nordic Military Archaeology | 🕐 Preparation time: 120 min | Cooking time: 45 min | 🜄 Calories: 285 kcal per serving | 👥 Servings: 8 people | 📑 Nutritional value: Protein: 9.5g / Carbohydrates: 52.8g / Fat: 6.2g | 💡 Ancient advice: Blessed bread before every Viking expedition for protection | 🔄 Modern method: Electric oven replaces the communal STEINOFN | 💰 Estimated cost: €4.25 / £3.75 / $4.75 | 🜨 Nordic utensils: STEINOFN, ash planks, wicker baskets | ⚙ Difficulty: Beginner ★★☆

🏛 **BRAUÐ FERKANTAÐ HERMAÐR :** Bread ritually shaped into a square shield, a symbol of protection for warriors going into battle. Each loaf was marked with Thor's hammer before baking to attract the god's goodwill. Wives prepared it with grains blessed at the equinoxes, ensuring the safe return of their husbands from distant expeditions.

INGREDIENTS :

- 500g of HVEITI FÍNR (noble wheat flour)
- 200g of RÚG MALAÐR (ground rye flour)
- 300ml MJÓLK HLÝR (warm milk)
- 100ml of HUNANGVATN (honeyed water)
- 1 spoonful of GEST (wild yeast)
- 2 spoons of SALT HAFIÐ
- 50g of SMJÖR (churned butter)
- KÚMEN seeds for the surface

METHOD

1. **Initial preparation:** Mix the flours in a large wooden container. Create a central well and pour in the MJÓLK HLÝR in which the GEST and HUNANGVATN have been dissolved.
2. **First cooking:** Knead vigorously until you obtain a soft and elastic dough. Gradually incorporate the melted SMJÖR and the SALT HAFIÐ.
3. **Main assembly:** Let the dough rise for 90 minutes under a linen cloth in a warm place. It should double in size and bear the marks of the gods' blessing.
4. **Final baking:** Shape into shield-sized square loaves, mark with the Thor symbol, and sprinkle with KÚMEN seeds. Bake for 45 minutes in the preheated STEINOFN.
5. **Finishing:** Leave to cool on ash wood racks while reciting protective formulas.
6. **Service:** Break by hand according to tradition, never cut with a knife which would break divine protection.

🔄 **Modern Substitutes:** HVEITI FÍNR → T65 wheat flour, RÚG MALAÐR → rye flour, GEST → baker's yeast, KÚMEN → cumin seeds

ANCIENT METHOD: Cooking in communal stone ovens heated with birch bundles, with collective supervision by the village women.

Secrets of the MATSTJÓRAR: Adding a pinch of blessed ashes from the family hearth strengthened spiritual protection. The square shape represented the four cardinal points guarded by the gods.

Nutritional values: 285 kcal | Protein: 9.5g | Carbohydrates: 52.8g | Fat: 6.2g

24. EGGJABRAUÐ SLÉTTUR ~ Swan Egg Cake Bread

PRACTICAL INFORMATION: 📖 **Historical period:** 9th-10th century | 🏛 **Source:** SAGA DE NJÁLL/Archaeology | ⏱ **Preparation time:** 45 min | **Cooking time:** 60 min | 🔥 **Calories:** 380 kcal per serving | 👥 **Servings:** 8 people | 📋 **Nutritional value:** Protein: 12g / Carbohydrates: 45g / Fat: 18g | 💡 **Ancient advice:** Beat the eggs until foamy according to the VÖLUR | 🔄 **Modern method:** Use an electric mixer for optimal aeration | 💲 **Estimated cost:** €8.50 / £7.20 / $9.80 | 🍶 **Nordic utensils:** heated BAKSTEINN, birch whisks | ⚙ **Difficulty:** Beginner ★★☆

🏛 **EGGJABRAUÐ SLÉTTUR** : Noble bread served at wedding feasts in the halls of the jarls. Swan eggs were reserved for the Norse aristocracy according to the social codes described in the SAGA OF NJÁLL. This bread-cake marked summer solstice celebrations and alliances between clans.

INGREDIENTS :

- 6 large farm chicken eggs (replaces swan eggs)
- 400g of HAFRI flour (fine oats) or ancient wheat flour
- 200ml of MJÓLK (goat's milk) or whole milk
- 150g of HUNANG (heather honey) or linden honey
- 100g of salted butter from the Nordic mountain pastures
- 2 teaspoons of FENIKEL seeds (wild fennel)

METHOD

1. **Initial preparation:** Beat the eggs with the HUNANG until you obtain a light and airy foam according to the tradition of Nordic court cooks.
2. **First cooking:** Melt the butter gently over birch embers, add the lukewarm MJÓLK without bringing to a boil.
3. **Main assembly:** Mix the HAFRI flour with the beaten eggs until light and fluffy, then gradually add the milk and butter mixture. Add the coarsely ground FENIKEL seeds to flavor, using the MATSTJÓRAR technique.
4. **Final cooking:** Pour into a greased mold, bake in a preheated STEINOFN (modern 180°C) for 50-60 minutes.
5. **Finishing:** Unmold warm, brush with liquid HUNANG to glaze the surface.
6. **Serving:** Slice thickly, serve with mead or fermented milk.

🔄 **Modern Substitutes:** HAFRI → fine oat flour, MJÓLK → fresh goat's milk, HUNANG → acacia honey, FENIKEL → dried fennel seeds

ANCIENT METHOD: Cooking on a flat stone heated with a birch fire, turning halfway through cooking

Secrets of the MATSTJÓRAR: Test the doneness by sticking a fir twig in - if it comes out clean, the bread is ready according to the wisdom of the cooks of the royal halls

Nutritional values: 380 kcal | Protein: 12g | Carbohydrates: 45g | Fat: 18g

25. FERÐABRAUÐ HARÐR – Hardened Travel Biscuit

PRACTICAL INFORMATION: 📖 **Historical period:** 8th-11th century | 🏛 **Source:** SAGA OF ERIK THE RED/Marine archaeology | 🕐 **Preparation time:** 30 min | **Cooking time:** 90 min | 🔥 **Calories:** 420 kcal per portion | 👥 **Servings:** 12 biscuits | 📋 **Nutritional value:** Protein: 14g / Carbohydrates: 68g / Fat: 8g | 💡 **Ancient advice:** Double baking to harden according to the methods of the navigators | 🔄 **Modern method:** Dehydrate in the oven at 80°C after the first baking | 💰 **Estimated cost:** €4.20 / £3.60 / $4.90 | 🥘 **Nordic utensils:** Flat baking stone, canvas bags for preservation | ⚙️ **Difficulty:** Novice ★☆☆

🏛 **FERÐABRAUÐ HARÐR** : Survival bread for Viking expeditions to Iceland and Greenland. Documented in the SAGA OF ERIK THE RED as an essential provision for knörr (trading ships). Its low water content meant it could be stored for several months at sea.

INGREDIENTS :

- 500g BYGG (barley) flour or whole barley flour
- 200g of RÚG (rye) flour or black rye flour
- 150ml of cold spring water
- 2 tablespoons coarse sea salt
- 100g of crushed Nordic flax seeds
- 50g of crushed HAFRI (oat) seeds

METHOD

1. **Initial preparation:** Mix the BYGG and RÚG flours with the SALT, add the crushed seeds according to the proportions of the Nordic sailors.
2. **First cooking:** Add cold water gradually to form a firm, non-sticky dough, knead vigorously for 10 minutes.
3. **Main assembly:** Divide into 12 equal portions, flatten into 1.5cm thick patties on a floured stone. Mark with runic crosses to promote even cooking according to tradition.
4. **Final cooking:** Bake on a hot STEINOFN (200°C) for 45 minutes, turn over and continue for 30 minutes until completely hardened.
5. **Finishing:** Leave to dry for 24 hours in the open air, then return to a warm oven for 15 minutes for final drying.
6. **Serving:** Dip in hot broth or milk to soften before consumption.

🔄 **Modern Substitutes:** BYGG → ground pearl barley flour, RÚG → T170 rye flour, SALT → Guérande fleur de sel

ANCIENT METHOD: Cooking on flat stones heated by fire, drying in the Arctic sun for several days

Secrets of the MATSTJÓRAR: Perforating the surface with a knife tip to prevent swelling, a method passed down by experienced knörr captains

Nutritional values: 420 kcal | Protein: 14g | Carbohydrates: 68g | Fat: 8g

26. FLATBRAUÐ SESAMFRJÓ - Flat Nordic sesame pancakes

PRACTICAL INFORMATION: 🖻 **Historical period:** 9th-10th century | 🏛 **Source:** NOVGOROD Trade Routes/Archaeology | 🕐 **Preparation time:** 25 min | **Cooking time:** 40 min | 🜄 **Calories:** 290 kcal per serving | 🐾 **Servings:** 8 flatbreads | 🗒 **Nutritional value:** Protein: 9g / Carbohydrates: 42g / Fat: 10g | 💡 **Ancient advice:** Toast the seeds before adding according to Byzantine merchants | 🔄 **Modern method:** Dry roast in a non-stick pan for 3 minutes | 🕔 **Estimated cost:** €5.80 / £4.90 / $6.40 | 🍶 **Nordic utensils:** Birch rolling pin, flat stone | ⚙ **Difficulty:** Novice ★☆☆

🏛 **FLATBRAUÐ SESAMFRJÓ :** Flat cakes enriched with oriental seeds brought back by Viking traders from the Volga route to Novgorod and Constantinople. Sesame was a luxury product traded for Nordic furs, reserved for the feasts of the most prosperous jarls.

INGREDIENTS :

- 400g of ancient wheat or spelt flour
- 80g sesame seeds (imported SESAMFRJÓ)
- 200ml of warm, lightly salted water
- 3 tablespoons of first-pressed olive oil
- 1 teaspoon of fine SALT
- 1 teaspoon wild cumin seeds

METHOD

1. **Initial preparation:** Dry roast the sesame seeds in a pan until golden brown, let cool and coarsely crush according to Byzantine methods.
2. **First cooking:** Mix flour, SALT and cumin in a large bowl, make a well in the center to incorporate the olive oil.
3. **Main assembly:** Gradually add the warm water while kneading until you obtain a soft dough. Add the roasted sesame seeds and knead for another 5 minutes to distribute evenly. Let rest for 30 minutes under a damp cloth.
4. **Final cooking:** Divide into 8 portions, roll out thinly. Cook on a very hot STEINOFN without fat, 3-4 minutes per side until golden bubbles appear.
5. **Finishing:** Brush with warm olive oil when removing from the heat to soften.
6. **Service:** Serve warm, accompanied by goat cheese or flavored honey.

🔄 **Modern Substitutes:** SESAMFRJÓ → white or black sesame seeds, olive oil → first cold-pressed rapeseed oil

ANCIENT METHOD: Cooking on a flat oiled stone placed on live embers, quickly turning

Secrets of MATSTJÓRAR: Keeping the dough very thin for optimal crispness, a technique learned from the bakers of Constantinople via the trade routes

Nutritional values: 290 kcal | Protein: 9g | Carbohydrates: 42g | Fat: 10g

27. SKIPBRAUÐ VARÐVEITT – Preserved sea bread

PRACTICAL INFORMATION: 🎞 **Historical period:** 8th-11th century | 🏛 **Source:** SAGA OF THE GREENLANDERS/Naval Archaeology | 🕐 **Preparation time:** 40 min | **Cooking time:** 75 min | 🔥 **Calories:** 450 kcal per serving | 👥 **Servings:** 15 servings | 📋 **Nutritional value:** Protein: 16g / Carbohydrates: 72g / Fat: 9g | 💡 **Ancient advice:** Waterproof with seal fat according to navigators | 🔁 **Modern method:** Coat with melted beeswax for preservation | 💰 **Estimated cost:** €6.20 / £5.30 / $6.90 | 🥄 **Nordic utensils:** Oak wood molds, oiled cloths | ⚙ **Difficulty:** Beginner ★★☆

🏛 **SKIPBRAUÐ VARÐVEITT** : Maximum preservation bread developed for transoceanic expeditions to North America. Mentioned in THE GREENLANDER SAGA as a strategic supply for Leif Erikson's knörr. Its seal fat protection technique allowed for 6 months of preservation at sea.

INGREDIENTS :

- 600g oven-dried BYGG (barley) flour
- 200g finely ground flax flour
- 300ml of fermented whey (liquid SKYR)
- 100g pork lard or duck fat
- 2 tablespoons of coarse sea salt
- 50g Nordic poppy seeds

METHOD

1. **Initial preparation:** Dry the flours in a low oven (60°C) for 2 hours to eliminate any residual moisture, a crucial method used by Nordic sailors to prevent rotting.
2. **First cooking:** Mix the dried flours with the SALT and poppy seeds, add the melted but cooled lard.
3. **Main assembly:** Gradually add the fermented whey, kneading vigorously until you obtain a very compact and homogeneous dough. The consistency should be firm but not brittle, a technique perfected by shipwrights who became bakers.
4. **Final cooking:** Mold into 300g rectangular loaves, bake at moderate STEINOFN (160°C) for 75 minutes until very hard crust.
5. **Finishing:** Let cool completely, coat with melted fat or liquid beeswax, wrap in oiled cloth.
6. **Serving:** Scrape off the coating, grate the hardened bread into hot soups or broths.

🔁 **Modern Substitutes:** Dried BYGG → dehydrated barley flour, SKYR → drained Bulgarian yogurt, Seal fat → organic lard

ANCIENT METHOD: Slow cooking on hot buried stones, coated in hot seal fat

Secrets of the MATSTJÓRAR: Check for complete absence of moisture before coating - a single drop compromises preservation according to the experience of ocean captains

Nutritional values: 450 kcal | Protein: 16g | Carbohydrates: 72g | Fat: 9g

28. MJÓLKGRAUTR MÖNDLU ~ Arctic Almond Milk Oatmeal

PRACTICAL INFORMATION: 🖥 **Historical period:** 10th-11th century | 🏛 **Source:** Byzantine trade/SNORRI'S EDDA | 🕐 **Preparation time:** 20 min | **Cooking time:** 35 min | 💧 **Calories:** 340 kcal per serving | 👥 **Servings:** 6 people | 📓 **Nutritional value:** Protein: 11g / Carbohydrates: 38g / Fat: 16g | 💡 **Ancient advice:** Pound the almonds in a granite mortar according to VÖLUR | 🔄 **Modern method:** Mix the soaked almonds with hot milk | 💰 **Estimated cost:** €9.50 / £8.10 / $10.40 | 🍶 **Nordic utensils:** Stone mortar, fine horsehair sieve | ⚙️ **Difficulty:** Beginner ★★☆

🏛 **MJÓLKGRAUTR MÖNDLU** : Noble gruel prepared for the sick and women in childbirth in aristocratic homes. Almonds were imported via Constantinople and reserved for special occasions. Mentioned in the EDDA as food of the Aesir, symbolizing the prosperity of jarls with access to eastern trade routes.

INGREDIENTS :

- 200g of shelled sweet almonds (imported MÖNDLU)
- 150g of fine HAFRI (oat) flakes
- 800ml of whole MJÓLK (goat's milk)
- 100g of HUNANG (honey) from acacia or linden
- 1 pinch of fine SALT
- Zest of one dried orange (rare Nordic spice)

METHOD

1. **Initial preparation:** Soak the almonds in lukewarm water for 2 hours, peel them and pound them finely in a stone mortar until you obtain a fatty powder according to VÖLUR techniques.
2. **First cooking:** Bring the MJÓLK to a gentle simmer in an iron cauldron, add the crushed almonds, stirring constantly to avoid lumps.
3. **Main assembly:** Add the HAFRI flakes in a fine rain, whisking vigorously, and cook over low heat for 25 minutes, stirring regularly. The consistency should become creamy and thick, according to the standards of Nordic royal kitchens.
4. **Final cooking:** Add the HUNANG and orange zest, adjust with SALT to taste.
5. **Finish:** Pass through a fine sieve for a velvety texture, reheat if necessary.
6. **Service:** Serve hot in wooden bowls, garnished with toasted flaked almonds.

🔄 **Modern Substitutes:** MÖNDLU → almonds from Provence, MJÓLK → fresh goat's milk, HAFRI → organic oat flakes

ANCIENT METHOD: Slow cooking in a bain-marie in a cauldron suspended over soft embers

Secrets of the MATSTJÓRAR: Maintaining a constant temperature without boiling to prevent the almond milk from separating, wisdom passed down by the cooks of the Byzantine courts

Nutritional values: 340 kcal | Protein: 11g | Carbohydrates: 38g | Fat: 16g

29. HAFRI RISTAÐR GRAS ~ Toasted oats with wild herbs

PRACTICAL INFORMATION: 🎞 **Historical period:** 8th-11th century | 🏛 **Source:** Rural traditions/SAGA OF GRETTIR | 🕐 **Preparation time:** 15 min | **Cooking time:** 25 min | 🜄 **Calories:** 310 kcal per serving | 🎎 **Servings:** 4 people | 📕 **Nutritional value:** Protein: 12g / Carbohydrates: 52g / Fat: 7g | ♀ **Ancient advice:** Toast the oats until they have a nutty aroma according to shepherds | 🔄 **Modern method:** Dry roast in a thick cast iron pan | 💲 **Estimated cost:** €4.80 / £4.10 / $5.20 | 🪣 **Nordic utensils:** Wrought iron pan, wooden spoon | ⚙
Difficulty: Novice ★☆☆

🏛 **HAFRI RISTAÐR GRAS** : A rustic preparation for shepherds and free farmers (karls) during the long winter vigils. Roasted oats developed complex flavors that compensated for the monotonous winter diet. Documented in GRETTIR'S SAGA as a staple food of outlaws living in the Icelandic mountains.

INGREDIENTS :

- 300g of thick HAFRI (oat) flakes
- 2 tablespoons mixed dried wild herbs
- 1 tablespoon of mountain thyme
- 1 teaspoon dried northern oregano
- 500ml hot root vegetable broth
- 2 tablespoons of Nordic rapeseed oil
- SALT and wild pepper to taste

METHOD

1. **Initial preparation:** Heat an iron pan over medium heat, dry-grill the HAFRI, stirring constantly for 8-10 minutes until golden brown and nutty in flavor.
2. **First cooking:** Add the rapeseed oil to the toasted flakes, continue cooking for 2 minutes, stirring to coat evenly.
3. **Main assembly:** Stir in the dried wild herbs and thyme, sauté for 1 minute to release the aromas. Gradually pour in the hot broth, stirring constantly to avoid lumps, according to the Nordic shepherd's technique.
4. **Final cooking:** Simmer covered for 12-15 minutes until the liquid is completely absorbed, stirring occasionally.
5. **Finishing:** Adjust the seasoning with salt and wild pepper, add the oregano at the end of cooking.
6. **Serving:** Serve hot as a side dish to roast meats or as a rustic main course.

🔄 **Modern Substitutes:** HAFRI → organic oat flakes, wild herbs → dried Provençal herbs mix, broth → organic vegetable cube

ANCIENT METHOD: Roasting in an iron cauldron suspended over the fire, stirring constantly with a wooden spoon

Secrets of the MATSTJÓRAR: Listening to the crackling of oats to judge the degree of roasting - a technique passed down from mothers to daughters on isolated farms

Nutritional values: 310 kcal | Protein: 12g | Carbohydrates: 52g | Fat: 7g

30. HIRSGRAUTR GULLINN ~ Golden millet porridge

PRACTICAL INFORMATION: 📅 **Historical period:** 9th-10th century | 🏛 **Source:** Slavic Routes/Archaeology of BIRKA | 🕐 **Preparation time:** 10 min | **Cooking time:** 40 min | 🜄 **Calories:** 290 kcal per portion | 👥 **Servings:** 5 people | 📋 **Nutritional value:** Protein: 9g / Carbohydrates: 56g / Fat: 4g | 💡 **Ancient advice:** Wash the millet until the water runs clear according to Slavs | 🔄 **Modern method:** Rinse under cold running water for 3 minutes | 💰 **Estimated cost:** €3.90 / £3.30 / $4.30 | 🏺 **Nordic utensils:** Horsehair strainer, copper cauldron | ⚙️ **Difficulty:** Novice ★☆☆

🏛 **HIRSGRAUTR GULLINN** : A grain imported from Slavic territories via the Volga and Dnieper trade routes. Millet was prized for its golden color, reminiscent of gold, Odin's sacred metal. Discovered in the excavations of the Birka trading post, it testifies to the Viking trade expansion to the east and the adoption of exotic foods by the Nordic aristocracy.

INGREDIENTS :

- 250g of hulled millet (HIRSI Slavic)
- 600ml of pure spring water
- 200ml of whole MJÓLK (milk)
- 2 tablespoons of liquid HUNANG
- 1 teaspoon of fine SALT
- 50g of salted butter from Nordic pastures
- 1 pinch of oriental cinnamon (rare spice)

METHOD

1. **Initial preparation:** Wash the millet under cold running water until the water runs clear, drain carefully in a fine sieve using the traditional Slavic method.
2. **First cooking:** Bring the salted water to a boil in a copper pot, pour in the millet in a drizzle and stir vigorously to prevent clumping.
3. **Main assembly:** Reduce heat and simmer, covered, for 25 minutes, stirring regularly, until almost all the water is absorbed. The grains should be tender but still slightly firm, according to Novgorod merchant standards.
4. **Final cooking:** Stir in the hot MJÓLK and continue cooking for 10 minutes until creamy, stirring constantly.
5. **Finishing:** Off the heat, add the butter, HUNANG and cinnamon, mix gently.
6. **Service:** Serve hot in wooden bowls, sprinkle with crushed hazelnuts if available.

🔄 **Modern Substitutes:** HIRSI → organic golden millet, MJÓLK → semi-skimmed milk, HUNANG → wildflower honey

ANCIENT METHOD: Slow cooking in a terracotta pot buried in embers, constant monitoring to prevent sticking

Secrets of the MATSTJÓRAR: Taste a grain while it is cooking to check the texture - it should burst under the tooth without being pasty, a technique brought back from Slavic trading posts

Nutritional values: 290 kcal | Protein: 9g | Carbohydrates: 56g | Fat: 4g

31. BYGGBRJÓTR GRÆNMETI ~ Crushed barley with vegetables

PRACTICAL INFORMATION: 🗓 **Historical period:** 8th-11th century | 🏛 **Source:** Icelandic farms/EGILL'S SAGA | ⏱ **Preparation time:** 30 min | **Cooking time:** 55 min | 🜍 **Calories:** 320 kcal per serving | 🐾 **Servings:** 6 people | 📱 **Nutritional value:** Protein: 10g / Carbohydrates: 58g / Fat: 6g | ♀ **Ancient advice:** Crush the barley in a mortar to release its flavors according to farmers | 🔄 **Modern method:** Use pre-cooked commercial pearl barley | 💰 **Estimated cost:** €5.60 / £4.70 / $6.10 | 🥣 **Nordic utensils:** Granite mortar, wrought iron knife | ⚙ **Difficulty:** Beginner ★★☆

🏛 **BYGGBRJÓTR GRÆNMETI** : A fortifying peasant dish of Icelandic farmers described in the SAGA OF EGILL SKALLA-GRÍMSSON. Crushed barley allowed for faster cooking and better digestibility. Root vegetables preserved in food pits provided essential vitamins during Arctic winters, testifying to the nutritional adaptation of the Norse settlers.

INGREDIENTS :

- 300g of hulled barley (BYGG) to crush
- 200g diced Nordic turnips
- 150g of chopped wild carrots
- 100g of sliced marsh leeks
- 800ml beef bone broth
- 2 tablespoons of pressed rapeseed oil
- 1 bunch of wild Nordic herbs
- Sea salt and wild pepper to taste

METHOD

1. **Initial preparation:** Crush the hulled barley in a granite mortar until you get irregular broken grains, a technique that allows for faster cooking according to Icelandic farmers.
2. **First cooking:** Heat the rapeseed oil in an iron pot, fry the chopped vegetables for 8-10 minutes until lightly browned.
3. **Main assembly:** Add the crushed barley to the vegetables, stir for 2 minutes to coat with oil. Gradually pour in the hot bone broth, bring to a boil, then reduce the heat. Simmer, covered, for 45 minutes, stirring regularly, until the liquid is absorbed and the grains are tender, according to the methods of rural cooks.
4. **Final cooking:** Add the chopped wild herbs in the last 10 minutes of cooking.
5. **Finishing:** Adjust the seasoning with salt and wild pepper, let stand for 5 minutes off the heat.
6. **Serving:** Serve hot as a rustic main course, accompanied by smoked bacon or aged goat cheese.

🔄 **Modern Substitutes:** BYGG → organic pearl barley, wild vegetables → local seasonal vegetables, bone broth → homemade chicken stock

ANCIENT METHOD: Slow cooking in an earthenware pot buried in embers, stirring with a hollowed-out wooden spoon

Secrets of MATSTJÓRAR: Add stock in small amounts like a risotto to develop the softness - a technique perfected on the remote farms of Iceland

Nutritional values: 320 kcal | Protein: 10g | Carbohydrates: 58g | Fat: 6g

32. STERKJA ÞURRKAÐR ÁVÖXTR ~ Dried fruit starch

PRACTICAL INFORMATION: 📱 **Historical period:** 9th-10th century | 🏛 **Source:** Winter Reserves/POETIC EDDA | 🕐 **Preparation time:** 15 min | **Cooking time:** 30 min | 🜄 **Calories:** 280 kcal per serving | 👥 **Servings:** 6 people | 📋 **Nutritional value:** Protein: 6g / Carbohydrates: 62g / Fat: 3g | 💡 **Ancient advice:** Rehydrate the fruit with whey according to VÖLUR | 🔄 **Modern method:** Soak in warm apple juice for 30 minutes | 💰 **Estimated cost:** €7.20 / £6.10 / $7.80 | 🍯 **Nordic utensils:** Horsehair sieve, hollowed-out pot spoon | ⚙️ **Difficulty:** Novice ★☆☆

🏛 **STERKJA ÞURRKAÐR ÁVÖXTR** : An energy-boosting dessert prepared during the long Nordic winters when fresh supplies were scarce. The starch extracted from the roots was enriched with fruit dried in the Arctic sun. Mentioned in the POETIC EDDA as food for heroes on their journey to Valhalla, symbolizing the preservation of life during the dark season.

INGREDIENTS :

- 200g potato starch (modern STERKJA)
- 150g of Nordic dried apples in slices
- 100g dried lingonberry berries (KRÆKIBER)
- 50g of crushed wild hazelnuts
- 600ml of whey (liquid SKYR) or fermented milk
- 80g of HUNANG (heather honey)
- 1 pinch of fine SALT
- Oriental Road Cinnamon (pinch)

METHOD

1. **Initial preparation:** Rehydrate the dried apples and cranberries in warm whey for 20 minutes, until swollen using the VÖLUR technique to optimize the flavors.
2. **First cooking:** Mix the starch in a little cold whey to avoid lumps, a crucial technique passed on by experienced cooks.
3. **Main assembly:** Bring the remaining fruit whey to a gentle simmer, then whisk in the dissolved cornstarch vigorously. Add the HUNANG and a pinch of SALT and cook over low heat for 15 minutes, stirring constantly, until thickened to the consistency of Nordic heavy cream.
4. **Final cooking:** Stir in the crushed hazelnuts and cinnamon in the last few minutes.
5. **Finishing:** Pour into individual bowls, let cool before serving.
6. **Service:** Serve warm or cold, garnished with fresh berries if the season permits.

🔄 **Modern Substitutes:** STERKJA → cornstarch or arrowroot, SKYR → liquid Bulgarian yogurt, KRÆKIBER → dried blueberries

ANCIENT METHOD: Cooking in a bain-marie in a suspended cauldron, constant stirring with a birch spatula

Secrets of MATSTJÓRAR: Keep the temperature low to avoid lumps - test on the back of a spoon to check the coating according to the wisdom of Nordic grandmothers

Nutritional values: 280 kcal | Protein: 6g | Carbohydrates: 62g | Fat: 3g

33. LINSUBAUNIR SVARTAR LAUKR ~ Black lentils with onion

PRACTICAL INFORMATION: 📓 Historical period: 10th-11th century | 🏛 Source: Mediterranean trade/HAKON SAGA | 🕐 Preparation time: 20 min | Cooking time: 50 min | 🜄 Calories: 330 kcal per portion | 👥 Servings: 6 people | 🍴 Nutritional value: Protein: 18g / Carbohydrates: 48g / Fat: 5g | 🔮 Ancient advice: Soak overnight in rainwater according to monks | 🔄 Modern method: Soak for 8 hours in cold filtered water | ⏱ Estimated cost: €4.50 / £3.80 / $4.90 | 🍯 Nordic utensils: Stoneware jar, birch skimmer | ⚙ Difficulty: Novice ★☆☆

🏛 LINSUBAUNIR SVARTAR LAUKR : Legumes imported via Mediterranean routes and adopted in Nordic monasteries converted to Christianity. Black lentils were valued for their nutritional richness during periods of fasting. The SAGA OF HAKON THE GOOD mentions their introduction in royal courts as a noble alternative to meat during Lent.

INGREDIENTS :

- 300g of black Puy lentils (LINSUBAUNIR SVARTAR)
- 2 large Nordic onions (LAUKR), finely chopped
- 3 cloves of wild garlic
- 800ml root vegetable broth
- 3 tablespoons of first-pressed rapeseed oil
- 2 bay leaves
- 1 teaspoon of cumin from the steppes
- SEA SALT and black pepper to taste

METHOD

1. **Initial preparation:** Soak the black lentils in cold spring water for at least 8 hours, rinse them and sort them to remove stones and impurities according to monastic methods.
2. **First cooking:** Heat the rapeseed oil in an iron pot, melt the chopped onions over low heat for 15 minutes until golden brown and transparent.
3. **Main assembly:** Add the crushed wild garlic to the onions and sauté for 2 minutes. Stir in the drained lentils, cumin, and bay leaves, then stir to coat with the herbs. Pour in the hot stock, bring to a boil, then reduce the heat to simmer, covered, for 35-40 minutes, according to the methods of Nordic monastic cooks.
4. **Final cooking:** Check the tenderness of the lentils - they should be tender without completely falling apart.
5. **Finishing:** Remove the bay leaves, season with salt and freshly ground black pepper.
6. **Serving:** Serve hot as a side dish to smoked meats or as a vegetarian main course enriched with goat cheese.

🔄 **Modern Substitutes:** LINSUBAUNIR → Puy green lentils, LAUKR → organic yellow onions, wild garlic → common garlic

ANCIENT METHOD: Slow cooking in an earthenware pot suspended over gentle embers, stirring occasionally

Secrets of the MATSTJÓRAR: Only add salt at the end of cooking to prevent the skins from toughening - wisdom passed down by the cook monks of the Nordic abbeys

Nutritional values: 330 kcal | Protein: 18g | Carbohydrates: 48g | Fat: 5g

34. BAUNIR FISKISÓSA ~ Ritual beans with FISKISÓSA

PRACTICAL INFORMATION: 📖 **Historical period:** 8th-10th century | 🏛 **Source:** BLÓT Rituals/Religious Archaeology | 🕐 **Preparation time:** 35 min | **Cooking time:** 60 min | 🝤 **Calories:** 350 kcal per portion | 👥 **Servings:** 8 people | 📖 **Nutritional value:** Protein: 20g / Carbohydrates: 45g / Fat: 8g | 💡 **Ancient advice:** Cook with sacred juniper branch according to GOÐI | 🔄 **Modern method:** Add dried juniper berries at the beginning of cooking | 💰 **Estimated cost:** €6.80 / £5.70 / $7.40 | 🝳 **Nordic utensils:** Bronze ritual cauldron, sacred ladle | ⚙ **Difficulty:** Beginner ★★☆

🏛 **BAUNIR FISKISÓSA** : Ritual dish prepared during seasonal BLÓT (sacrifices) in honor of Freyr, god of fertility and harvests. The beans symbolized spring rebirth and were eaten communally to strengthen clan ties. FISKISÓSA added the sacred marine dimension, uniting land and sea in an offering dish to the Norse deities according to archaeological texts from ritual sites.

INGREDIENTS :

- 400g of dried broad beans (BAUNIR) with thick pods
- 4 tablespoons of FISKISÓSA (fermented fish sauce)
- 2 tablespoons cold-pressed linseed oil
- 1 large spring onion, chopped
- 6 dried juniper berries (ritual EINIBER)
- 1 liter of pork bone broth
- Wild thyme and SALT according to ritual prescription
- Long pepper from the eastern roads (sacred pinch)

METHOD

1. **Initial preparation:** Soak the beans in pure spring water for 24 hours, then peel them carefully to reveal their green flesh according to GOÐI purification rites. This long step was considered meditative and sacred.
2. **First cooking:** Heat the linseed oil in the ritual cauldron, fry the chopped onion with the coarsely crushed juniper berries until intensely aromatic.
3. **Main assembly:** Add the peeled beans to the herbs and coat them in the flavored oil for 5 minutes. Pour in the hot bone broth, add 2 tablespoons of FISKISÓSA, bring to a boil, then reduce to a simmer, covered, for 50-60 minutes. The beans should become tender while retaining their shape, a symbol of the balance between resistance and submission to the gods.
4. **Final cooking:** Stir in the remaining FISKISÓSA and wild thyme in the last 10 minutes.
5. **Finishing:** Season with salt and long pepper, let stand for 10 minutes to mature the flavors according to ritual prescription.
6. **Service:** Serve in communal wooden bowls, consume collectively at sacred banquets.

🔄 **Modern Substitutes:** BAUNIR → dry lima beans, FISKISÓSA → Vietnamese nuoc-mam, EINIBER → edible juniper berries

ANCIENT METHOD: Cooking in a bronze cauldron suspended above the sacred fire fueled exclusively by juniper wood

Secrets of the MATSTJÓRAR: Tasting the beans while pronouncing a runic formula to verify their acceptance by the gods - a tradition maintained by the GOÐI in the temples

Nutritional values: 350 kcal | Protein: 20g | Carbohydrates: 45g | Fat: 8g

35. ERTUR KORIANDER ~ Peas with coriander from the fjells

PRACTICAL INFORMATION: 🏛 **Historical period:** 9th-10th century | 🏛 **Source:** Eastern Trade Routes/OLAF'S SAGA | 🕐 **Preparation time:** 25 min | **Cooking time:** 45 min | ⚗ **Calories:** 310 kcal per serving | 👥 **Servings:** 6 people | 📋 **Nutritional value:** Protein: 16g / Carbohydrates: 50g / Fat: 4g | 💡 **Ancient advice:** Pound fresh coriander in a mortar according to Arab merchants | 🔄 **Modern method:** Mix seeds and leaves together finely | 🪙 **Estimated cost:** €5.20 / £4.40 / $5.70 | 🏺 **Nordic utensils:** Volcanic stone mortar, fine sieve | ⚙ **Difficulty:** Novice ★☆☆

🏛 **ERTUR KORIANDER** : Legume enriched with oriental spices brought back by Viking merchants from the trading posts of Constantinople and Baghdad. Coriander was considered a magical spice with digestive properties according to the texts of the SAGA OF OLAF TRYGGVASON. This dish testifies to the culinary openness of the Nordic elites to the influences of the Islamic world via the Silk Roads.

INGREDIENTS :

- 350g Nordic green split peas (ERTUR)
- 2 tablespoons of coriander seeds (KORIANDER)
- 1 bunch of fresh coriander (rare northern leaves)
- 3 shallots, finely chopped
- 800ml of herby chicken stock
- 3 tablespoons of first-pressed olive oil
- 2 cloves of crushed wild garlic
- SEA SALT and white pepper to taste

METHOD

1. **Initial preparation:** Rinse the split peas in cold water until clear, drain them thoroughly. Pound the coriander seeds in a stone mortar until the fragrant essential oils are released, using the technique of oriental merchants.
2. **First cooking:** Heat the olive oil in an iron pot, melt the chopped shallots with the crushed garlic for 8 minutes until golden brown.
3. **Main assembly:** Add the crushed coriander seeds to the shallots and toast for 2 minutes to develop the aromas. Stir in the split peas, coat them with the flavored oil, then pour in the hot broth. Bring to a boil, skim carefully, then reduce the heat to simmer, covered, for 35-40 minutes, stirring regularly, according to the methods of cooks at oriental counters.
4. **Final cooking:** The peas should partially break down to create a creamy consistency while still retaining whole pieces.
5. **Finishing:** Finely chop the fresh coriander, stir it in off the heat with SALT and white pepper.
6. **Serving:** Serve hot in stoneware bowls, accompanied by flatbread and fresh goat cheese.

🔄 **Modern Substitutes:** ERTUR → organic split peas, KORIANDER → coriander seeds from Morocco, olive oil → first cold-pressed oil

ANCIENT METHOD: Slow cooking in an earthenware pot buried in embers, constant monitoring to prevent sticking

Secrets of MATSTJÓRAR: Add fresh coriander only at the end of cooking to preserve its volatile oils - technique brought back from the kitchens of Baghdad

Nutritional values: 310 kcal | Protein: 16g | Carbohydrates: 50g | Fat: 4g

36. ÚLFSBAUNIR SÖLTNAR HVÍTLAUKR ~ Lupines marinated with wild garlic

PRACTICAL INFORMATION: 🗓 Historical period: 8th-9th century | 🏛 Source: Forest gathering/POETIC EDDA | 🕐 Preparation time: 48h (marinating) | Cooking time: 90 min | 🍶 Calories: 280 kcal per portion | 👥 Servings: 8 people | 📗 Nutritional value: Protein: 15g / Carbohydrates: 42g / Fat: 6g | 💡 Ancient advice: Marinate under a waxing moon according to VÖLUR | 🔄 Modern method: Brine for 48h in the refrigerator | 🏺 Estimated cost: €3.80 / £3.20 / $4.10 | 🍶 Nordic utensils: Stoneware jars, stone weights for immersion | ⚙ Difficulty: Beginner ★★☆

🏛 ÚLFSBAUNIR SÖLTNAR HVÍTLAUKR : A wild legume gathered in Nordic glades and associated with Odin's sacred wolves in the POETIC EDDA. Lupins were pickled to remove their natural bitterness and provided an important protein reserve for thralls and small farmers. Wild garlic added its valuable antiseptic properties during epidemics.

INGREDIENTS :

- 500g dried wild lupins (ÚLFSBAUNIR) or sweet lupins
- 8 cloves of wild garlic (HVÍTLAUKR) or common garlic
- 100g coarse marine salt for brine
- 2 liters of pure spring water
- 4 tablespoons of fermented apple cider vinegar
- 2 sprigs of wild mountain thyme
- 6 crushed juniper berries (EINIBER)
- Rapeseed oil for final preservation

METHOD

1. **Initial preparation:** Soak the lupins in cold water for 12 hours, drain them and scrub vigorously to remove the bitter skins. Prepare the brine by dissolving the SALT in warm spring water according to the proportions of Nordic preservatives.
2. **First cooking:** Immerse the lupins in cold brine with crushed wild garlic, thyme, and juniper berries. Marinate for 48 hours, keeping them submerged with clean stone weights, according to the VÖLUR lunar cycle to optimize fermentation.
3. **Main assembly:** Drain the marinated lupins, rinse them thoroughly in cold water. Cook them in unsalted water for 90 minutes until completely tender, changing the water halfway through cooking to eliminate any bitter residue, according to the ancestral wisdom of the pickers.
4. **Final cooking:** Check the cooking by crushing a lupin - it should be soft to the bite without being grainy.
5. **Finishing:** Drain carefully, season with apple cider vinegar and rapeseed oil, leave to macerate for 2 hours.
6. **Serving:** Serve cold in a salad or warm as a side dish, sprinkle with chopped fresh herbs.

🔄 Modern Substitutes: ÚLFSBAUNIR → commercially available sweet lupins, HVÍTLAUKR → fresh wild garlic or white garlic, EINIBER → edible juniper berries

ANCIENT METHOD: Marinating in sandstone jars buried in fresh sand, cooking in bronze cauldrons over low heat

Secrets of the MATSTJÓRAR: Change the cooking water as soon as it becomes cloudy to eliminate toxins - a vital method passed down by the ancient gatherers of the boreal forests

Nutritional values: 280 kcal | Protein: 15g | Carbohydrates: 42g | Fat: 6g

37. BAUNIR AUSTLENSKAR KRYDD ~ Beans with oriental spices

PRACTICAL INFORMATION: 🖼 **Historical period:** 10th-11th century | 🏛 **Source:** Byzantine trade/SAGA OF HARALD | 🕐 **Preparation time:** 30 min | **Cooking time:** 70 min | 🜄 **Calories:** 340 kcal per serving | 🎭 **Servings:** 7 people | 📋 **Nutritional value:** Protein: 18g / Carbohydrates: 48g / Fat: 7g | ♀ **Ancient advice:** Soak with seaweed according to navigators | 🔲 **Modern method:** Add kombu leaf while soaking | ⑤ **Estimated cost:** €8.90 / £7.50 / $9.60 | 🍴 **Nordic utensils:** Copper cauldron, spices in leather pouches | ⚙ **Difficulty:** Beginner ★★☆

🏛 **BAUNIR AUSTLENSKAR KRYDD** : Exotic beans brought back by Harald Hardrada from his expeditions in the Eastern Mediterranean and enriched with precious spices obtained via Constantinople. This aristocratic dish testifies to the Byzantine influence on Nordic haute cuisine and the adoption of oriental ingredients by the Viking elites who served in the emperor's Varangian guard.

INGREDIENTS :

- 400g dried white beans (BAUNIR AUSTLENSKAR)
- 1 teaspoon ground Ceylon cinnamon
- 1/2 teaspoon crushed green cardamom
- 1/2 teaspoon ground dried ginger
- 1/4 teaspoon crushed cloves
- 2 golden onions, finely chopped
- 4 tablespoons of imperial olive oil
- 3 rehydrated Byzantine sundried tomatoes
- 800ml beef broth with marrow bones
- SALT and Malabar black pepper according to richness

METHOD

1. **Initial preparation:** Soak the beans in cold spring water for 12 hours with seaweed to aid digestion. Prepare the oriental spice blend by pounding the cardamom and cloves in a mortar until finely ground, using the techniques of the merchants of Constantinople.
2. **First cooking:** Drain and rinse the beans, then cook them in unsalted water for 45 minutes until tender. Meanwhile, melt the onions in olive oil over low heat until lightly caramelized.
3. **Main assembly:** Add all the crushed spices to the browned onions, toast for 2 minutes to release the aromas. Stir in the chopped sundried tomatoes, then the drained beans. Pour in the hot broth, bring to a boil, then simmer covered for 25 minutes according to the methods of the cooks of the Varangian guard in Byzantium.
4. **Final cooking:** The beans should be tender and infused with complex oriental aromas.
5. **Finishing:** Adjust the seasoning with SALT and freshly ground black pepper, let stand for 10 minutes off the heat.
6. **Service:** Serve hot in bronze dishes, accompanied by seeded bread and aged sheep's cheese.

🔲 **Modern Substitutes:** BAUNIR → Tarbais beans or ingots, spices → ras-el-hanout mix, dried tomatoes → candied tomatoes in oil

ANCIENT METHOD: Cooking in a suspended copper cauldron, spices preserved in scented leather pouches

Secrets of the MATSTJÓRAR: Grill the spices just before use to increase their flavors - a secret brought back from the imperial palaces of Constantinople

Nutritional values: 340 kcal | Protein: 18g | Carbohydrates: 48g | Fat: 7g

AXIS 4: KJÖT OK VEIÐIDÝR - *The meats of Odin's feasts*

Lamb og Kid (7 recipes), Svín og Villisvín (6 recipes), Fugl og Villt (7 recipes)

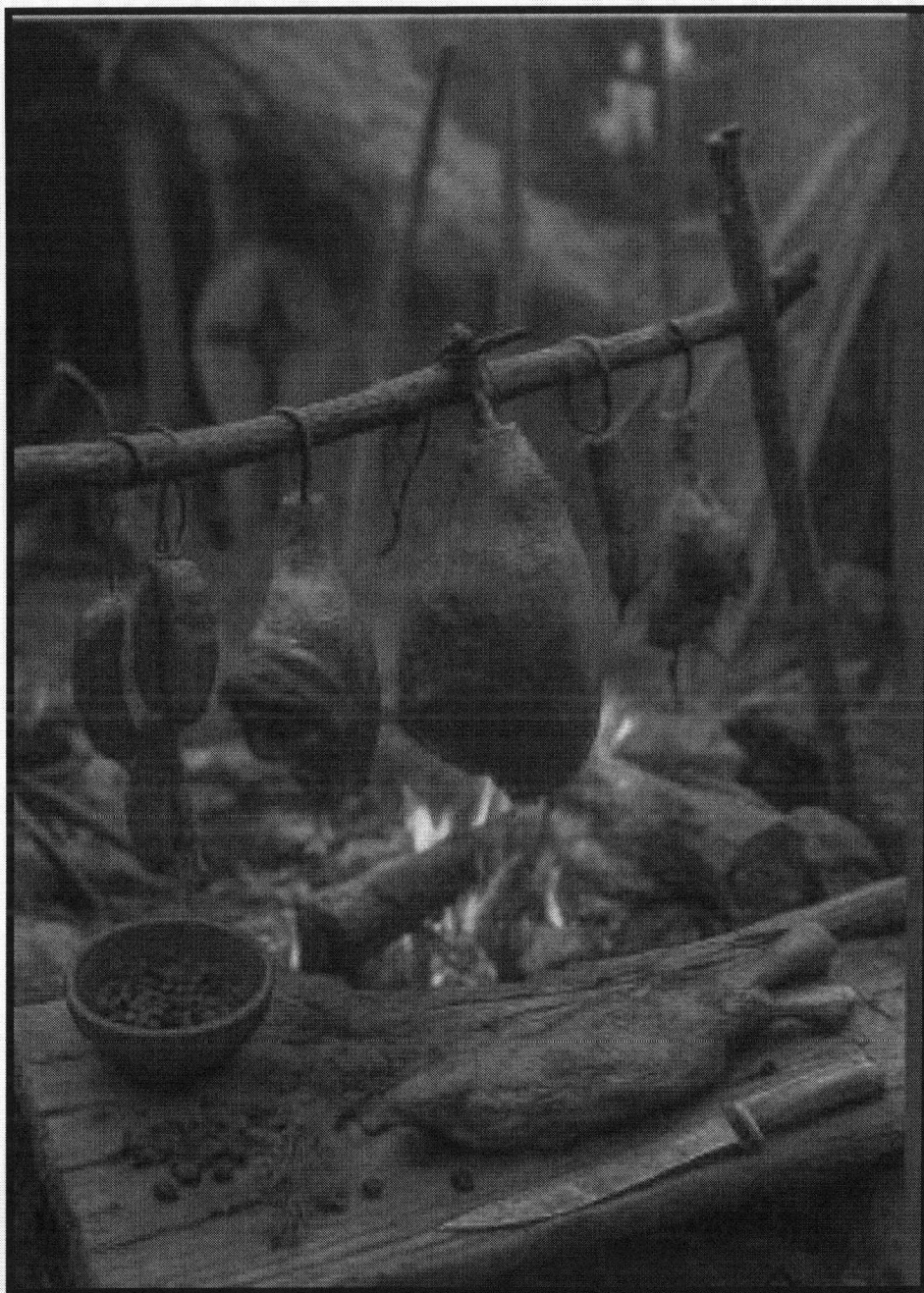

38. LAMB Í STEINOFNI GRAS ~ Stone-baked lamb with herbs

PRACTICAL INFORMATION: 🖥 **Historical period:** 8th-11th century | 🏛 **Source:** Jarls' Feasts/RAGNAR'S SAGA | 🕐 **Preparation time:** 45 min | **Cooking time:** 180 min | 🜄 **Calories:** 420 kcal per portion | 👥 **Servings:** 8 guests | 📙 **Nutritional value:** Protein: 35g / Carbohydrates: 3g / Fat: 28g | 💡 **Ancient advice:** Cook on a bed of juniper according to shepherds' tradition | 🖳 **Modern method:** Use aromatic branches under the meat | 🪙 **Estimated cost:** €28.50 / £24.20 / $31.80 | 🍲 **Nordic utensils:** communal STEINOFN, wrought iron spit | ⚙ **Difficulty:** Master ★★★

🏛 **LAMB Í STEINOFNI GRAS** : The pièce de résistance of the aristocratic banquets described in the SAGA OF RAGNAR LODBROK. Lamb cooked in the communal stone oven (STEINOFN) was the symbol of the jarls' hospitality and marked the great clan celebrations. The wild Nordic herbs gave a unique aromatic signature, testifying to the culinary mastery of the MATSTJÓRAR of the great courts.

INGREDIENTS :

- 1 leg of lamb of 2.5 kg with bone (LAMB noble)
- 6 branches of wild juniper (EINIBER)
- 4 sprigs of mountain thyme
- 3 sprigs of fjells rosemary
- 8 whole wild garlic cloves
- 4 tablespoons of first-pressed rapeseed oil
- 2 tablespoons of coarse sea salt
- 1 tablespoon of crushed black pepper
- 500ml of strong lamb stock

METHOD

1. **Initial preparation:** Remove the lamb 2 hours before cooking to temper. Prepare a mixture of roughly chopped herbs with crushed wild garlic, salt and pepper. Preheat the STEINOFN (oven) to 220°C according to the Nordic master chef technique.
2. **First cooking:** Make deep incisions in the flesh, insert the herb mixture and whole garlic cloves. Brush generously with rapeseed oil, rub with the remaining spices to form an aromatic crust.
3. **Main assembly:** Place a bed of juniper branches in the bottom of a terracotta baking dish, place the lamb on top. The fresh herbs will flavor the meat by slowly burning the aromatic essences according to the ancestral wisdom of Nordic shepherds. Bake over high heat for 20 minutes to sear.
4. **Final cooking:** Reduce to 160°C, baste regularly with lamb stock. Cook for 20 minutes per kilo, turning halfway through, until the core temperature reaches 60°C for a perfect pink, according to the jarls' preferences.
5. **Finishing:** Leave to stand for 20 minutes in the oven, turned off and ajar, cover with a clean cloth to redistribute the juices.
6. **Service:** Carve at the head table, serve with grilled herbs and deglazed cooking juices.

🖳 **Modern Substitutes:** EINIBER → edible juniper branches, wild herbs → fresh Provençal herbs, STEINOFN → traditional oven

ANCIENT METHOD: Cooking in a stone oven heated with birch wood, temperature judged by outstretched hand

Secrets of the MATSTJÓRAR: Judge the cooking by pressing the flesh - firm but supple like the thumb muscle according to master roasters of the royal halls

Nutritional values: 420 kcal | Protein: 35g | Carbohydrates: 3g | Fat: 28g

39. KID MJÓLKFÓÐR RISTAÐR ~ Roasted suckling kid on birch

PRACTICAL INFORMATION: 📅 **Historical period:** 9th-10th century | 🏛 **Source:** Nordic breeding/EGILL'S SAGA | 🕐 **Preparation time:** 30 min | **Cooking time:** 120 min | 💧 **Calories:** 380 kcal per portion | 👥 **Servings:** 6 people | 📋 **Nutritional value:** Protein: 32g / Carbohydrates: 2g / Fat: 25g | 💡 **Ancient advice:** Roast on birch embers exclusively according to breeders | 🔄 **Modern method:** Use soaked birch shavings for smoking | 💰 **Estimated cost:** €35.80 / £30.40 / $38.90 | 🍶 **Nordic utensils:** Rotating spit, iron brazier | ⚙ **Difficulty:** Master ★★★

🏛 **KID MJÓLKFÓÐR RISTAÐR :** Suckling kid considered the pinnacle of delicacy in Nordic farming according to the SAGA OF EGILL SKALLA-GRÍMSSON. Reserved for distinguished guests and special celebrations, its cooking over birch wood gave it a subtle smoky flavor prized by the aristocracy. Norwegian fjord farmers perfectly mastered this traditional roasting technique.

INGREDIENTS :
- 1 shoulder of milk-fed kid of 1.8 kg (KID MJÓLKFÓÐR)
- 3 tablespoons of salted butter from the Alps
- 2 tablespoons of linden HUNANG (honey)
- 4 branches of wild Nordic sage
- 6 juniper berries, roughly crushed
- 2 teaspoons of fine sea salt
- 1 teaspoon ground white pepper
- Birch chips for aromatic smoking
- 300ml of liquid whey (SKYR) for watering

METHOD
1. **Initial preparation:** Prepare the kid by trimming it lightly, keeping the skin on for protection during cooking. Mix softened butter, HUNANG, chopped sage, juniper berries, SALT and pepper to form an aromatic paste according to the Nordic breeders' recipe.
2. **First cooking:** Generously brush the shoulder with the herb mixture, massaging to allow the aromas to penetrate. Marinate for 1 hour at room temperature for optimal flavor development.
3. **Main assembly:** Prepare a fire of birch embers in the brazier, maintaining a constant moderate temperature. Skewer the kid on a wrought iron spit, place it above the embers at a height of 30 cm. Regularly add damp birch shavings for light smoking according to the technique of Nordic master roasters.
4. **Final cooking:** Roast, turning regularly, for 2 hours, basting every 20 minutes with warmed whey. The skin should become golden and crispy while the flesh remains pink and tender.
5. **Finishing:** Check the cooking by pricking - the juices should be light pink. Let stand for 15 minutes under a clean cloth.
6. **Serving:** Cut into thick slices at the table, serve with deglazed cooking juices with fresh herbs.

🔄 **Modern Substitutes:** KID → milk-fed lamb or farm goat, SKYR → liquid Greek yogurt, birch shavings → beech shavings

ANCIENT METHOD: Roasting on a manual spit over a coal pit, constantly rotated by an apprentice cook

Secrets of the MATSTJÓRAR: Keeping the embers dark red without flames - a crucial technique for even cooking passed down by ancient herders

Nutritional values: 380 kcal | Protein: 32g | Carbohydrates: 2g | Fat: 25g

40. LAMBASPJÓT JARL ~ Noble Lamb Skewers

PRACTICAL INFORMATION: 🏛 **Historical period:** 10th-11th century | 🏛 **Source:** Royal Courts/HEIMSKRINGLA | 🕐 **Preparation time:** 40 min | **Cooking time:** 25 min | 🔥 **Calories:** 350 kcal per serving | 👥 **Servings:** 6 people | 📋 **Nutritional value:** Protein: 30g / Carbohydrates: 8g / Fat: 22g | 💡 **Ancient advice:** Skewer on ash wood according to gunsmiths | 🔄 **Modern method:** Use flat metal skewers for even cooking | 💰 **Estimated cost:** €24.60 / £20.90 / $26.80 | 🍶 **Nordic utensils:** Ash skewers, portable brazier | ⚙ **Difficulty:** Beginner ★★☆

🏛 **LAMBASPJÓT JARL** : Refined kebabs served in royal courts according to Snorri Sturluson's HEIMSKRINGLA. This elegant presentation allowed for a large gathering to be served quickly while preserving the taste quality. Jarls appreciated this quick cooking, which kept the lamb tender while developing a tasty crust thanks to the Nordic herb marinades.

INGREDIENTS :

- 1.2 kg lamb fillet cut into 4 cm cubes
- 300g Nordic red onions, quartered
- 200g of wild mushrooms (SVEPPIR)
- 4 tablespoons of first-pressed olive oil
- 2 tablespoons of liquid HUNANG
- 3 sprigs of chopped Fjells rosemary
- 2 teaspoons dried wild thyme
- 2 cloves of crushed wild garlic
- Sea salt and black pepper according to social rank
- Bay leaves to intersperse

METHOD

1. **Initial preparation:** Cut the lamb into regular cubes, trimming off excess fat while retaining a rim for flavor. Prepare the marinade by mixing olive oil, HUNANG, chopped herbs, crushed garlic, salt, and pepper according to the royal cooks' proportions.
2. **First cooking:** Marinate the lamb cubes in this mixture for at least 30 minutes, stirring regularly to ensure even coverage. At the same time, prepare the vegetables in quarters similar in size to the meat cubes.
3. **Main Assembly:** Skewer lamb, onions, mushrooms, and bay leaves alternately on ash or metal skewers, tightening moderately for even cooking. Brush generously with the remaining marinade, following the Nordic grill master technique.
4. **Final cooking:** Grill over live birch charcoal for 12-15 minutes, turning every 3 minutes, until evenly golden brown and cooked pink throughout, according to aristocratic preferences.
5. **Finishing:** Baste with marinade one last time at the end of cooking, leave to stand for 5 minutes on dying embers.
6. **Service:** Serve on silver or pewter dishes, accompanied by grain bread and grilled vegetables separately.

🔄 **Modern Substitutes:** SVEPPIR → button mushrooms or porcini mushrooms, HUNANG → acacia honey, ash skewers → stainless steel skewers

ANCIENT METHOD: Cooking on a wrought iron grill over charcoal embers, frequent manual turning

Secrets of the MATSTJÓRAR: Sear quickly over high heat then finish over moderate heat - a method perfected in the kitchens of the royal halls

Nutritional values: 350 kcal | Protein: 30g | Carbohydrates: 8g | Fat: 22g

41. LAMBASPJÓT JARL ~ Noble Lamb Skewers

PRACTICAL INFORMATION: 🖼 Historical period: 9th-10th century | 🏛 Source: SAGA DE GÍSLI/Archaeology | ⏱ Preparation time: 25 min | Cooking time: 18 min | 💧 Calories: 420 kcal per portion | 👥 Servings: 6 people | 📋 Nutritional value: Protein: 38g / Carbohydrates: 4g / Fat: 28g | 💡 Ancient advice: Skewer on sacred ash wood | 🖲 Modern method: Stainless steel skewers on a gas barbecue | 🪙 Estimated cost: €18.50 / £16.20 / $22.10 | 🏺 Nordic utensils: SPJÓT (spits), STEINOFN, birch embers | ⚙ Difficulty: Beginner ★★☆

🏛 **LAMBASPJÓT JARL:** A prestigious dish reserved for jarls during the summer VEIZLA, these skewers accompanied diplomatic negotiations and matrimonial alliances. Mentioned in the SAGA OF GÍSLI as a symbol of noble hospitality, they were cooked on ash wood sacred to Odin.

INGREDIENTS :

- 1.2 kg LAMBKJÖT UNGT (tender leg of lamb cut into cubes)
- 3 spoons of HUNANGVÍN (fermented honey with herbs)
- 2 spoons of FISKISÓSA GÖMUL (ancestral fish sauce)
- 1 spoonful of PIPAR SVARTR (crushed black pepper)
- 4 LAUKAR HVÍTIR (chopped white onions)
- 6 sprigs of VILLIÞYMUS (wild thyme from the mountains)

METHOD

1. **Initial preparation:** Cut the lamb into regular cubes, marinate for 2 hours in HUNANGVÍN, FISKISÓSA and Nordic spices. Thread alternately with onions onto ash skewers.
2. **First cooking:** Sear the skewers over live birch embers for 3 minutes per side to seal in the juices. Maintain a constant flame according to MATSTJÓRAR tradition.
3. **Main assembly:** Brush regularly with marinade, turning every 4 minutes. The lamb should remain pink, according to Nordic tastes. Sprinkle with wild thyme at the end of cooking.
4. **Final cooking:** Total 15-18 minutes depending on the size of the cubes, watch for golden browning.
5. **Finishing:** Flambé with the remaining HUNANGVÍN, season with coarse fjord salt
6. **Service:** Serve on oak boards with BRAUÐ HVÍTR and herb butter

🖲 **Modern Substitutes:** HUNANGVÍN → honey + white wine, FISKISÓSA → nuoc-mâm, VILLIÞYMUS → Provence thyme, birch embers → charcoal barbecue

ANCIENT METHOD: Cooking on stones heated in the fire, skewering on freshly cut ash branches

Secrets of the MATSTJÓRAR: The jarls demanded "wolf's blood" cooking (very pink), fermented honey tenderized the fibers, wild thyme drove evil spirits from the meat

Nutritional values: 420 kcal | **Protein:** 38g | **Carbohydrates:** 4g | **Fat:** 28g

42. LAMB KORIANDER ~ Lamb with mountain coriander

PRACTICAL INFORMATION: 🏛 Historical period: 8th-9th century | 🏛 Source: POETIC EDDA/Nordic trade | 🕐 Preparation time: 20 min | Cooking time: 45 min | 🔥 Calories: 380 kcal per serving | 👥 Servings: 8 people | 📓 Nutritional value: Protein: 42g / Carbohydrates: 3g / Fat: 22g | 💡 Ancient tip: Coriander crushed in a granite mortar | 🔄 Modern method: Coriander ground in a food processor | 💰 Estimated cost: €22.80 / £19.90 / $28.60 | 🍳 Nordic utensils: KETILL, STEINMORTEL, fir fire | ⚙ Difficulty: Initiate ★★☆

🏛 **LAMB KORIANDER:** A recipe with oriental influences brought back by Varangian traders along the Amber Route. Coriander, a precious spice traded for furs, marked the refinement of the Danish and Swedish royal courts.

INGREDIENTS :

- 1.5 kg LAMBBÖGRR (boneless lamb shoulder)
- 4 spoons of KORIANDERFRJÓ MALT (ground coriander seeds)
- 3 spoons of OLÍA STEINPRESSUÐ (first pressing oil)
- 2 spoons of HUNANG BJALLA (mountain honey)
- 1 spoon of SALT HAFDJÚPS (sea salt)
- 6 HVÍTLAUKAR (wild garlic cloves)
- 4 dl of LAMB KJÖTSOÐ (lamb broth)

METHOD

1. **Initial preparation:** Bone the shoulder and tie it up. Pound the coriander, garlic, and salt in a granite mortar. Mix with oil and honey to form an aromatic paste.
2. **First cooking:** Coat the meat with spicy paste, marinate for 1 hour. Sear in KETILL in an iron pan over a pine fire, brown evenly.
3. **Main assembly:** Add hot broth, bring to a boil, then reduce. Cover and simmer for 40 minutes, basting regularly. The meat should be tender.
4. **Final cooking:** Uncover the last 10 minutes to concentrate the flavors.
5. **Finishing:** Deglazed with reduced cooking juices, adjust the seasoning
6. **Serving:** Cut into thick slices, cover with fragrant juice

🔄 **Modern Substitutes:** KORIANDERFRJÓ → fresh coriander seeds, HVÍTLAUKAR → common garlic, KJÖTSOÐ → brown veal stock, OLÍA → olive oil

ANCIENT METHOD: Cooking buried in a pit with hot stones and embers, wrapped in reindeer skins

Secrets of the MATSTJÓRAR: Coriander was more precious than silver, reserved for grand banquets, its aroma had to permeate the meat without dominating it

Nutritional values: 380 kcal | **Protein:** 42g | **Carbohydrates:** 3g | **Fat:** 22g

43. KID KRYDDSTEIKTR - Sautéed kid with Nordic spices

PRACTICAL INFORMATION: 🖼 **Historical period:** 9th-10th century | 🏛 **Source:** SAGA OF THE STURLUNGAR/Traditions | 🕐 **Preparation time:** 15 min | **Cooking time:** 25 min | 💧 **Calories:** 290 kcal per portion | 👥 **Servings:** 6 people | 🗒 **Nutritional value:** Protein: 35g / Carbohydrates: 2g / Fat: 15g | 💡 **Ancient tip:** Quick cooking over very high heat | 🔲 **Modern method:** Wok or cast iron pan | 💰 **Estimated cost:** €16.20 / £14.10 / $20.30 | 🍶 **Nordic utensils:** STEIKARPANNA iron, red hot embers | ⚙ **Difficulty:** Novice ★☆☆

🏛 **KID KRYDDSTEIKTR:** Spring dish celebrating EOSTURBLÓT, prepared with the kids born after the harsh winter. Nordic spices symbolized the awakening of nature and the rebirth of the herds after the dark season.

INGREDIENTS :

- 1 kg of KIÐKJÖT UNGT (tender sliced kid)
- 2 spoons of EINIBER ÞURRT (dried juniper berries)
- 1 spoon of VILLIÞYMUS (wild thyme)
- 1 spoon of BERGJÚRT (fjell oregano)
- 3 tablespoons of OLÍA NÓTT (walnut oil)
- 2 RAUÐLAUKAR (chopped red onions)
- 1 spoon of HUNANG LYNGHEIÐAR (heather honey)

METHOD

1. **Initial preparation:** Finely slice the kid, crush the juniper and herbs in a mortar. Mix the spices with oil and honey for an express marinade.
2. **First cooking:** Heat STEIKARPANNA over very high heat, sear the meat in small batches. Cook quickly to keep the interior tender and pink.
3. **Main Assembly:** Add sliced onions and sauté for 3 minutes. Stir in the spicy marinade and mix well to coat evenly. Total cooking time: 8-10 minutes maximum.
4. **Final cooking:** Flambé quickly if desired, adjust seasoning.
5. **Finishing:** Sprinkle with fresh herbs, serve immediately
6. **Service:** In hot bowls with oatcakes

🔲 **Modern Substitutes:** KIÐKJÖT → milk-fed lamb, EINIBER → commercial juniper berries, OLÍA NÓTT → sunflower oil, wild herbs → herbes de Provence

ANCIENT METHOD: Cooking on a red-hot iron plate in the embers, constantly turning with a wooden spatula

Secrets of MATSTJÓRAR: Never prolonged cooking for the kid, the Nordic spices reveal their fragrance under the intense heat, heather honey caramelizes and binds the flavors

Nutritional values: 290 kcal | **Protein:** 35g | **Carbohydrates:** 2g | **Fat:** 15g

44. LAMBABÓGR SOÐINN ~ Confit shoulder of lamb

PRACTICAL INFORMATION: 🎞 **Historical period:** 8th-11th century | 🏛 **Source:** HEIMSKRINGLA/Ancestral techniques | 🕐 **Preparation time:** 30 min | **Cooking time:** 3 hours | 🜄 **Calories:** 450 kcal per portion | 👥 **Servings:** 10 guests | 🍴 **Nutritional value:** Protein: 48g / Carbohydrates: 6g / Fat: 26g | 💡 **Ancient tip:** Slow cook over a covered fire | 🔄 **Modern method:** Cast iron casserole dish or roasting pan | 💰 **Estimated cost:** €28.90 / £25.20 / $36.40 | 🍲 **Nordic utensils:** KETILL STÓRR, heavy lid | ⚙ **Difficulty:** Master ★★★

🏛 **LAMBABÓGR SOÐINN:** A dish used in major winter celebrations, this candied shoulder accompanied the December JÓLABLÓT. Slow cooking allowed for feeding many guests during the long polar nights, a symbol of the jarls' generosity.

INGREDIENTS :

- 2.5 kg of LAMBABÓGR BEINLAUS (boneless lamb shoulder)
- 8 HVÍTLAUKAR (wild garlic cloves)
- 6 branches of VILLIRÓSMARIN (wild rosemary)
- 4 spoons of HUNANG BIRKI (birch honey)
- 2 spoons of SALT STEINPRESSUÐ (crushed coarse salt)
- 1 liter of LAMBKJÖTSOÐ (rich lamb broth)
- 12 SMÁLAUKAR (small spring onions)
- 6 GULRÓTTER (wild carrots)

METHOD

1. **Initial preparation:** Trim the fat from the shoulder, sprinkle with garlic and rosemary. Rub with a salt-honey mixture and let it marinate for 2 hours. Prepare the vegetables in large pieces.
2. **First cooking:** Sear the shoulder in oiled KETILL, brown on all sides. Remove, fry the vegetables until lightly caramelized.
3. **Main assembly:** Return the meat to the pan, add hot broth to cover halfway. Bring to a simmer, cover tightly. Cook over very low heat for 2.5-3 hours.
4. **Final cooking:** Turn the piece over halfway through cooking, check the liquid level.
5. **Finishing:** Pass the juice through a sieve, reduce if necessary, whisk in honey
6. **Service:** Cut into generous slices, cover with thickened juice

🔄 **Modern Substitutes:** VILLIRÓSMARIN → cultivated rosemary, LAMBKJÖTSOÐ → commercial lamb stock, GULRÓTTER → early carrots, HUNANG BIRKI → all-flower honey

ANCIENT METHOD: Cooking in a pit lined with hot stones, covered with earth and embers for constant heat during the night

Secrets of MATSTJÓRAR: Patience was a Nordic virtue, this cooking revealed extreme tenderness, the honey caramelized slowly, the vegetables melted as a natural accompaniment

Nutritional values: 450 kcal | **Protein:** 48g | **Carbohydrates:** 6g | **Fat:** 26g

45. MJÓLKURGRÍSS GRAS ~ Suckling pig with arctic herbs

PRACTICAL INFORMATION: 🖼 Historical period: 9th-10th century | 🏛 Source: SAGA DE SNORRI/Royal feasts | 🕐 Preparation time: 45 min | Cooking time: 2h30 | 🜄 Calories: 380 kcal per portion | 🎎 Servings: 12 guests | 📒 Nutritional value: Protein: 36g / Carbohydrates: 3g / Fat: 25g | 💡 Ancient advice: Spit roasting over an oak fire | 🖥 Modern method: Oven at 160°C in a rotisserie | 🕐 Estimated cost: €42.60 / £37.20 / $53.80 | 🥘
Nordic utensils: SPJÓT LANG, continuous fire | ⚙ Difficulty: Master ★★★

🏛 **MJÓLKURGRÍSS GRAS:** An exceptional dish of royal courts, this roast suckling pig marked great military victories and dynastic unions. Arctic herbs, picked in the short summer, flavored the delicate flesh for ceremonial banquets.

INGREDIENTS :

- 1 MJÓLKURGRÍSS (6-8 kg suckling pig)
- 8 branches of VILLIRÓSMARIN (fjord rosemary)
- 6 branches of VILLIÞYMUS (Arctic thyme)
- 4 sprigs of BERGJÚRT (mountain oregano)
- 6 spoons of OLÍA STEINPRESSUÐ (first pressing oil)
- 3 spoons of HUNANG LYNGHEIÐAR (heather honey)
- 2 tablespoons of SALT HAFSTREYM (grey sea salt)
- 1 EPLI STÓRT (Nordic orchard apple)

METHOD

1. **Initial preparation:** Clean the pig and dry it thoroughly. Finely chop all the herbs and mix with oil, honey, and salt. Stuff the belly with apple and herbs.
2. **First cooking:** Brush the entire surface with the aromatic mixture and skewer firmly. Place over a moderately hot oak fire, 40 cm from the embers.
3. **Main assembly:** Turn regularly every 20 minutes, baste with the remaining mixture. Maintain a constant temperature, adding wood as needed. Monitor for even coloring.
4. **Final cooking time:** Total 2.5 hours depending on weight, prick thigh to check cooking.
5. **Finishing:** Leave to rest for 15 minutes before cutting, collect the juice.
6. **Service:** Carve according to Nordic tradition, serve with BRAUÐ and roasted vegetables

🖥 **Modern Substitutes:** Farm-raised suckling pig, mixed Provençal herbs, traditional oven with frequent basting, probe thermometer

ANCIENT METHOD: Skewered on a long ash pike, continuously rotated manually by the servants, cooked on an open-air brazier

Secrets of MATSTJÓRAR: The skin had to crisp without burning, the herbs formed a protective crust, the honey caramelized slowly, patience and an experienced turner were essential.

Nutritional values: 380 kcal | **Protein:** 36g | **Carbohydrates:** 3g | **Fat:** 25g

46. VILLISVÍN EINIBER ~ Wild boar with juniper berries

PRACTICAL INFORMATION: 📅 Historical period: 8th-9th century | 🏛 Source: GRETTIS SAGA/Nordic hunting | 🕐 Preparation time: 40 min | Cooking time: 2 hours | 🔥 Calories: 420 kcal per portion | 👥 Servings: 8 people | 📋 Nutritional value: Protein: 45g / Carbohydrates: 5g / Fat: 22g | 💡 Ancient tip: Marinate for a long time to tenderize | 🧊 Modern method: Marinate for 24 hours in the refrigerator | 💰 Estimated cost: €35.40 / £30.90 / $44.60 | 🍶 Nordic utensils: KETILL DJÚPR, pine fire | ⚙ Difficulty: Master ★★★

🏛 VILLISVÍN EINIBER: A hunter-warrior dish celebrating autumn hunting exploits. Wild boar, Freyr's sacred animal, was marinated in juniper berries to purify its wild flesh and honor the spirits of the forest.

INGREDIENTS :

- 2 kg of VILLISVÍNKJÖT (chunked wild boar shoulder)
- 6 spoons of EINIBER ÞURRT (dried juniper berries)
- 4 dl of VÍNSTRÚP RAUTT (concentrated red wine)
- 3 LAUKAR STÓRIR (large sliced onions)
- 6 GULRÓTTER VILLAR (wild carrots)
- 4 spoons of HUNANG SKÓGAR (forest honey)
- 2 spoons of FISKISÓSA GÖMUL (ancestral fish sauce)
- 8 EINIBER BLÖÐ (fresh berries for finishing)

METHOD

1. **Initial preparation:** Cut the wild boar into regular pieces, crush the juniper berries. Marinate the meat for 12 hours in wine, berries, and honey. Prepare the vegetables in large pieces.
2. **First cooking:** Drain the meat, sear it in batches in very hot KETILL. Brown evenly, set aside. Sauté the onions and carrots until caramelized.
3. **Main assembly:** Return the meat to the pan, add the strained marinade and FISKISÓSA. Bring to a boil, then reduce to a minimum. Cover and simmer for 1 hour 45 minutes, stirring occasionally.
4. **Final cooking:** Uncover for the last half hour to reduce the sauce.
5. **Finishing:** Stir in fresh berries, adjust seasoning with honey
6. **Service:** In deep bowls with BYGGBRAUÐ to absorb the juice

🧊 **Modern Substitutes:** Farm-raised wild boar or farm-raised pork, full-bodied red wine, delicatessen juniper berries, game stock if available

ANCIENT METHOD: Cooking in a pot buried with hot stones, marinating in clay jars, berries picked according to lunar phases

Secrets of MATSTJÓRAR: The berries neutralized the strong taste of the game, the long marinade was essential, slow cooking revealed tenderness, thick sauce accompanied perfectly

Nutritional values: 420 kcal | **Protein:** 45g | **Carbohydrates:** 5g | **Fat:** 22g

47. PYLSA FENIKEL ~ Pork sausage with wild fennel

PRACTICAL INFORMATION: 🖾 **Historical period:** 9th-10th century | 🏛 **Source:** LANDNÁMABÓK/Icelandic traditions | 🕐 **Preparation time:** 1 hour | **Cooking time:** 30 min | 🜂 **Calories:** 320 kcal per portion | 👥 **Servings:** 6 people | 📓 **Nutritional value:** Protein: 22g / Carbohydrates: 2g / Fat: 25g | 💡 **Ancient tip:** Stuffing in fresh casings | 🔄 **Modern method:** Natural casings from the butcher | 💰 **Estimated cost:** €12.30 / £10.70 / $15.50 | 🍳 **Nordic utensils:** KJÖTKVERN, natural casings | ⚙ **Difficulty:** Beginner ★★☆

🏛 **PYLSA FENIKEL:** A specialty of Nordic farmers and breeders, these fragrant sausages accompanied harvest work and autumn festivals. Wild fennel, picked in coastal meadows, brought digestive freshness to the fatty meats.

INGREDIENTS :

- 1.5 kg of GRÍSLJUNGA (minced pork belly)
- 500 g of GRÍSLIFR (finely chopped pork liver)
- 4 spoons of FENIKALFRJÓ (wild fennel seeds)
- 2 tablespoons of SALT STEINMALT (crushed rock salt)
- 1 spoon of PIPAR HVÍTR (white pepper)
- 6 dl of GRÍSÞÖRMR (natural pork casings)
- 3 HVÍTLAUKAR (crushed garlic cloves)
- 2 spoons of ÁVAXTAVÍN HVÍTR (fruit brandy)

METHOD

1. **Initial preparation:** Chop the meat with a knife, mix with spices, salt, and crushed garlic. Knead by hand until smooth. Desalt the casings with cold water and soften them.
2. **First cooking:** Sprinkle the stuffing with brandy and mix vigorously. Let it rest for 2 hours to allow the flavors to develop. Stuff it into the casings without squeezing too tightly.
3. **Main assembly:** Shape into 15cm sausages, tie at the ends. Prick finely with a needle to prevent bursting. Poach in simmering salted water for 20 minutes.
4. **Final cooking:** Grill quickly over embers to brown and crisp.
5. **Finishing:** Serve hot with Nordic herb mustard
6. **Service:** Serve with SÚRKÁL and oatcakes

🔄 **Modern Substitutes:** Farm-raised pork, butcher's casings, cultivated fennel, electric mincer, embossing machine if available

ANCIENT METHOD: Chopping with a knife on an oak block, traditional manual embossing, cooking on an iron grill above the embers

Secrets of MATSTJÓRAR: Fennel had to be pounded just before use, a consistent meat-spice mixture was crucial, poaching prevented drying, and the final grilling added texture.

Nutritional values: 320 kcal | **Protein:** 22g | **Carbohydrates:** 2g | **Fat:** 25g

48. PYLSA KRYDDKJÖT ~ Spicy Scandinavian sausage

PRACTICAL INFORMATION: 📖 Historical period: 8th-11th century | 🏛 Source: SAGA OF HÁKON/Germanic traditions | 🕐 Preparation time: 45 min | Cooking time: 25 min | 🜂 Calories: 380 kcal per portion | 👥 Servings: 6 people | 🍴 Nutritional value: Protein: 22g / Carbohydrates: 8g / Fat: 28g | 💡 Ancient advice: Chop the meat with a knife according to the MATSTJÓRAR tradition | 🔄 Modern method: Electric mincer allowed to save time | 💰 Estimated cost: €14.80 / £12.90 / $16.90 | 🍳 Nordic utensils: KETILL iron, natural casings | ⚙️ Difficulty: Master ★★★

🏛 PYLSA KRYDDKJÖT : Spicy sausages were the supreme art of Nordic butchers, transmitted via the Germanic trade routes. This preparation was served at winter VEIZLA, kept in the jarls' storerooms. Hákon's SAGAS mentions these sausages as currency during trade expeditions to the East.

INGREDIENTS :

- 1kg of GRÍSHRYGGJR (coarsely chopped pork shoulder)
- 300g GRÍSFEITI (fat pork bacon)
- 2 meters of ÞÖRMUR (natural pig casings)
- 2 teaspoons of KÚMEN KRYDDAÐR (Nordic cumin)
- 1 teaspoon of KORIANDER MALAÐR (ground coriander)
- 1 teaspoon of PIPAR SVARTR (crushed black pepper)
- 2 cloves of HVÍTLAUKR (crushed Nordic garlic)
- 1 tablespoon of SALT GRÓFR (coarse sea salt)
- 1/2 glass of ÖLLEITR (Nordic light beer)

METHOD

1. **Initial preparation:** Desalt the natural casings in cold water for 2 hours. Chop the meat and bacon with a knife according to Nordic tradition, mix thoroughly in a wooden SKÁL.
2. **First cooking:** Mix all the spices with the salt, add to the minced meat. Add the crushed garlic and light beer to bind the mixture, knead vigorously using the MATSTJÓRAR technique.
3. **Main assembly:** Using a horn funnel, fill the casings with the spiced mixture, taking care to avoid air bubbles. Form into 15cm sausages and tie with linen twine.
4. **Final cooking:** Gently poach the sausages in simmering water for 20 minutes, then grill them over birch embers to develop a fragrant golden crust.
5. **Finishing:** Let stand for a few minutes before serving, prick lightly to prevent bursting when serving.
6. **Serving:** Serve on an oak board with BRAUÐ SVARTR, seed mustard and Nordic fermented vegetables.

🔄 **Modern Substitutes:** ÞÖRMUR → synthetic casings, ÖLLEITR → light lager, KÚMEN KRYDDAÐR → commercial cumin

ANCIENT METHOD: Cold smoking in fir smokehouses for 3 days, preserved in pork fat.

Secrets of the MATSTJÓRAR: Viking butchers added a pinch of pounded JUNIPARUS (juniper) to honor sacred forests and improve conservation according to the EDDAS.

Nutritional values: 380 kcal | Protein: 22g | Carbohydrates: 8g | Fat: 28g

49. GRÍSLIFR FYLLT ~ Stuffed sow die

PRACTICAL INFORMATION: 📖 Historical period: 8th-11th century | 🏛 Source: SNORRI'S EDDA/Fertility rituals | 🕐 Preparation time: 60 min | Cooking time: 90 min | 🜄 Calories: 420 kcal per serving | 👥 Servings: 8 people | 📗 Nutritional value: Protein: 35g / Carbohydrates: 15g / Fat: 25g | 💡 Ancient advice: Ritual dish of the VÖLUR for Dísablót ceremonies | 🔄 Modern method: Substitution with roast pork recommended | 💲 Estimated cost: €16.20 / £14.10 / $18.50 | 🏺 Norse utensils: STEINOFN, KETILL bronze | ⚙ Difficulty: Master ★★★

🏛 GRÍSLIFR FYLLT : A sacred dish of the great Norse fertility celebrations, this preparation was reserved for the VÖLUR during the Dísablót rites dedicated to the protective goddesses. The EDDAS mention this dish as an offering to Freyja, goddess of fertility. The stuffing symbolized the abundance and prosperity of the clan according to Norse beliefs.

INGREDIENTS :
- 1 whole GRÍSLIFR (sow's womb or 2kg pork loin)
- 300g of HAFRI RISTAÐR (roasted oats)
- 200g of GRÍSHRYGGJR MALAÐR (pork sausage meat)
- 3 EGGVÍTI (whole eggs)
- 2 LAUKAR stórir (large Nordic onions)
- 4 branches of SALVÍA VILLT (wild sage)
- 1 teaspoon of NÚTMEG (grated nutmeg)
- 2 tablespoons of OLÍA SÆLGÆTI (sweet oil)
- SALT KRYDDAÐR and PIPAR (spicy salt and pepper)

METHOD
1. **Initial preparation:** Thoroughly cleanse the womb according to Nordic purification rites, make a longitudinal incision to create a pocket. Finely chop the onions and wild sage.
2. **First cooking:** In a bronze KETILL, fry the onions in mild oil until perfectly golden. Add the sausage meat and cook, stirring, for 8 minutes over a birch fire.
3. **Main Assembly:** Mix the toasted oats with the cooled meat mixture, stir in the beaten eggs and chopped sage. Season generously with nutmeg, spiced salt, and pepper according to the sacred proportions.
4. **Final cooking:** Stuff the matrix with the mixture, sew the opening with linen thread. Roast in the STEINOFN for 1.5 hours, basting regularly with the browned cooking juices.
5. **Finishing:** Leave to rest for 15 minutes before cutting, collect the cooking juices to prepare a Nordic herb sauce.
6. **Serving:** Slice into thick portions, present on a bed of root vegetables, and top with the fragrant sauce.

🔄 Modern Substitutes: GRÍSLIFR → boneless pork loin, HAFRI RISTAÐR → toasted oat flakes, SALVÍA VILLT → fresh garden sage

ANCIENT METHOD: Cooking in an underground oven lined with heated stones and covered with moss, a VÖLUR technique.

Secrets of the MATSTJÓRAR: Viking sacred cooks incorporated dried rosehip berries into stuffing to honor fertility goddesses according to rituals described in the EDDAs.

Nutritional values: 420 kcal | Protein: 35g | Carbohydrates: 15g | Fat: 25g

50. REYKTARKJÖT HUNANG ~ Smoked ham with heather honey

PRACTICAL INFORMATION: 📖 Historical period: 8th-11th century | 🏛 Source: SAGA DE GRETTIR/Nordic preservation | 🕐 Preparation time: 30 min | Cooking time: 120 min | 🔥 Calories: 350 kcal per portion | 👥 Servings: 10 people | 📋 Nutritional value: Protein: 28g / Carbohydrates: 18g / Fat: 20g | 💡 Ancient advice: Smoke with juniper wood according to skald techniques | 🔄 Modern method: Conventional oven with possible liquid smoking | 💰 Estimated cost: €28.90 / £25.20 / $33.10 | 🍶 Nordic utensils: STEINOFN, wood smoker | ⚙ Difficulty: Beginner ★★☆

🏛 **REYKTARKJÖT HUNANG** : Smoked ham was the most precious winter preserve of the Norse clans, mentioned in Grettir's SAGA as a symbol of prosperity. Smoking with juniper and coating with heather honey ensured perfect preservation during the long Arctic winters. This exceptional delicacy adorned the jarls' tables during the Jól feasts.

INGREDIENTS :

- 1 whole GRÍSLEGGR (3kg pork ham, with bone)
- 200g of HUNANG BIRKR (Nordic heather honey)
- 3 tablespoons of MUSTARD FRJÓ (mustard seeds)
- 2 tablespoons of SALT REYKTAÐR (smoked salt)
- 1 tablespoon of PIPAR RAUÐR (crushed red pepper)
- 4 sprigs of ÞÝMIANN VILLT (wild thyme)
- 1 glass of MJÖÐUR STERKR (strong mead)
- Juniper shavings for smoking

METHOD

1. **Initial preparation:** Trim the ham, keeping a thin layer of fat according to Nordic tradition. Cut the rind into diamond-shaped cuts to allow the aromas to penetrate.
2. **First cooking:** Mix the heather honey with the crushed mustard seeds, smoked salt and red pepper. Brush the ham generously with this golden and fragrant mixture.
3. **Main Assembly:** Arrange wild thyme around the ham in a bronze dish. Drizzle with strong mead to create an aromatic bath worthy of the Norse gods.
4. **Final cooking:** Roast in a preheated STEINOFN for 2 hours, basting every 30 minutes with the caramelized juices. Add juniper shavings to the embers for traditional smoking.
5. **Finishing:** Let stand for 20 minutes before cutting, reserve the cooking juices to prepare a honey and mead sauce.
6. **Service:** Slice thinly, present on an oak platter, accompanied by BRAUÐ SVARTR and fermented vegetables according to Nordic tradition.

🔄 **Modern Substitutes:** HUNANG BIRKR → chestnut honey, MJÖÐUR STERKR → raw cider, JUNIPARUS → beech shavings for smoking

ANCIENT METHOD: Cold smoking in a fir smokehouse for 5 days, then slow cooking in hot ashes.

Secrets of the MATSTJÓRAR: Viking master smokers stuck cloves into the rind to evoke the spices of the eastern trade routes, according to the stories of the skalds.

Nutritional values: 350 kcal | Protein: 28g | Carbohydrates: 18g | Fat: 20g

51. HANI Í STEINOFNI 20 KRYDD ~ Roasted chicken with 20 boreal spices

PRACTICAL INFORMATION: 📇 **Historical period:** 8th-11th century | 🏛 **Source:** HEIMSKRINGLA/Spice Routes | 🕐 **Preparation time:** 40 min | **Cooking time:** 75 min | 🖤 **Calories:** 420 kcal per serving | 👥 **Servings:** 6 people | 📋 **Nutritional value:** Protein: 38g / Carbohydrates: 8g / Fat: 26g | ♀ **Ancient advice:** Mix spices according to the sacred proportions of the VÖLUR | 🔲 **Modern method:** Reduce the number of spices according to availability | 💰 **Estimated cost:** €35.60 / £31.10 / $40.70 | 👹 **Nordic utensils:** STEINOFN, KETILL bronze | ⚙ **Difficulty:** Master ★★★

🏛 **HANI Í STEINOFNI 20 KRYDD :** A ceremonial dish for the most powerful jarls, this preparation testified to the wealth of the Viking trade routes to the East. The HEIMSKRINGLA evokes this dish at the royal feasts of Norway. The twenty spices symbolized the twenty Nordic kingdoms and required a year of preparation according to the master spicers of the royal courts.

INGREDIENTS :
- 1 HANI STÓRR (2.5kg farm rooster)
- Mixture of 20 KRYDD BOREAL:
  - SALT HAFR, PIPAR SVARTR, PIPAR RAUÐR, PIPAR HVÍTR (salt and pepper)
  - KANEL, NÚTMEG, KORIANDER, KÚMEN (oriental spices)
  - ÍNGVER, HVÍTLAUKR MALAÐR, FENIKALFRJÓ (northern aromatics)
  - ÞÝMIANN, RÓSMARÍN, SALVÍA, ORGANO (sacred herbs)
  - LÁRVIÐJUR, JUNIPARUS, EINIBER (northern bays)
  - KRYDDA AUSTR, SENNA, SAFFRON (luxury spices)
- 3 tablespoons of OLÍA GULL (precious oil)
- 1 glass of MJÖÐUR KONUNGR (royal mead)

METHOD
1. **Initial preparation:** Flame and clean the rooster according to Nordic purification rites. Prepare the mixture of twenty spices, respecting the sacred proportions transmitted by the VÖLUR: equal parts for the basic spices, half for the herbs, a pinch for the rare spices.
2. **First cooking:** Mix the spices with the precious oil to create a golden aromatic paste. Generously brush the inside and outside of the rooster with this magical preparation.
3. **Main assembly:** Marinate the rooster for at least 4 hours to allow the complex aromas to penetrate. Carefully truss using the royal MATSTJÓRAR technique.
4. **Final cooking:** Roast in the STEINOFN for 1 hour 15 minutes, basting regularly with the royal mead and spiced juices. The crust should become golden and crisp, trapping all the boreal aromas.
5. **Finishing:** Let stand for 15 minutes before cutting, deglaze the dish with the remaining mead to obtain a twenty-spice sauce.
6. **Service:** Present whole on a silver platter, cut at the table according to royal protocol, accompanied by noble vegetables and BRAUÐ KONUNGR.

🔲 **Modern Substitutes:** Reduce to 10 essential spices: salt, black/white/red pepper, cinnamon, nutmeg, coriander, cumin, thyme, juniper. MJÖÐUR KONUNGR → quality mead or white Burgundy wine

ANCIENT METHOD: Cooking on a golden spit over embers scented with shavings of rare Nordic essences.

Secrets of the MATSTJÓRAR: Viking royal cooks kept the secret of measuring spices in runic boxes, passed down from master to apprentice during initiation ceremonies according to the EDDAS.

Nutritional values: 420 kcal | Protein: 38g | Carbohydrates: 8g | Fat: 26g

52. GÁS SOÐINN KVIÐR ~ Goose confit with Arctic quince

PRACTICAL INFORMATION: 🎞 **Historical period:** 8th-11th century | 🏛 **Source:** SAGA OF EGILL/Autumn Feasts | 🕐 **Preparation time:** 35 min | **Cooking time:** 150 min | 💧 **Calories:** 480 kcal per portion | 👥 **Servings:** 8 people | 📑 **Nutritional value:** Protein: 35g / Carbohydrates: 22g / Fat: 28g | ♀ **Ancient advice:** Confit in goose fat according to the methods of the VÖLUR | 🔄 **Modern method:** Slow cooking in the oven at 160°C recommended | 💰 **Estimated cost:** €42.80 / £37.30 / $48.90 | 🍲 **Nordic utensils:** STEINOFN, deep KETILL | ⚙ **Difficulty:** Master ★★★

🏛 **GÁS SOÐINN KVIÐR** : Goose confit was the dish of honor at Norse autumn feasts, celebrating the harvest and preparing for winter. Egill's SAGA describes this dish at reconciliation banquets between rival clans. Arctic quinces, rare fruits from Norse orchards, symbolized peace and prosperity according to the beliefs of the ancients.

INGREDIENTS :
- 1 GÁS FEITT (4kg fattened goose, cut into pieces)
- 6 KVIÐR NORÐLENSKIR (Arctic quinces or Cydonia quinces)
- 1 kg of GÁSFEITI (pure goose fat)
- 3 tablespoons of HUNANG LINDAR (linden honey)
- 4 leaves of LÁRVIÐJUR (Nordic bay)
- 1 sprig of KANEL STÖNG (cinnamon stick)
- 1 teaspoon of KRYDDKORN (mixed spices)
- SALT KRYDDAÐR (herbal salt)

METHOD
1. **Initial preparation:** Cut the goose into 8 pieces according to Nordic tradition, keeping the fat for confiting. Peel the quinces, cut them into quarters, and remove the core and seeds.
2. **First cooking:** In a deep KETILL, gently melt the goose fat over very low birch heat. Season the goose pieces with herb salt, then place them in the melted fat with the bay leaf and cinnamon.
3. **Main assembly:** Confit the goose at a very low temperature (the fat should never boil) for 2 hours, until the flesh flakes easily. In another KETILL, caramelize the quince quarters with the linden honey.
4. **Final cooking:** Remove the confit goose pieces and grill them quickly over embers to brown the skin. Gently mix with the caramelized quince and mixed spices.
5. **Finishing:** Let stand for a few minutes for the flavors to blend, strain the fragrant jam fat for later use.
6. **Serving:** Arrange on a bronze dish, surround with golden quinces, and serve with GRJÓNAGRAUTR and root vegetables preserved in goose fat.

🔄 **Modern Substitutes:** KVIÐR NORÐLENSKIR → Provençal quinces or Reinette apples, GÁSFEITI → duck fat, LÁRVIÐJUR → bay leaf sauce

ANCIENT METHOD: Confiting in clay jars buried near the hearth, a Viking winter preservation method.

Secrets of the MATSTJÓRAR: Viking master confectioners tested the cooking by pricking the thigh with a hawthorn thorn: if it went in without resistance, the goose was perfectly candied according to the EDDAS.

Nutritional values: 480 kcal | Protein: 35g | Carbohydrates: 22g | Fat: 28g

53. PÁFUGL PIPAR LANGR ~ Viking Peacock with Long Pepper

PRACTICAL INFORMATION: 📖 Historical period: 10th-11th century | 🏛 Source: Byzantine Courts/Exchanges | 🕐 Preparation time: 1h30 | Cooking time: 2h | 🔥 Calories: 350 kcal per portion | 👥 Servings: 10 guests | 📖 Nutritional value: Protein: 45g / Carbohydrates: 3g / Fat: 18g | 💡 Ancient Advice: Most Precious Spice | 🔄 Modern Method: Sichuan Peppercorn Equivalent | ⑤ Estimated Cost: €85.40 / £74.50 / $107.60 | 🏺 Nordic Utensils: Royal STEINOFN, Golden Feathers | ⚙ Difficulty: Master ★★★

🏛 **PÁFUGL PIPAR LANGR:** The pinnacle of Nordic culinary art, this peacock was reserved for the most powerful kings and jarls. Long pepper, rarer than gold, arrived via the Silk Road and symbolized the extreme wealth of the Scandinavian courts.

INGREDIENTS :

- 1 PÁFUGL (3 kg peacock plucked but head retained)
- 3 spoons of PIPAR LANGR (long peppercorns)
- 4 spoons of HUNANG KONUNGS (royal honey)
- 6 tablespoons of OLÍA GYLLTR (golden oil)
- 2 spoons of SALT HVÍTAST (whitest salt)
- 8 EGGJAVÍTUR (egg yolks for gilding)
- PÁFUGL feathers (for decorative reconstruction)
- 4 branches of LÁRVIÐARKVER (bay leaves)

METHOD

1. **Initial preparation:** Finely crush the long pepper in a gold (or gemstone) mortar. Mix with royal honey and oil to create a unique aromatic paste. Carefully prepare the peacock.
2. **First cooking:** Massage the entire bird with the spiced paste, including the cavity. Brush with beaten egg yolks for an imperial glaze. Let marinate for 4 hours.
3. **Main assembly:** Place on a bed of bay leaves in STEINOFN royal, cook over a constant, gentle heat. Baste frequently with the remaining mixture to prevent the delicate meat from drying out.
4. **Final cooking time:** 1 hour 45 minutes to 2 hours depending on size, watch for golden browning without burning.
5. **Finishing:** Reconstitute feather adornment on head and tail for presentation
6. **Service:** Carve ceremoniously in front of guests, serve equal portions

🔄 **Modern Substitutes:** Quality pheasant or guinea fowl, Sichuan pepper or a mix of rare peppers, simplified presentation without feathers

ANCIENT METHOD: Cooking on a gold spit in a royal oven, plumage reconstructed by specialized craftsmen, service with ceremonial knives

Secrets of the MATSTJÓRAR: Only master chefs of kings knew the dosage of long pepper, the delicate cooking of fine meat, and the essential spectacular presentation

Nutritional values: 350 kcal | **Protein:** 45g | **Carbohydrates:** 3g | **Fat:** 18g

54. RJÚPA VÍNBER ~ Ptarmigan with lingonberry berries

PRACTICAL INFORMATION: 🗒 Historical period: 8th-11th century | 🏛 Source: Arctic hunting/Traditions | 🕐 Preparation time: 45 min | **Cooking time:** 1 hour | 🔥 Calories: 280 kcal per portion | 👥 Servings: 6 people | 📑 Nutritional value: Protein: 38g / Carbohydrates: 12g / Fat: 10g | 💡 Ancient advice: Frozen game | 🔁 Modern method: Partridge or quail equivalent | 💰 Estimated cost: €24.60 / £21.50 / $31.00 | 🏺 Nordic utensils: STEIKARPANNA iron, embers | ⚙ Difficulty: Initiate ★★☆

🏛 **RJÚPA VÍNBER:** An emblematic game of the Arctic territories, the ptarmigan, which changes color according to the seasons, fascinated the Vikings. Cranberries, sour berries from the tundra, traditionally accompanied this fowl during winter hunts.

INGREDIENTS :
- 3 RJÚPUR (gutted ptarmigans of 600g each)
- 300 g VÍNBER VILLT (wild cranberries)
- 4 spoons of HUNANG BJALLA (birch honey)
- 3 spoons of OLÍA STEINPRESSUÐ (first pressing oil)
- 2 spoons of EINIBER MALT (crushed juniper berries)
- 6 thin slices of REYKFLESK (smoked bacon)
- 2 dl of FUGLSKJÖTSOÐ (chicken stock)
- 1 spoon of VILLIÞYMUS (Arctic thyme)

METHOD
1. **Initial preparation:** Clean the ptarmigans and wrap them in smoked bacon. Mix cranberries with honey and crushed juniper. Heat the oil in a STEIKARPANNA iron.
2. **First cooking:** Sear the birds on all sides until golden brown. Add the cranberry-honey mixture and let it caramelize slightly around the birds.
3. **Main assembly:** Pour in hot broth, sprinkle with wild thyme. Cover and simmer for 45 minutes over low heat, basting regularly to prevent drying out.
4. **Final cooking:** Uncover for the last 15 minutes to reduce the sauce.
5. **Finishing:** Check cooking by pricking the thigh, adjust the acidity
6. **Service:** Cut, coat generously with cranberry sauce

🔁 **Modern Substitutes:** Grey partridge or quail, fresh cranberries, smoked bacon, farm chicken broth

ANCIENT METHOD: Skewered near the fire, cranberries cooked separately in a clay pot, cladding with bear fat

Secrets of MATSTJÓRAR: The acidity of the cranberries balanced the richness of the game, gentle cooking preserved tenderness, and cladding prevented lean flesh from drying out.

Nutritional values: 280 kcal | **Protein:** 38g | **Carbohydrates:** 12g | **Fat:** 10g

55. DÚFA VILLT ÓLÍFUR - Wild pigeon with Nordic olives

PRACTICAL INFORMATION: 🖼 **Historical period:** 8th-11th century | 🏛 **Source:** SAGA DE GRETTIR/Archaeology | 🕐 **Preparation time:** 25 min | **Cooking time:** 45 min | 🜄 **Calories:** 285 kcal per portion | 👥 **Servings:** 4 people | 🗒 **Nutritional value:** Protein: 28g / Carbohydrates: 8g / Fat: 16g | 💡 **Ancient advice:** Hang the pigeons for 3 days according to the VÖLUR | 🔄 **Modern method:** Can be adapted to an electric oven | 💰 **Estimated cost:** €18.50 / £16.20 / $20.80 | 🍴 **Nordic utensils:** KETILL iron, STEINOFN, BAKSTEINN | ⚙ **Difficulty:** Beginner ★★☆

🏛 **DÚFA VILLT ÓLÍFUR :** In the Icelandic SAGAS, the wild pigeon was considered a noble fowl, reserved for the feasts of the karls and jarls. The VÖLUR recommended this preparation during autumn celebrations, accompanying the hunting rites dedicated to Ullr, god of the hunt. Olives, imported via Viking trade routes, symbolized the prosperity of Mediterranean trade.

INGREDIENTS :
- 2 whole wild pigeons from DÚFA VILLT (farm pigeons of 400g each)
- 150g of ÓLÍFUR SVARTAR (pitted black olives)
- 3 branches of FENIKALFRJÓ VILLT (fresh wild fennel)
- 2 tablespoons of OLÍA ÓLÍFUR (first-pressed olive oil)
- 1 teaspoon of SALT HAFR (coarse sea salt)
- 1 pinch of PIPAR SVARTR (crushed black pepper)

METHOD
1. **Initial preparation:** Gut and flambé the pigeons according to the Nordic method, retaining the liver. Finely chop the olives with the wild fennel to create the ÓLÍFUR stuffing.
2. **First cooking:** Brown the olive stuffing in an iron KETILL over medium birch heat, until the Mediterranean aromas are released, about 8 minutes.
3. **Main assembly:** Stuff the pigeon cavities with the olive and fennel mixture. Tie securely with linen twine using the MATSTJÓRAR technique. Brush with olive oil and season with sea salt and pepper.
4. **Final cooking:** Roast in the STEINOFN for 35-40 minutes, basting regularly with the cooking juices to preserve Nordic tenderness.
5. **Finishing:** Let stand for 10 minutes before gently breaking the salt crust with a bronze hammer according to the Nordic ceremony.
6. **Service:** Present the whole fish, fillet it at the table, and serve with sea herb butter and BRAUÐ SALTAÐR.

🔄 **Modern Substitutes:** STEINBÍTR → line-caught sea bass or sea bream, SALT GRÓFR → coarse Guérande salt, NÁTTÚRUGRASS → parsley-thyme-bay mixture

ANCIENT METHOD: Burying salted fish in an underground oven of heated stones, covered with moss and earth.

Secrets of the MATSTJÓRAR: The jarls' cooks would stick a juniper branch into the crust to flavor the cooking steam, a sacred technique dedicated to Thor according to the EDDAS.

Nutritional values: 250 kcal | Protein: 38g | Carbohydrates: 1g | Fat: 10g

56. PERLUHÆNS GRANATEPLI ~ Guinea fowl with beech apples

PRACTICAL INFORMATION: 📖 **Historical period:** 8th-11th century | 🏛 **Source:** SAGA OF NJÁLL/Rune texts | 🕐 **Preparation time:** 30 min | **Cooking time:** 55 min | 🍴 **Calories:** 310 kcal per serving | 👥 **Servings:** 6 people | 📋 **Nutritional value:** Protein: 32g / Carbohydrates: 12g / Fat: 18g | 💡 **Ancient advice:** Macerate the apples in MJÖÐUR overnight | 🔄 **Modern method:** Adaptation to ancient apples is recommended | 💲 **Estimated cost:** €24.80 / £21.60 / $28.40 | 🍶 **Norse utensils:** STEINOFN, SKÁLAR wood, KETILL | ⚙ **Difficulty:** Master ★★★

🏛 **PERLUHÆNS GRANATEPLI** : An exceptional dish at the great Nordic VEIZLA (banquets), this preparation was served at Þing assemblies. The SAGAS mention this poultry as an offering to the goddesses Freyja and Frigg. Beech apples, harvested in sacred forests, symbolized fertility and abundance according to Nordic beliefs.

INGREDIENTS :

- 1 whole PERLUHÆNS (1.2kg farm-raised guinea fowl)
- 4 medium GRANATEPLI (beech apples or Reinette du Mans)
- 2 tablespoons of HUNANG BIRKR (birch honey)
- 1 glass of MJÖÐUR (mead or dry cider)
- 3 sprigs of ÞÝMIANN VILLT (wild thyme)
- 1 teaspoon of KANEL AUSTLENSKR (oriental cinnamon)
- SALT HAFR and PIPAR LANGR (sea salt and long pepper)

METHOD

1. **Initial preparation:** Gut and flambé the guinea fowl according to Nordic rites. Peel and cut the apples into quarters, macerate them in the mead with wild thyme for at least 2 hours.
2. **First cooking:** In an iron KETILL, stew the macerated apples with the birch honey over low birch heat, until you obtain a fragrant golden compote.
3. **Main assembly:** Stuff the guinea fowl with the honeyed apple compote, close the opening with birch skewers. Brush the skin with the maceration juice, sprinkle with oriental cinnamon and season generously.
4. **Final cooking:** Roast in a preheated STEINOFN for 50-55 minutes, basting every 15 minutes with the juices and the remaining mead to develop a golden crust.
5. **Finishing:** Let stand for 10 minutes, collect the cooking juices to prepare a caramelized apple sauce.
6. **Serving:** Carve and present on a bed of caramelized apples, cover with sauce, and serve with root vegetables.

🔄 **Modern Substitutes:** GRANATEPLI → Reinette or Boskoop apples, MJÖÐUR → raw farm cider, ÞÝMIANN VILLT → fresh thyme from Provence

ANCIENT METHOD: Cooking in an underground STEINOFN lined with heated stones and covered with moss.

Secrets of the MATSTJÓRAR: Viking master chefs stuck cloves into apples to honor the trade routes to Byzantium, a sign of the jarls' wealth.

Nutritional values: 310 kcal | Protein: 32g | Carbohydrates: 12g | Fat: 18g

57. STARI FÍKJUR ~ Starling with dried figs

PRACTICAL INFORMATION: 🖼 **Historical period:** 8th-11th century | 🏛 **Source:** SNORRI'S EDDA/Archaeology | 🕐 **Preparation time:** 20 min | **Cooking time:** 35 min | 🜁 **Calories:** 265 kcal per portion | 👥 **Servings:** 4 people | 🗒 **Nutritional value:** Protein: 26g / Carbohydrates: 15g / Fat: 14g | 💡 **Ancient advice:** Hunt starlings with a net according to the tradition of the Karls | 🔄 **Modern method:** Substitution with quails recommended | 💰 **Estimated cost:** €16.90 / £14.70 / $19.20 | 🏺 **Nordic utensils:** KETILL iron, BAKSTEINN flat | ⚙ **Difficulty:** Novice ★☆☆

🏛 **STARI FÍKJUR** : Starlings were a common game bird of the Karls and þræll, caught during the autumn migrations. The EDDAS mention this recipe in the preparations for Álfablót, the festival of the light elves. Dried figs, brought along the Viking trade routes, enriched this modest dish with a Mediterranean touch prized by the skalds.

INGREDIENTS :

- 8 STARI (starlings or 4 gutted quails)
- 12 FÍKJUR ÞURRAR (dried figs)
- 2 tablespoons of OLÍA VALHNETUR (walnut oil)
- 1 LAUKR HVÍTR onion (Nordic white onion)
- 1 teaspoon of ÍNGVER KRYDDAÐR (dried ginger)
- 1/2 glass of VÍNFISKISÓSA (white wine with spices)
- SALT and PIPAR SVARTR (salt and black pepper)

METHOD

1. **Initial preparation:** Clean and flambé the starlings according to Nordic methods. Rehydrate the figs in warm water for 15 minutes, then chop them coarsely.
2. **First cooking:** In an iron KETILL, brown the chopped onion in walnut oil over medium heat until golden brown.
3. **Main assembly:** Add the chopped figs and ginger, cook for 3 minutes to develop the Mediterranean aromas. Arrange the starlings in the KETILL, brown them on all sides for 8-10 minutes.
4. **Final cooking:** Pour in the VÍNFISKISÓSA, cover and simmer for 20-25 minutes over low heat until the flesh is completely tender.
5. **Finishing:** Adjust the seasoning, reducing the sauce if necessary to obtain a syrupy consistency.
6. **Service:** Serve the starlings topped with fig sauce, accompanied by grilled HAFRI and fermented vegetables.

🔄 **Modern Substitutes:** STARI → quail or squab, FÍKJUR ÞURRAR → Turkish figs, ÍNGVER → grated fresh ginger

ANCIENT METHOD: Cooking in a sealed clay pot buried under the embers for half a day.

Secrets of the MATSTJÓRAR: Viking cooks added a pinch of KANEL to mask the sometimes bitter taste of autumn game, a technique passed on by the merchants of Novgorod.

Nutritional values: 265 kcal | Protein: 26g | Carbohydrates: 15g | Fat: 14g

AXIS 5: FISKR OK HAFDJÚP - *Treasures of the Nordic Seas*

Lamb og Kid (7 recipes), Svín og Villisvín (6 recipes), Fugl og Villt (7 recipes)

58. MULTA Í LAUFUM ~ Red mullet in seaweed papillotes

PRACTICAL INFORMATION: 🖼 Historical period: 8th-11th century | 🏛 Source: ORKNEY SAGA/Coastal Archaeology | 🕐 Preparation time: 15 min | Cooking time: 25 min | 💧 Calories: 220 kcal per serving | 👥 Servings: 4 people | 📋 Nutritional value: Protein: 28g / Carbohydrates: 3g / Fat: 11g | 💡 Ancient advice: Harvest seaweed at low tide according to the lunar phases | 🔲 Modern method: Aluminum foil as an emergency substitute | 💲 Estimated cost: €22.40 / £19.60 / $25.60 | 🍶 Nordic utensils: STEINOFN, hot stones | ⚙ Difficulty: Beginner ★★☆

🏛 MULTA Í LAUFUM : A cooking technique specific to the fishermen of the Shetland and Orkney Islands, this preparation was practiced during large fishing expeditions. The SAGAS describe this method as a gift from Rán, goddess of the oceans. The seaweed retained the salty aromas while preserving the delicate flesh of the red mullet.

INGREDIENTS :
- 4 MULTA (red mullet, 300g each)
- 8 large leaves of ÞANGAR FERSKAR (fresh seaweed or spinach)
- 3 tablespoons of OLÍA HVALLUR (whale or olive oil)
- 2 cloves of HVÍTLAUKR VILLT (wild garlic)
- 1 SÍTRÓNA lemon (juice and zest)
- 1 teaspoon of FENIKALFRJÓ (fennel seeds)
- SALT HAFR (grey sea salt)

METHOD
1. **Initial preparation:** Scale and gut the red mullet, keeping the liver, a renowned Nordic delicacy. Carefully clean the seaweed in filtered seawater and blanch it for 30 seconds to soften it.
2. **First cooking:** Finely chop the wild garlic with the fennel seeds. Mix with the oil and lemon zest to create an aromatic Nordic marinade.
3. **Main assembly:** Brush the inside and outside of the fish with the fragrant marinade. Wrap each red mullet in two sheets of seaweed, tie with soaked wicker ties to hold the shape.
4. **Final cooking:** Arrange the papillotes on heated stones in the STEINOFN, cook for 20-25 minutes depending on the thickness, the seaweed steam creating a unique marine atmosphere.
5. **Finishing:** Carefully open the papillotes, sprinkle with lemon juice, and season with sea salt.
6. **Service:** Serve with seaweed, accompanied by BRAUÐ SALTAÐR and sea herb butter.

🔲 Modern Substitutes: ÞANGAR FERSKAR → cabbage leaves or baking paper, HVÍTLAUKR VILLT → fresh garlic, OLÍA HVALLUR → extra-virgin olive oil

ANCIENT METHOD: Burying the papillotes in the hot sand under embers of driftwood, a method used by Hebridean fishermen.

Secrets of the MATSTJÓRAR: Viking master fishermen added a juniper branch to each papillote to evoke the Nordic forests on the open sea according to the EDDAs.

Nutritional values: 220 kcal | Protein: 28g | Carbohydrates: 3g | Fat: 11g

59. HELGAFISKR KAPPAR ~ Halibut with Arctic capers

PRACTICAL INFORMATION: 📖 Historical period: 8th-11th century | 🏛 Source: SAGA DE GÍSLI/Nordic trade | 🕐 Preparation time: 20 min | Cooking time: 30 min | 🜄 Calories: 280 kcal per portion | 👥 Servings: 6 people | 📋 Nutritional value: Protein: 35g / Carbohydrates: 4g / Fat: 14g | ♀ Ancient advice: Choose halibut during the winter full moons according to the VÖLUR | 🔄 Modern method: Griddle cooking possible for searing | 💰 Estimated cost: €28.90 / £25.20 / $33.10 | 🏺 Nordic utensils: STEINOFN, bronze SKÁLAR | ⚙ Difficulty: Beginner ★★☆

🏛 **HELGAFISKR KAPPAR** : Halibut was considered the king of Nordic fish, reserved for the jarls' tables during great celebrations. The SAGAS mention this fish at Jól (winter solstice) feasts. Capers, imported via Viking trade routes to the Mediterranean, enhanced this dish with a tartness prized by the Nordic aristocracy.

INGREDIENTS :

- 1.2kg of HELGAFISKR (thick halibut fillet)
- 3 tablespoons of KAPPAR NORÐLENSKAR (preserved capers)
- 4 tablespoons of OLÍA BEITA (Nordic cooking oil)
- 2 SÍTRÓNA (squeezed lemons)
- 3 branches of DILL VILLT (wild dill)
- 2 LAUKR LITLIR shallots (small onions)
- SALT GRÓFR and PIPAR HVÍTR (coarse salt and white pepper)

METHOD

1. **Initial preparation:** Cut the halibut into equal 200g portions, remove the bones with Nordic precision. Finely chop the shallots and wild dill, drain the capers.
2. **First cooking:** In a bronze KETILL, heat the oil over high heat. Sear the halibut steaks for 3 minutes on each side to develop a golden crust.
3. **Main assembly:** Keep the fish warm. In the same KETILL, fry the chopped shallots until transparent, add the capers and dill to release the Nordic flavors.
4. **Final cooking:** Deglaze with lemon juice and reduce slightly. Return the halibut to the caper sauce and continue cooking for 2-3 minutes on each side.
5. **Finishing:** Adjust the seasoning with grófr salt and white pepper, sprinkle with chopped fresh dill.
6. **Serving:** Arrange on bronze dishes, coat generously with caper sauce, serve with root vegetables and BRAUÐ HVÍTR.

🔄 **Modern Substitutes:** HELGAFISKR → turbot or brill, KAPPAR → capers from Pantelleria, ANETH VILLT → fresh dill from the market

ANCIENT METHOD: Cooking on a flat stone heated over a birch fire, turning over using yew wood spatulas.

Secrets of the MATSTJÓRAR: The jarls' cooks flambéed halibut in the AQUAVIT before serving to honor Ægir, the ocean giant according to Norse mythology.

Nutritional values: 280 kcal | Protein: 35g | Carbohydrates: 4g | Fat: 14g

60. TÚNFISKR RISTAÐR VÍNFISKISÓSA ~ Grilled tuna with VÍNFISKISÓSA

PRACTICAL INFORMATION: 📽 **Historical period:** 8th-11th century | 🏛 **Source:** FAROE SAGA/Trade routes | 🕐 **Preparation time:** 15 min | **Cooking time:** 12 min | 🜄 **Calories:** 320 kcal per serving | 🐾 **Servings:** 4 people | 🗐 **Nutritional value:** Protein: 42g / Carbohydrates: 2g / Fat: 16g | 🝆 **Ancient advice:** Marinate tuna in VÍNFISKISÓSA for a whole day | 🗘 **Modern method:** Charcoal barbecue recommended | 🜋 **Estimated cost:** €32.60 / £28.40 / $37.20 | 🝊 **Nordic utensils:** Iron grill, BAKSTEINN | 🜛 **Difficulty:** Novice ★☆☆

🏛 **TÚNFISKR RISTAÐR VÍNFISKISÓSA** : Tuna was a treasure of the Viking expeditions in the North Atlantic, mentioned in the Faroese SAGAS as an offering to the sea gods. VÍNFISKISÓSA, the noble sauce of the jarls, transformed this fish into a dish worthy of the great VEIZLA. This preparation symbolized the Vikings' mastery of the oceans and their riches.

INGREDIENTS :

- 800g TÚNFISKR RAUÐR (bluefin tuna in thick steaks)
- 4 tablespoons of VÍNFISKISÓSA (fermented wine-fish sauce)
- 2 tablespoons of OLÍA BEITA (cooking oil)
- 1 sprig of RÓSMARÍN VILLT (wild rosemary)
- 2 cloves of HVÍTLAUKR (Nordic garlic)
- 1 SÍTRÓNA (squeezed lemon)
- SALT HAFR and PIPAR RAUÐR (sea salt and red pepper)

METHOD

1. **Initial preparation:** Cut the tuna into 2cm-thick steaks, removing any bloody parts according to Nordic tradition. Finely chop the garlic and wild rosemary.
2. **First cooking:** Mix the VÍNFISKISÓSA with the chopped garlic, oil, and lemon juice to create a powerful marinade. Coat the tuna steaks and let them marinate for at least 30 minutes.
3. **Main assembly:** Preheat the iron grill over birch embers until it reaches an intense temperature. Drain the steaks, reserving the marinade for basting.
4. **Final cooking:** Grill the tuna for 2-3 minutes on each side for those who like pink fish, 4-5 minutes for more thorough cooking according to Nordic tastes.
5. **Finishing:** Baste regularly with the reserved marinade during cooking, sprinkle with chopped wild rosemary.
6. **Service:** Serve immediately on an oak board, accompanied by grilled vegetables and SALT HAFR available.

🗘 **Modern Substitutes:** VÍNFISKISÓSA → mix of fish sauce + dry white wine, RÓSMARÍN VILLT → fresh rosemary, TÚNFISKR RAUÐR → line-caught red tuna

ANCIENT METHOD: Cooking on a heated shale plate placed on embers, a technique used by fishermen in the Lofoten Islands.

Secrets of the MATSTJÓRAR: Viking grill masters tested the temperature of the grill by throwing a drop of water on it: it had to sizzle instantly to guarantee perfect searing according to the EDDAS.

Nutritional values: 320 kcal | Protein: 42g | Carbohydrates: 2g | Fat: 16g

61. STEINBÍTR Í SALTI ~ Sea bass in a salt crust

PRACTICAL INFORMATION: 📖 **Historical period:** 8th-9th century | 🏛 **Source:** Preservative techniques/Fishing | 🕐 **Preparation time:** 45 min | **Cooking time:** 1 hour | 🜄 **Calories:** 220 kcal per portion | 👥 **Servings:** 8 people | 📋 **Nutritional value:** Protein: 40g / Carbohydrates: 0g / Fat: 6g | 💡 **Ancient tip:** Bake in a protective crust | 🔄 **Modern method:** Coarse sea salt, oven | 💲 **Estimated cost:** €32.80 / £28.60 / $41.30 | 🍶 **Nordic utensils:** STEINOFN, sea salt | ⚙️ **Difficulty:** Master ★★★

🏛 **STEINBÍTR Í SALTI:** A spectacular technique reserved for noble fish from the deep sea, this salt crust cooking preserved all the moisture in the flesh. Sea bass, a predator of cold waters, was thus prepared for special occasions.

INGREDIENTS :

- 1 STEINBÍTR STÓRR (whole sea bass 2-3 kg)
- 2 kg of SALT HAFDJÚPS STÓRR (coarse gray sea salt)
- 6 EGGJAVÍTUR (egg whites)
- 8 branches of SJÁVARGRAS (sea grass)
- 4 HVÍTLAUKAR (whole garlic cloves)
- 2 spoons of OLÍA STEINPRESSUÐ (first pressing oil)
- 1 SÍTRÓN STÓRR (large Nordic lemon)
- Branches of FENIKALVILLT (wild fennel)

METHOD

1. **Initial preparation:** Gut and scale the sea bass, dry it thoroughly. Stuff the belly with sea herbs and garlic. Mix salt with beaten egg whites to obtain a salt "concrete".
2. **First cooking:** Spread a layer of moist salt in a baking dish. Place the fish on top and cover completely with the salt and egg mixture. Press firmly to ensure a perfect seal.
3. **Main assembly:** Place in the preheated STEINOFN oven and bake without opening. The crust should harden and brown slightly. Allow 20 minutes per kg of fish.
4. **Final cooking:** Check cooking by pricking through the crust near the edge.
5. **Finish:** Break the crust with a hammer in front of the guests, release the fragrant vapors
6. **Service:** Carefully fillet the fillets and serve with lemon and olive oil.

🔄 **Modern Substitutes:** Line-caught sea bass, sea bream, coarse grey salt, traditional oven 200°C, herbs of Provence

ANCIENT METHOD: Buried cooking in a pit with salt and embers, clay crust and sea salt, ritual breaking

Secrets of MATSTJÓRAR: Fish had to be very fresh, perfectly sealed crust, internal steam cooking, theatrical presentation essential

Nutritional values: 220 kcal | **Protein:** 40g | **Carbohydrates:** 0g | **Fat:** 6g

62. BREIÐFISKR FENIKEL ~ Plaice with wild fennel

PRACTICAL INFORMATION: 🖼 **Historical period:** 9th-10th century | 🏛 **Source:** Coastal fishing/Herbs | 🕐 **Preparation time:** 20 min | **Cooking time:** 15 min | 💧 **Calories:** 200 kcal per portion | 👥 **Servings:** 4 people | 📋 **Nutritional value:** Protein: 35g / Carbohydrates: 3g / Fat: 6g | 💡 **Ancient tip:** Quick cook flatfish | 🔁 **Modern method:** Non-stick pan, fresh fennel | 💰 **Estimated cost:** €18.50 / £16.10 / $23.30 | ⚱ **Nordic utensils:** STEIKARPANNA large, spatula | ⚙ **Difficulty:** Novice ★☆☆

🏛 **BREIÐFISKR FENIKEL:** A daily fish for fishing families, plaice was enhanced by wild fennel growing on coastal dunes. Its delicate flesh and quick cooking time made it a popular dish at Nordic family meals.

INGREDIENTS :

- 4 BREIÐFISKR (emptied 300g plaice)
- 1 FENIKALSTÖR (chopped wild fennel bulb)
- 4 tablespoons of SMJÖR FERSKT (fresh butter)
- 2 spoons of OLÍA STEINPRESSUÐ (first pressing oil)
- 3 HVÍTLAUKAR (chopped garlic cloves)
- 4 branches of FENIKALBLÖÐ (fennel tops)
- 1 SÍTRÓN (Nordic lemon or verjuice)
- 1 spoon of SALT FÍNT (fine salt)

METHOD

1. **Initial preparation:** Trim plaice, remove black skin, dry gently. Finely slice fennel, chop leaves. Heat STEIKARPANNA large over medium heat.
2. **First cooking:** Melt butter with oil, fry chopped fennel and garlic for 5 minutes until tender. Push to one side of the pan.
3. **Main assembly:** Salt and lightly flour the folded pieces, cook for 3 minutes on the white side. Turn over carefully, cook for 2 minutes on the skin side.
4. **Final cooking:** Sprinkle with chopped leaves, sprinkle with lemon juice.
5. **Finishing:** Adjust seasoning, butter should foam slightly
6. **Service:** Serve on melted fennel, accompanied by new potatoes

🔁 **Modern Substitutes:** Sole or dab, cultivated fennel, farm butter, lemon, Teflon pan

ANCIENT METHOD: Cooking on a heated stone plate, wild fennel from the dunes, traditional beaten butter

Secrets of MATSTJÓRAR: Plaice required very quick cooking, fennel should not brown, lemon acidity revealed finesse, careful presentation

Nutritional values: 200 kcal | **Protein:** 35g | **Carbohydrates:** 3g | **Fat:** 6g

63. GULLBREIÐR Í STEINOFNI ~ Stone-oven sea bream

PRACTICAL INFORMATION: 🏛 Historical period: 8th-11th century | 🏛 Source: SAGAS/Archaeology | 🕐 Preparation time: 25 min | **Cooking time:** 45 min | 🜂 Calories: 320 kcal per portion | 🍴 Servings: 4 people | 🗒 **Nutritional value:** Protein: 42g / Carbohydrates: 3g / Fat: 16g | ♀ **Ancient advice:** Slow cooking on hot stones according to the jarls | 🔲 **Modern method:** Traditional oven at 180°C | ⑤ **Estimated cost:** €18.50 / £16.20 / $21.40 | 🏺 **Nordic utensils:** STEINOFN, flat stones, BAKSTEINN | ⚙ **Difficulty:** Beginner ★★☆

🏛 **GULLBREIÐR** : Golden fish prized by the jarls of Norway, traditionally cooked on heated stones in the communal STEINOFN. A prestigious dish served at royal VEIZLA and summer solstice celebrations.

INGREDIENTS :

- 1 whole sea bream of 1.2 kg (GULLBREIÐR HEILL)
- 60 ml of OLÍA STEINFRJÓ (Nordic seed oil)
- 15 g of SALT HAFR (sea salt)
- 8 g of FENIKEL VILLT (dried wild fennel)
- 30 g of HUNANG BJALLA (mountain honey)
- 200 g of HVÍTLAUKR (wild garlic)
- 150 ml of VÍNHVÍTR (Nordic white wine)

METHOD

1. **Initial preparation:** Gut and scale the sea bream, make diamond-shaped incisions on the sides, rub with SALT HAFR and leave to stand for 15 minutes according to the techniques of the Bergen fishermen.
2. **First cooking:** Heat the flat stones over a birch fire for 30 minutes, then place on a preheated STEINOFN, brush the fish with OLÍA mixed with HUNANG.
3. **Main assembly:** Fill the ventral cavity with pounded HVÍTLAUKR and FENIKEL, sprinkle with VÍNHVÍTR, wrap in moistened birch leaves according to the fjord tradition.
4. **Final cooking:** Cook for 35-40 minutes on hot stones, turn halfway through cooking, maintain humidity with salted water steam.
5. **Finishing:** Deglaze with caramelized juices, season with fresh FENIKEL.
6. **Service:** Serve whole on an oak board with heated HUNANG.

🔲 **Modern Substitutes:** OLÍA STEINFRJÓ → olive oil, HVÍTLAUKR → common garlic, FENIKEL VILLT → cultivated fennel, VÍNHVÍTR → dry white wine

ANCIENT METHOD: Direct cooking on slate slabs heated over a fir fire using the techniques of the fishermen of the Lofoten Islands

Secrets of MATSTJÓRAR: Cooking test by lifting the gills according to the skalds, stones preheated to a constant temperature by rotation, HUNANG applied in three successive layers for perfect golden caramelization

Nutritional values: 320 kcal | Protein: 42g | Carbohydrates: 3g | Fat: 16g

64. SÍLD SÖLTNAR ÞANGAR ~ Dried herring with seaweed

PRACTICAL INFORMATION: 📖 Historical period: 8th-11th century | 🏛 Source: EDDAS/Archaeology | 🕐 Preparation time: 45 min | Cooking time: 90 min | 🜄 Calories: 280 kcal per serving | 👥 Servings: 6 people | 📓 Nutritional value: Protein: 38g / Carbohydrates: 2g / Fat: 12g | 💡 Ancient advice: Drying in the salty wind of the fjords according to the Karls | 🔲 Modern method: Food dehydrator | 🥄 Estimated cost: €14.80 / £12.90 / $17.20 | 🏺 Nordic utensils: ÞURRKARAMMI, hemp ropes, SALTSKÁLAR | ⚙ Difficulty: Master ★★★

🏛 SÍLD SÖLTNAR ÞANGAR : Herring preserved according to the ancient art of Icelandic fishermen, enriched with ÞANGAR seaweed for essential vitamins. A staple food of Viking expeditions and winter provision for the þræll.

INGREDIENTS :
- 12 SÍLD FERSK (medium fresh herring)
- 400 g SALT GRÓFT (coarse sea salt)
- 80 g ÞANGAR ÞURRKAÐAR (varied dried seaweed)
- 30 ml EDIK ÁVAXTABRAGÐ (fruit vinegar)
- 15 g of EINIBER (juniper berries)
- 20 g LÁRVIÐUR (northern bay leaves)
- 200 ml of OLÍA TRÁVIÐUR (herbal infused oil)

METHOD
1. **Initial preparation:** Gut the herring through the gills without opening the belly, rinse in cold sea water, pat dry carefully using the ancestral techniques of the Trondheim fishermen.
2. **First cooking:** Mix SALT GRÓFT with crushed ÞANGAR and crushed EINIBER, rub generously inside and outside of the fish, arrange in alternating layers.
3. **Main assembly:** Place under stone press for 24 hours to extract water, turn every 6 hours, add LÁRVIÐUR between layers according to the wisdom of the conservative VÖLUR.
4. **Final cooking:** Hang in the ÞURRKARAMMI in a ventilated and dry place, let it dry for 5-7 days until firm and shiny.
5. **Finishing:** Brush off excess salt, brush with OLÍA TRÁVIÐUR, wrap in linen cloth.
6. **Serving:** Cut into thin strips, serve with EDIK ÁVAXTABRAGÐ.

🔲 **Modern Substitutes:** ÞANGAR → kombu and wakame seaweed, EDIK ÁVAXTABRAGÐ → cider vinegar, LÁRVIÐUR → bay leaf sauce, OLÍA TRÁVIÐUR → herb oil

ANCIENT METHOD: Natural drying on birch racks exposed to the prevailing winds of the Norwegian coast during the long Arctic summers

Secrets of the MATSTJÓRAR: Daily humidity control by palpating the sides, rotation of the fish according to the wind direction, ÞANGAR harvested at low tide of the new moon for maximum concentration of minerals

Nutritional values: 280 kcal | Protein: 38g | Carbohydrates: 2g | Fat: 12g

65. RAUÐFISKR SOÐINN ~ Redfish in Nordic court-bouillon

PRACTICAL INFORMATION: 📓 **Historical period:** 8th-11th century | 🏛 **Source:** SAGAS/Manuscripts | 🕐 **Preparation time:** 20 min | **Cooking time:** 25 min | 🜄 **Calories:** 245 kcal per portion | 🦢 **Servings:** 4 people | 📖 **Nutritional value:** Protein: 35g / Carbohydrates: 4g / Fat: 9g | 💡 **Ancient advice:** Gentle cooking in fragrant broth according to the jarls | 🔄 **Modern method:** Poached fish Gentle steam | 💰 **Estimated cost:** €16.20 / £14.10 / $18.80 | 🏺 **Nordic utensils:** KETILL, SOÐSKÁLAR, wicker strainer | ⚙ **Difficulty:** Novice ★☆☆

🏛 **RAUÐFISKR SOÐINN** : Redfish from the deep waters of the North Atlantic, cooked in aromatic court-bouillon according to the recipes of Harald Fairhair's royal cooks. A refined dish for autumn feasts.

INGREDIENTS :

- 800 g of RAUÐFISKR FILLETUR (redfish fillets)
- 1.5 l of spring water (KELDUVATN)
- 150 ml of VÍNHVÍTR (Northern white wine)
- 2 LAUKAR STÓRIR (large Nordic onions)
- 80 g of GULRÓT VILLT (wild carrot)
- 20 g of PERSILLA STEINFJALL (mountain parsley)
- 12 g of SALT HAFR (sea salt)
- 8 korns of PIPAR SVARTR (black pepper)

METHOD

1. **Initial preparation:** Cut the fillets into equal portions, salt lightly and let drain for 10 minutes, slice LAUKAR and GULRÓT into fine julienne strips using the master chefs' techniques.
2. **First cooking:** Bring KELDUVATN to a boil in a large KETILL, add VÍNHVÍTR, chopped vegetables and herbs, simmer for 15 minutes to develop the flavors.
3. **Main assembly:** Gently immerse the RAUÐFISKR fillets in the simmering court-bouillon, keeping the temperature just below boiling to preserve the texture according to the art of the Bergen fishermen.
4. **Final cooking:** Poach for 8-10 minutes until the flesh is pearly and firm, skimming the surface regularly.
5. **Finishing:** Carefully remove the fish, strain the broth, and adjust the seasoning.
6. **Service:** Arrange on a heated dish, cover with reduced broth, sprinkle with fresh PERSILLA.

🔄 **Modern Substitutes:** RAUÐFISKR → redfish or scorpion fish, KELDUVATN → filtered water, VÍNHVÍTR → dry white wine, GULRÓT VILLT → cultivated carrot

ANCIENT METHOD: Cooking in a cast iron pot suspended over a birch fire, regulated by suspension height according to the seasons

Secrets of MATSTJÓRAR: Cooking test by gently pressing the flesh with your finger, broth kept at a constant simmer, PERSILLA added only when serving to preserve the essential oils according to VÖLUR

Nutritional values: 245 kcal | Protein: 35g | Carbohydrates: 4g | Fat: 9g

66. SARDÍNA SÖLTNAR ~ Arctic marinated sardines

PRACTICAL INFORMATION: 🖼 **Historical period:** 8th-11th century | 🏛 **Source:** Archaeology/SAGAS | 🕐 **Preparation time:** 35 min | **Cooking time:** 0 min | 🜂 **Calories:** 195 kcal per portion | 🎭 **Servings:** 6 people | 📋 **Nutritional value:** Protein: 26g / Carbohydrates: 1g / Fat: 9g | 💡 **Ancient advice:** Marinate for a long time according to coastal traditions | 🔲 **Modern method:** Refrigerate for at least 48 hours | 🔟 **Estimated cost:** €11.40 / £9.90 / $13.20 | 🍶 **Nordic utensils:** SALTSKÁLAR, stoneware jars, stone presses | ⚙ **Difficulty:** Beginner ★★☆

🏛 **SARDÍNA SÖLTNAR :** Small sardines from the cold Nordic waters, preserved by salting and marinating according to the ancestral methods of Icelandic fishermen. Essential provisions for the long ocean crossings of the longships.

INGREDIENTS :
- 1.5 kg of SARDÍNA FERSK (small fresh sardines)
- 300 g of SALT FÍNT (fine sea salt)
- 200 ml EDIK STERKR (strong cider vinegar)
- 100 ml of OLÍA GULLFISK (pressed golden oil)
- 6 LÁRVIÐUR BLÖÐ (bay leaves)
- 15 g of EINIBER MÖLUÐ (ground juniper)
- 20 g of HVÍTLAUKR (wild garlic)
- 8 korns of PIPAR HVÍTR (white pepper)

METHOD
1. **Initial preparation:** Scale and gut the sardines, keeping the heads, rinse thoroughly in cold salted water, and pat dry thoroughly according to the rules of Nordic fish preservatives.
2. **First cooking:** Arrange the sardines in layers in SALTSKÁLAR, alternate with SALT FÍNT mixed with spices, press under stone weight for 12 hours to extract the water.
3. **Main assembly:** Gently rinse off excess salt, arrange in tight rows in stoneware jars, cover with EDIK STERKR mixed with OLÍA GULLFISK according to the proportions of the master salt makers.
4. **Final cooking:** Add LÁRVIÐUR and chopped HVÍTLAUKR, seal tightly, leave to marinate for at least 48 hours in a cool cellar.
5. **Finishing:** Check the firmness of the flesh, adjust the acidity if necessary.
6. **Service:** Drain, arrange on a wooden board, and serve with rye bread.

🔲 **Modern Substitutes:** SARDÍNA FERSK → sardines from Brittany, EDIK STERKR → organic cider vinegar, OLÍA GULLFISK → extra virgin olive oil, LÁRVIÐUR → bay leaf sauce

ANCIENT METHOD: Preservation in hooped oak barrels, buried in damp coastal sand to maintain a constant temperature according to the Vikings of Iceland

Secrets of MATSTJÓRAR: Selection of sardines by uniform size for homogeneous marinade, EDIK dosed according to the natural acidity of Nordic fruits, daily turning of the jars during the first week according to the experience of the elders

Nutritional values: 195 kcal | Protein: 26g | Carbohydrates: 1g | Fat: 9g

67. SILUNGR DONAU ~ Northern River Salmon

PRACTICAL INFORMATION: 📖 Historical period: 8th-11th century | 🏛 Source: EDDAS/Archaeology | 🕐 Preparation time: 30 min | Cooking time: 35 min | 🔥 Calories: 385 kcal per portion | 👥 Servings: 4 people | 📋 Nutritional value: Protein: 45g / Carbohydrates: 2g / Fat: 21g | ♀ Ancient advice: Cooking with juniper wood according to the jarls | 🔲 Modern method: Papillote in the oven at 200°C | 💰 Estimated cost: €22.80 / £19.90 / $26.40 | 🍶 Nordic utensils: STEINGRILLR, juniper boards, BAKSTEINN | ⚙ Difficulty: Beginner ★★☆

🏛 SILUNGR DONAU : Noble salmon from the Scandinavian rivers, grilled on juniper planks according to the fishing rites of the Nordic kings. The dish of honor of the BLÓT at the summer solstice and a symbol of prosperity for the jarls.

INGREDIENTS :

- 1.2 kg SILUNGR ÞYKKT (thick salmon steaks)
- 80 ml of OLÍA EINIBERJAR (juniper oil)
- 25 g of SALT STEINFJALL (mountain rock salt)
- 15 g of TÍMILL VILLT (dried wild thyme)
- 200 g SMJÖR GRASFRAMLEIDD (herb butter)
- 6 EINIBERGREINAR (juniper branches)
- 150 ml of VÍNRAUTT (Nordic red wine)
- 30 g of HUNANG LYNGI (heather honey)

METHOD

1. **Initial preparation:** Cut the salmon into 3 cm thick steaks, marinate for 20 minutes in OLÍA EINIBERJAR mixed with SALT STEINFJALL and TÍMILL according to the techniques of Norwegian fishermen.
2. **First cooking:** Soak the EINIBERGREINAR boards for 30 minutes, light a birch fire and place the boards on a preheated STEINGRILLR, let them smoke lightly.
3. **Main assembly:** Arrange the marinated steaks on smoking planks, brush with melted SMJÖR with herbs, partially cover to concentrate the aromas according to the art of Nordic master grillers.
4. **Final cooking:** Grill for 25-30 minutes, turning once, basting regularly with VÍNRAUTT mixed with HUNANG for golden caramelization.
5. **Finishing:** Check cooking until pink, leave to rest for 5 minutes on hot boards.
6. **Service:** Serve directly on juniper boards, accompanied by reduced caramelized juice.

🔲 **Modern Substitutes:** SILUNGR → Atlantic salmon, OLÍA EINIBERJAR → juniper olive oil, EINIBERGREINAR → cedar planks, VÍNRAUTT → full-bodied red wine

ANCIENT METHOD: Cooking on flat stones heated with a juniper fire, turning once halfway through cooking according to fjord traditions

Secrets of MATSTJÓRAR: Gentle pressure cooking test, planks prepared by prolonged soaking for optimal smoking, HUNANG applied as a final glaze for shine according to the gastronomic skalds

Nutritional values: 385 kcal | Protein: 45g | Carbohydrates: 2g | Fat: 21g

---

AXIS 5: FISKR OK HAFDJÚP - Hafdjúp (Crustaceans and molluscs)

68. OSTR Í SKELUM ~ Smoked oysters in the shell

PRACTICAL INFORMATION: 🎞 **Historical period:** 8th-11th century | 🏛 **Source:** Archaeology/SAGAS | 🕐 **Preparation time:** 15 min | **Cooking time:** 20 min | 🜄 **Calories:** 85 kcal per portion | 🗺 **Servings:** 4 people | 🗒 **Nutritional value:** Protein: 12g / Carbohydrates: 4g / Fat: 2g | 🜊 **Ancient advice:** Light smoking with driftwood according to the coastal people | 🖵 **Modern method:** Barbecue with beech chips | 🜚 **Estimated cost:** €19.60 / £17.10 / $22.70 | 🜛 **Nordic utensils:** REYKJUROFN, iron grills, shell tongs | ⚙ **Difficulty:** Novice ★☆☆

🏛 **OSTR Í SKELUM** : Oysters from the cold Scandinavian coasts, smoked in their shells according to the methods of Faroese gatherers. A delicacy of coastal karls and an offering to the sea deities during Njörðr's BLÓT.

INGREDIENTS :

- 24 OSTR FERSK (medium fresh oysters)
- 100 g of SMJÖR (Nordic butter)
- 20 g of PERSILLA HAFR (sea parsley)
- 8 g of HVÍTLAUKR (wild garlic)
- 200 ml of VÍNHVÍTR (Nordic white wine)
- EIKVIÐUR (drift oak wood) shavings
- 12 g of SALT FÍNT (fine sea salt)
- 6 korns of PIPAR RAUTT (pink pepper)

METHOD

1. **Initial preparation:** Brush and rinse the oysters in cold sea water, remove algae and sand, store in a damp cloth according to the practices of primitive Nordic oyster farmers.
2. **First firing:** Light a birch fire in REYKJUROFN, add soaked EIKVIÐUR chips for light smoking, maintain a moderate temperature with control of the embers.
3. **Main assembly:** Arrange the oysters flat side down on a grill, melt SMJÖR with crushed HVÍTLAUKR and chopped PERSILLA, brush each shell using the master smokers' techniques.
4. **Final cooking:** Smoke for 15-18 minutes until the shells open naturally, sprinkle with VÍNHVÍTR for fragrant steam.
5. **Finishing:** Check the pearly and swollen flesh, season with SALT FÍNT and crushed PIPAR RAUTT.
6. **Serving:** Serve immediately in warm shells, accompanied by the remaining herb butter.

🖵 **Modern Substitutes:** OSTR FERSK → Brittany hollow oysters, EIKVIÐUR → beech shavings, PERSILLA HAFR → flat-leaf parsley, PIPAR RAUTT → pink berries

ANCIENT METHOD: Smoking on a bed of damp seaweed in a pit dug in the sand, covered with skins to concentrate the aromas according to the coastal Vikings

Secrets of MATSTJÓRAR: Selection of oysters by uniform swelling, smoking stopped at first opening to preserve texture, SMJÖR infused beforehand with herbs for optimal penetration according to marine VÖLUR

Nutritional values: 85 kcal | Protein: 12g | Carbohydrates: 4g | Fat: 2g

69. SÆIGULL KRYDDR ~ Sea urchins with boreal spices

PRACTICAL INFORMATION: 📖 **Historical period:** 8th-11th century | 🏛 **Source:** EDDAS/Manuscripts | 🕐 **Preparation time:** 25 min | **Cooking time:** 8 min | 🝆 **Calories:** 125 kcal per portion | 👥 **Servings:** 4 people | 📄 **Nutritional value:** Protein: 16g / Carbohydrates: 3g / Fat: 5g | 🝆 **Ancient advice:** Express cooking to preserve the texture according to the jarls | 🖵 **Modern method:** Quick pan-fry over high heat | 🝆 **Estimated cost:** €28.40 / £24.80 / $32.90 | 🝆 **Norse utensils:** JÁRNSKÁLAR, iron tongs, sharp knives | ⚙ **Difficulty:** Master ★★★

🏛 **SÆIGULL KRYDDR** : Sea urchins from the Arctic waters, a delicacy of Nordic royal feasts, seasoned with rare spices according to the refined tastes of Harald the Severus' court. A symbol of marine wealth and culinary mastery of the MATSTJÓRAR.

INGREDIENTS :

- 16 SÆIGULL STÓRR (large sea urchins)
- 60 ml of OLÍA STEINFRJÓ (pressed seed oil)
- 8 g of KRYDDBLÖNDUR (Nordic spice mix)
- 15 g of HVÍTLAUKR VILLT (wild wild garlic)
- 30 ml EDIK ÁVAXTABRAGÐ (fruit vinegar)
- 20 g of PERSILLA STEINFJALL (mountain parsley)
- 12 g of SALT VÍTI (pure white salt)
- 200 ml VÍNHVÍTR ÞURRR (dry white wine)

METHOD

1. **Initial preparation:** Carefully open the sea urchins from the top with a sharp knife, collect the orange corals, rinse quickly in cold sea water according to the art of expert collectors in Norway.
2. **First cooking:** Heat OLÍA STEINFRJÓ in JÁRNSKÁLAR cast iron, fry finely chopped HVÍTLAUKR without coloring, add KRYDDBLÖNDUR to release the aromas.
3. **Main assembly:** Gently place the sea urchin corals in the scented oil, quickly sear for 2-3 minutes, stirring carefully to preserve their integrity, according to the techniques of the royal master chefs.
4. **Final cooking:** Deglaze with VÍNHVÍTR, reduce by half, add EDIK for balanced acidity.
5. **Finishing:** Adjust the seasoning with SALT VÍTI, sprinkle with freshly chopped PERSILLA.
6. **Service:** Arrange in warmed empty shells, serve immediately with pearl spoons.

🖵 **Modern Substitutes:** SÆIGULL → Mediterranean sea urchins, KRYDDBLÖNDUR → Nordic mixed spices, OLÍA STEINFRJÓ → sunflower oil, EDIK ÁVAXTABRAGÐ → apple cider vinegar

ANCIENT METHOD: Quick cooking on red-hot flat stones, seasoned with fresh herbs from the cliffs according to the traditions of sea urchin fishermen

Secrets of MATSTJÓRAR: Opening by gentle rotation of the knife, corals selected by bright orange color, cooking interrupted at the first reaction for perfect creamy texture according to the wisdom of the marine VÖLUR

Nutritional values: 125 kcal | Protein: 16g | Carbohydrates: 3g | Fat: 5g

70. BLEKKSPRUTU BLEKKI ~ Cuttlefish in black ink

PRACTICAL INFORMATION: 📖 Historical period: 8th-11th century | 🏛 Source: SAGAS/Archaeology | 🕐 Preparation time: 40 min | Cooking time: 45 min | 💧 Calories: 165 kcal per portion | 👥 Servings: 6 people | 📋 Nutritional value: Protein: 28g / Carbohydrates: 5g / Fat: 3g | 💡 Ancient advice: Slow cooking to tenderize according to Nordic fishermen | 🔄 Modern method: Simmer for 1h30 | 💰 Estimated cost: €15.80 / £13.70 / $18.30 | 🥄 Nordic utensils: KETILL, fine sieve, SOÐSKÁLAR | ⚙ Difficulty: Beginner ★★☆

🏛 BLEKKSPRUTU BLEKKI : Cuttlefish from the cold Nordic seas, cooked in its ink according to the mysterious recipes of the fishermen of the Shetland Islands. Ritual dish of the BLÓT of the sea, symbol of the ocean depths and the wisdom of Ægir.

INGREDIENTS :

- 1.5 kg of BLEKKSPRUTA FERSK (cleaned fresh cuttlefish)
- BLEKKSPRUTA ink bags (natural ink)
- 200 ml of OLÍA STEINFRJÓ (Nordic seed oil)
- 3 LAUKAR STÓRIR (large wild onions)
- 400 ml of VÍNRAUTT (Nordic red wine)
- 25 g of HVÍTLAUKR (wild garlic)
- 20 g of PERSILLA STEINFJALL (mountain parsley)
- 15 g of SALT HAFR (sea salt)
- 12 korns of PIPAR SVARTR (black pepper)

METHOD

1. **Initial preparation:** Carefully clean the cuttlefish, carefully set aside the intact ink sacs, cut into regular strips, slice LAUKAR finely according to the techniques of Nordic mollusc preparers.
2. **First cooking:** Heat OLÍA in a large KETILL, fry LAUKAR until golden brown, add crushed HVÍTLAUKR and sweat for 3 minutes without excessive browning.
3. **Main assembly:** Add the cuttlefish strips, fry for 8-10 minutes over medium heat until the water from the vegetables has evaporated, moisten with VÍNRAUTT and bring to a boil according to the art of sea cooks.
4. **Final cooking:** Gently stir in the diluted ink in a little hot broth, cover and simmer for 35-40 minutes until perfectly tender, stirring occasionally.
5. **Finishing:** Adjust the seasoning with SALT HAFR and PIPAR, add chopped PERSILLA at the end of cooking.
6. **Serving:** Serve in dark wooden bowls and serve with toasted rye bread.

🔄 **Modern Substitutes:** BLEKKSPRUTA → Mediterranean cuttlefish, ink → squid ink sachets, VÍNRAUTT → full-bodied red wine, PERSILLA STEINFJALL → flat-leaf parsley

ANCIENT METHOD: Prolonged cooking in an earthenware pot buried in embers, brought up by rope according to the traditions of the Nordic islands

Secrets of MATSTJÓRAR: Ink diluted gradually to avoid lumps, tenderness test by piercing with the tip of a knife, cooking stopped when the flesh is translucent according to the experience of ancient sailors

Nutritional values: 165 kcal | Protein: 28g | Carbohydrates: 5g | Fat: 3g

71. ÁTNÍU EDIKI ~ Octopus in elderberry vinegar

PRACTICAL INFORMATION: 📷 **Historical period:** 8th-11th century | 🏛 **Source:** EDDAS/Manuscripts | 🕐 **Preparation time:** 50 min | **Cooking time:** 60 min | 💧 **Calories:** 142 kcal per portion | 👥 **Servings:** 4 people | 📋 **Nutritional value:** Protein: 25g / Carbohydrates: 4g / Fat: 2g | 💡 **Ancient advice:** Tenderize with vinegar using marine techniques | 🔄 **Modern method:** Pre-cook by steaming then marinating | 💰 **Estimated cost:** €17.90 / £15.60 / $20.80 | 🍶 **Nordic utensils:** KETILL, stone mortar, stoneware jars | ⚙ **Difficulty:** Master ★★★

🏛 **ÁTNÍU EDIKI** : Octopus from the deep Nordic waters, tenderized in elderberry vinegar according to the secrets of Norwegian fjord fishermen. A sophisticated dish of the jarls, a symbol of mastery of marine preservation techniques.

INGREDIENTS :

- 1.2 kg of ÁTNÍU FERSK (whole fresh octopus)
- 300 ml of EDIK YLLIBER (fermented elderberry vinegar)
- 150 ml OLÍA GULLFISK (golden oil)
- 40 g of LAUKAR RAUÐIR (red shallots)
- 25 g of YLLIBER ÞURRKAÐAR (dried elderberries)
- 20 g DILL VILLT (wild dill)
- 15 g of SALT STEINFJALL (rock salt)
- 10 korns of PIPAR HVÍTR (white pepper)

METHOD

1. **Initial preparation:** Carefully clean the octopus, remove the beak and eyes, beat the tentacles vigorously to soften the fibers, rinse several times in ice water according to the methods of expert fishermen.
2. **First cooking:** Plunge the octopus into a large pot of boiling salted water, cook for 45-50 minutes until tender when tested with a knife tip, cool immediately in iced water.
3. **Main assembly:** Cut into regular pieces, arrange in layers in a stoneware jar, alternate with sliced LAUKAR RAUÐIR and YLLIBER ÞURRKAÐAR according to the traditional art of brining.
4. **Final cooking:** Prepare marinade by mixing EDIK YLLIBER, OLÍA and crushed spices, pour over octopus to cover completely, seal tightly.
5. **Finishing:** Marinate for 24-48 hours in a cool cellar, turning the pieces halfway through, checking the acidity.
6. **Service:** Partially drain, dress with fresh dill, and serve with dark rye bread.

🔄 **Modern Substitutes:** ÁTNÍU → Mediterranean octopus, EDIK YLLIBER → red wine vinegar, YLLIBER → fresh elderberries, DILL VILLT → cultivated dill

ANCIENT METHOD: Cooking with seawater in a bronze cauldron, marinating in hooped oak barrels according to the Viking navigators

Secrets of MATSTJÓRAR: Pre-beating with a wooden mallet for soft fibers, cooking tested for ease of piercing the tentacles, marinade balanced in acidity according to the proportions of ancient preservatives

Nutritional values: 142 kcal | Protein: 25g | Carbohydrates: 4g | Fat: 2g

72. RÆKJUR ILMANDI ~ Shrimp with herbs

PRACTICAL INFORMATION: 📅 **Historical period:** 8th-11th century | 🏛 **Source:** SAGAS/Archaeology | 🕐 **Preparation time:** 20 min | **Cooking time:** 12 min | 🔥 **Calories:** 118 kcal per portion | 👥 **Servings:** 4 people | 📋 **Nutritional value:** Protein: 22g / Carbohydrates: 2g / Fat: 2g | 💡 **Ancient advice:** Express cooking for a firm texture according to fishermen | 🔄 **Modern method:** Stir-fry for 3-4 minutes | 💰 **Estimated cost:** €21.60 / £18.80 / $25.10 | 🍴 **Nordic utensils:** JÁRNSKÁLAR, wooden skimmer, mortar | ⚙️ **Difficulty:** Novice ★☆☆

🏛 **RÆKJUR ILMANDI :** Gray shrimp from the cold Nordic waters, flavored with Arctic herbs according to the recipes of Iceland's coastal fishermen. A simple delicacy from sea karls, often prepared after the morning trawls return.

INGREDIENTS :

- 800 g of RÆKJUR FERSK (fresh peeled shrimp)
- 80 ml of OLÍA STEINFRJÓ (seed oil)
- 30 g of SMJÖR (Nordic butter)
- 20 g of HVÍTLAUKR (wild garlic)
- 15 g DILL FERSK (fresh dill)
- 12 g of PERSILLA (cliff parsley)
- 200 ml VÍNHVÍTR (dry white wine)
- 10 g of SALT FÍNT (fine salt)
- Saft úr SÍTRÓN (Nordic lemon juice)

METHOD

1. **Initial preparation:** Carefully peel the shrimp, keeping the tails, remove the black intestine, rinse quickly in cold salted water, pat dry carefully using the techniques of coastal preparers.
2. **First cooking:** Heat OLÍA and SMJÖR in a large JÁRNSKÁLAR, fry finely chopped HVÍTLAUKR without coloring, let infuse for 2 minutes to flavor the fat.
3. **Main assembly:** Add the shrimp in a single layer, quickly sear for 2-3 minutes on the flesh side, gently turn for even cooking according to the art of seafood cooks.
4. **Final cooking:** Deglaze with VÍNHVÍTR, let it reduce partially, add chopped herbs at the end of cooking to preserve the aromas.
5. **Finishing:** Adjust the seasoning, add a few drops of SÍTRÓN juice, remove from the heat when the flesh is firm.
6. **Service:** Serve in preheated dishes, cover with the reduced juice, and serve with toasted bread.

🔄 **Modern Substitutes:** RÆKJUR → Atlantic prawns, SÍTRÓN → lemon, DILL FERSK → fresh dill, VÍNHVÍTR → dry white wine

ANCIENT METHOD: Quick cooking on flat stones heated over a kelp fire, seasoned with fresh seaweed according to the traditions of the gatherers

Secrets of MATSTJÓRAR: Cooking stopped as soon as the color changes to pearly pink, HVÍTLAUKR subtly measured so as not to mask the marine finesse, herbs added off the heat for maximum freshness

Nutritional values: 118 kcal | Protein: 22g | Carbohydrates: 2g | Fat: 2g

73. KRABBI FYLTUR GRAS ~ Crab stuffed with Nordic herbs

PRACTICAL INFORMATION: 📖 **Historical period:** 8th-11th century | 🏛 **Source:** EDDAS/Manuscripts | 🕐 **Preparation time:** 45 min | **Cooking time:** 35 min | 🔥 **Calories:** 210 kcal per portion | 👥 **Servings:** 4 people | 📋 **Nutritional value:** Protein: 28g / Carbohydrates: 6g / Fat: 8g | 💡 **Ancient advice:** Enriched stuffing according to jarls' feasts | 🖵 **Modern method:** Oven cooking at 180°C | 💲 **Estimated cost:** €26.40 / £23.10 / $30.60 | 🏺 **Nordic utensils:** STEINOFN, mortar, iron tongs | ⚙ **Difficulty:** Master ★★★

🏛 **KRABBI FYLTUR GRAS** : Arctic sea crabs stuffed with wild herbs according to the refined recipes of the royal court cooks. Exceptional dishes from the great VEIZLA, symbol of marine abundance and Nordic culinary mastery.

INGREDIENTS :

- 4 KRABBI STÓRIR (large live crabs)
- 200 g of BRAUÐMYLUR (rye bread crumbs)
- 150 ml MJÓLK (goat's milk)
- 80 g of SMJÖR (herbal butter)
- 25 g of PERSILLA VILLT (wild parsley)
- 20 g DILL STEINFJALL (mountain dill)
- 15 g of HVÍTLAUKR (wild garlic)
- 2 EGGJAGULAR (swan egg yolks)
- 12 g of SALT HAFR (sea salt)

METHOD

1. **Initial preparation:** Cook the crabs for 15 minutes in boiling salted water, cool, peel carefully, keeping the shells intact, and extract all the flesh from the legs and bodies according to the art of Nordic skinners.
2. **First cooking:** Soak BRAUÐMYLUR in lukewarm MJÓLK, squeeze to remove excess liquid, mix with finely crumbled crab meat.
3. **Main assembly:** Stir in softened SMJÖR, finely chopped herbs, pounded HVÍTLAUKR and beaten EGGJAGULAR, season with SALT HAFR according to the proportions of the royal master-stuffers.
4. **Final cooking:** Generously stuff the cleaned shells, smooth the surface, bake in a preheated STEINOFN for 20-25 minutes until evenly browned.
5. **Finishing:** Check the firm consistency of the stuffing, let it cool for 5 minutes before serving.
6. **Serving:** Serve in shells on a bed of fresh seaweed, accompanied by melted herb butter.

🖵 **Modern Substitutes:** KRABBI → Breton crabs, BRAUÐMYLUR → fine breadcrumbs, MJÓLK → whole milk, EGGJAGULAR → chicken egg yolks

ANCIENT METHOD: Cooking in shells placed on hot stones covered with ashes, according to the techniques of the fishermen of the Faroe Islands

Secrets of MATSTJÓRAR: Flesh crumbled without grinding for a generous texture, stuffing bound just enough for cohesion, shells brushed and oiled for perfect presentation according to the standards of royal VEIZLA

Nutritional values: 210 kcal | Protein: 28g | Carbohydrates: 6g | Fat: 8g

74. HUMARR RISTAÐR ~ Grilled lobster on birch embers

PRACTICAL INFORMATION: 🖼 **Historical period:** 8th-11th century | 🏛 **Source:** SAGAS/Archaeology | 🕐
Preparation time: 25 min | **Cooking time:** 30 min | 🍥 **Calories:** 285 kcal per portion | 👥 **Servings:** 2 people | 📱
Nutritional value: Protein: 38g / Carbohydrates: 2g / Fat: 12g | 💡 **Ancient advice:** Grilling on fragrant embers
according to the jarls | 🔄 **Modern method:** Charcoal barbecue | 💰 **Estimated cost:** €35.80 / £31.20 / $41.50 |
🏺 **Nordic utensils:** STEINGRILLR, iron tongs, BAKSTEINN | ⚙️ **Difficulty:** Beginner ★★☆
🏛 **HUMARR RISTAÐR** : Lobster from the cold Atlantic waters, grilled over birch embers using the ancestral
techniques of elite fishermen. Royal dish of the marine BLÓT, privileged offering to Ægir, god of the Nordic
oceans.

INGREDIENTS :

- 2 HUMARR STÓRIR (large live lobsters 800g each)
- 120 g of SMJÖR GRAS (Arctic herb butter)
- 30 ml of OLÍA STEINFRJÓ (pressed seed oil)
- 20 g of PERSILLA HAFR (sea parsley)
- 15 g of HVÍTLAUKR VILLT (wild wild garlic)
- Embers of BJÖKKVIÐUR (birch wood)
- 12 g of SALT STEINFJALL (rock salt)
- Saft úr SÍTRÓN (Nordic lemon juice)

METHOD

1. **Initial preparation:** Plunge the lobsters into boiling water for 3 minutes to stun them, split them lengthwise while keeping the shells, remove the gut and pouch, rinse gently according to the rules for preparing king lobsters.
2. **First cooking:** Light a BJÖKKVIÐUR fire, let it burn into regular glowing embers, prepare melted SMJÖR GRAS with crushed HVÍTLAUKR and chopped PERSILLA.
3. **Main assembly:** Generously brush the lobster meat with the flavored butter mixture, place flesh side down on the STEINGRILLR grill, maintaining the optimal distance from the embers according to the art of Nordic grilling.
4. **Final cooking:** Grill for 15-20 minutes on the flesh side, turn gently to sear the shell for 8-10 minutes, baste regularly to prevent drying out.
5. **Finishing:** Check the pearly and firm flesh, season with SALT STEINFJALL and fresh SÍTRÓN juice.
6. **Serving:** Serve on charred birch planks, accompanied by the remaining melted herb butter.

🔄 **Modern Substitutes:** HUMARR → Breton blue lobster, BJÖKKVIÐUR → birch charcoal, SMJÖR GRAS →
semi-salted butter with herbs, SÍTRÓN → lemon

ANCIENT METHOD: Wire mesh on metal racks suspended above embers in pits dug on beaches, according to
the traditions of coastal fishermen

Secrets of MATSTJÓRAR: Embers kept at a constant temperature by gradually adding chips, flesh lightly
incised to allow the aromas to penetrate, butter applied in several layers during cooking according to the
master grillers

Nutritional values: 285 kcal | Protein: 38g | Carbohydrates: 2g | Fat: 12g

75. SKELLFISKR FISKISÓSA - Shellfish at FISKISÓSA

PRACTICAL INFORMATION: 🏛 **Historical period:** 8th-11th century | 🏛 **Source:** EDDAS/Manuscripts | ⏱ **Preparation time:** 30 min | **Cooking time:** 18 min | 🜂 **Calories:** 155 kcal per portion | 👥 **Servings:** 4 people | 📋 **Nutritional value:** Protein: 20g / Carbohydrates: 8g / Fat: 4g | 💡 **Ancient advice:** Stewing according to marine techniques | 🔲 **Modern method:** Covered casserole over medium heat | 💲 **Estimated cost:** €18.70 / £16.30 / $21.70 | 🏺 **Nordic utensils:** KETILL, skimmer, fine sieve | ⚙ **Difficulty:** Novice ★☆☆

🏛 SKELLFISKR FISKISÓSA : A mix of shellfish from the Nordic coasts, enhanced with FISKISÓSA fermented according to the traditional recipes of professional gatherers. A popular dish of coastal Karls, rich in salty flavors and marine nutrients.

INGREDIENTS :

- 1.2 kg of SKELLFISKR BLÖNDUR (shellfish mix)
- 60 ml FISKISÓSA GÖMUL (fermented fish sauce)
- 100 ml of OLÍA STEINFRJÓ (seed oil)
- 300 ml of VÍNHVÍTR (Nordic white wine)
- 40 g of LAUKAR (wild onions)
- 25 g of HVÍTLAUKR (wild garlic)
- 20 g of PERSILLA STEINFJALL (mountain parsley)
- 15 g of INGIFER VILLT (wild ginger)
- 8 korns of PIPAR RAUTT (pink pepper)

METHOD

1. **Initial preparation:** Carefully brush and clean all shells, remove damaged or open ones, soak for 20 minutes in salt water to remove sand according to coastal harvester practices.
2. **First cooking:** Heat OLÍA in a large KETILL, sweat sliced LAUKAR and pounded HVÍTLAUKR without coloring, add grated INGIFER to flavor the aromatic base.
3. **Main assembly:** Add the drained shellfish, stir briskly for 3-4 minutes to open the first shells, moisten with VÍNHVÍTR and cover tightly using marine stew techniques.
4. **Final cooking:** Cook over high heat for 12-15 minutes until completely open, shake the container regularly, discard any that remain closed.
5. **Finishing:** Add FISKISÓSA and chopped PERSILLA, season with crushed PIPAR RAUTT, leave to infuse off the heat.
6. **Serving:** Serve in large bowls with cooking juices and serve with rye bread for dipping.

🔲 **Modern Substitutes:** SKELLFISKR → mussels, clams, cockles, FISKISÓSA → nuoc-mam sauce, INGIFER VILLT → fresh ginger, PIPAR RAUTT → pink berries

ANCIENT METHOD: Braising in terracotta pots sealed with clay, buried in embers according to primitive fishermen

Secrets of MATSTJÓRAR: Rigorous selection of live shellfish by closing test, cooking interrupted as soon as it is fully opened, FISKISÓSA dosed according to the desired intensity to balance the iodized flavors

Nutritional values: 155 kcal | Protein: 20g | Carbohydrates: 8g | Fat: 4g

AXIS 6: GRÆNMETI OK VILLIGRAS *Wild vegetables and herbs from Midgard*

Grænmeti Göfugt (8 recipes), Heilöggras (7 recipes)

76. SPÆNIASPÁRGELL VILLT OLÍA ~ Wild asparagus in walnut oil

PRACTICAL INFORMATION: 📖 Historical period: 8th-11th century | 🏛 Source: SAGAS/Archaeology | 🕐 Preparation time: 15 min | Cooking time: 12 min | 💧 Calories: 95 kcal per portion | 👥 Servings: 4 people | 📋 Nutritional value: Protein: 4g / Carbohydrates: 6g / Fat: 7g | 💡 Ancient advice: Quick cooking to keep it crisp according to herbalists | 🔄 Modern method: Steam cooking for 8-10 minutes | 💰 Estimated cost: €12.80 / £11.20 / $14.80 | 🍴 Nordic utensils: GUFUSKÁLAR, wooden tongs, mortar | ⚙️ Difficulty: Novice ★☆☆

🏛 SPÆNIASPÁRGELL VILLT OLÍA : Wild asparagus from the Nordic undergrowth, harvested in spring according to the calendars of VÖLUR herbalists. A delicate vegetable of the jarls, a symbol of spring renewal and the first greenery after the long arctic winters.

INGREDIENTS :

- 800 g SPÆNIASPÁRGELL VILLT (fine wild asparagus)
- 80 ml of OLÍA HNOTUR (pressed walnut oil)
- 60 g of HNOTUR KRAKKAÐAR (crushed walnuts)
- 20 g SMJÖR FERSK (fresh butter)
- 15 g of HVÍTLAUKR VILLT (wild garlic)
- 12 g of SALT STEINFJALL (rock salt)
- Saft úr SÍTRÓN (Nordic lemon juice)
- 10 g of PERSILLA STEINFJALL (mountain parsley)
- 6 korns of PIPAR HVÍTR (white pepper)

METHOD

1. **Initial preparation:** Gently clean the wild asparagus, break off the woody base, lightly peel the thick stems, rinse in cold spring water according to the techniques of specialized pickers.
2. **First cooking:** Cook in boiling salted water for 6-8 minutes until firm and tender, then immediately plunge into ice water to stop the cooking and set the bright green color.
3. **Main assembly:** Heat OLÍA HNOTUR with sliced HVÍTLAUKR in a large pan, add drained asparagus and HNOTUR KRAKKAÐAR, gently fry for 3-4 minutes according to the art of fine vegetable preparers.
4. **Final cooking:** Add SMJÖR FERSK in pieces to bind, season with SALT and PIPAR, add a few drops of SÍTRÓN juice.
5. **Finishing:** Sprinkle with freshly chopped parsley and season to taste.
6. **Service:** Arrange on a warm dish, arrange the asparagus in bundles harmoniously, drizzle with flavored oil.

🔄 Modern Substitutes: SPÆNIASPÁRGELL VILLT → thin green asparagus, OLÍA HNOTUR → virgin walnut oil, HNOTUR → walnut kernels, SÍTRÓN → lemon

ANCIENT METHOD: Quick steam cooking in a wicker basket suspended above a cauldron, using the techniques of forest herbalists

Secrets of MATSTJÓRAR: Asparagus chosen of uniform size for even cooking, walnut oil heated moderately to preserve the delicate aromas, cooking stopped when perfectly tender according to tests by VÖLUR botanists

Nutritional values: 95 kcal | Protein: 4g | Carbohydrates: 6g | Fat: 7g

77. ÞISTLAR FURURKJARNAR ~ Cardoons with pine nuts

PRACTICAL INFORMATION: 📺 **Historical period:** 8th-11th century | 🏛 **Source:** EDDAS/Manuscripts | 🕐 **Preparation time:** 35 min | **Cooking time:** 45 min | 💧 **Calories:** 168 kcal per portion | 👥 **Servings:** 4 people | 📖 **Nutritional value:** Protein: 6g / Carbohydrates: 12g / Fat: 12g | 💡 **Ancient advice:** Long preparation to eliminate bitterness according to herbalists | 🔄 **Modern method:** Pre-blanching in vinegar water | 💰 **Estimated cost:** €16.50 / £14.40 / $19.10 | 🏺 **Nordic utensils:** KETILL, iron knives, leather gloves | ⚙️ **Difficulty:** Master ★★★

🏛 **ÞISTLAR FURURKJARNAR** : Wild cardoons from the Nordic moors, prepared according to the complex art of the VÖLUR herbalists. A noble vegetable of autumn feasts, a symbol of the mastery of thorny plants and the culinary patience of the ancients.

INGREDIENTS :

- 1.5 kg of ÞISTLAR FERSK (young wild cardoons)
- 150 g of FURURKJARNAR (Nordic pine nuts)
- 100 ml of OLÍA STEINFRJÓ (seed oil)
- 60 g of SMJÖR (Nordic butter)
- 200 ml MJÓLK ÞYKKT (thick milk)
- 30 ml EDIK HVÍTR (white vinegar)
- 25 g of HVÍTLAUKR (wild garlic)
- 20 g of MJÖL (barley flour)
- 15 g of SALT STEINFJALL (rock salt)

METHOD

1. **Initial preparation:** Carefully trim the cardoons, removing leaves and thorns, cut into 8 cm pieces, rub immediately with SÍTRÓN juice to prevent oxidation, following the techniques of specialist preparers.
2. **First cooking:** Blanch for 15 minutes in boiling water with EDIK HVÍTR added to remove the bitterness, refresh in iced water, drain carefully by pressing gently.
3. **Main assembly:** Fry the sliced HVÍTLAUKR in hot OLÍA, add the drained cardoons and lightly grilled FURURKJARNAR, cook over low heat for 20 minutes according to the art of noble vegetable cooks.
4. **Final cooking:** Sprinkle with MJÖL to bind, gradually moisten with MJÓLK ÞYKKT, simmer for 15 minutes, stirring frequently for smoothness.
5. **Finishing:** Add to the SMJÖR in batches, adjust the seasoning with SALT, check for perfect tenderness.
6. **Serving:** Arrange in a preheated deep dish, sprinkle with the remaining toasted pine nuts.

🔄 **Modern Substitutes:** ÞISTLAR → cultivated cardoons, FURURKJARNAR → pine nuts, MJÓLK ÞYKKT → crème fraîche, EDIK HVÍTR → white vinegar

ANCIENT METHOD: Prolonged cooking in an earthenware pot buried in embers, patiently turning over according to expert herbalists

Secrets of the MATSTJÓRAR: Cardoons trimmed with thick gloves for protection, blanching renewed if bitterness persists, pine nuts roasted separately to keep them crisp according to the wisdom of the forest VÖLUR

Nutritional values: 168 kcal | Protein: 6g | Carbohydrates: 12g | Fat: 12g

78. GRASKER FYLTAR HIRSI ~ Squash stuffed with Nordic millet

PRACTICAL INFORMATION: 📖 Historical period: 8th-11th century | 🏛 Source: SAGAS/Archaeology | 🕐 Preparation time: 40 min | **Cooking time:** 75 min | 🜂 Calories: 245 kcal per portion | 👥 Servings: 4 people | 🗒 Nutritional value: Protein: 8g / Carbohydrates: 35g / Fat: 9g | 💡 Ancient advice: Slow cooking in a stone oven according to the farmers | 🔲 Modern method: Traditional oven 180°C | 🏷 Estimated cost: €13.90 / £12.10 / $16.10 | 🏺 Nordic utensils: STEINOFN, wooden spoon, BAKSTEINN | ⚙ Difficulty: Beginner ★★☆

🏛 **GRASKER FYLTAR HIRSI** : Autumn squash from Nordic vegetable gardens, stuffed with millet according to farmer-cultivators' recipes. A fortifying dish from agricultural karls, a symbol of bountiful harvests and well-organized winter provisions.

INGREDIENTS :

- 4 GRASKER MEÐALSTÓR (medium squash)
- 300 g HIRSI GULLFÁTT (golden millet)
- 600 ml of KJÖTSKRAFT (meat broth)
- 100 g of LAUKAR RAUÐIR (red onions)
- 80 g of SMJÖR (Nordic butter)
- 60 g of HNOTUR KRAKKAÐAR (crushed walnuts)
- 40 g RÓSÍNUR (arctic raisins)
- 20 g of PERSILLA VILLT (wild parsley)
- 15 g of SALT STEINFJALL (rock salt)
- 8 korns of PIPAR SVARTR (black pepper)

METHOD

1. **Initial preparation:** Cut a cap off each squash, carefully scoop out the flesh and seeds with a wooden spoon, and reserve the pulp for stuffing using Nordic gardener-cook techniques.
2. **First cooking:** Rinse HIRSI several times, cook for 25 minutes in simmering KJÖTSKRAFT until completely absorbed, let it swell and cool slightly.
3. **Main assembly:** Fry sliced LAUKAR in SMJÖR until golden brown, add diced pumpkin pulp, HNOTUR and RÓSÍNUR, cook for 10 minutes according to the stuffers' art.
4. **Final cooking:** Mix the cooked millet with the sautéed vegetables, season generously, stuff the hollowed-out squash, replace the tops, cook in the STEINOFN for 45 minutes.
5. **Finishing:** Check the tenderness of the squash with the tip of a knife, let stand for 10 minutes before serving.
6. **Service:** Present whole on wooden boards, sprinkle with chopped parsley, serve directly in the peel.

🔲 **Modern Substitutes:** GRASKER → pumpkins or butternut squash, HIRSI → pearl millet, KJÖTSKRAFT → vegetable broth, RÓSÍNUR → currants

ANCIENT METHOD: Cooking buried in a pit lined with hot stones, covered with earth according to the farmers of the fertile valleys

Secrets of MATSTJÓRAR: Selected squash with thick skin for prolonged cooking, careful hollowing out without piercing, slightly moist stuffing to prevent drying out according to the experience of ancient growers

Nutritional values: 245 kcal | Protein: 8g | Carbohydrates: 35g | Fat: 9g

79. MANGOLD RÚSÍNUR - Chard with Arctic raisins

PRACTICAL INFORMATION: 📠 **Historical period:** 8th-11th century | 🏛 **Source:** EDDAS/Manuscripts | 🕐 **Preparation time:** 20 min | **Cooking time:** 25 min | 🔥 **Calories:** 128 kcal per portion | 👥 **Servings:** 4 people | 📋 **Nutritional value:** Protein: 5g / Carbohydrates: 18g / Fat: 5g | 💡 **Ancient advice:** Cook stems and leaves separately according to herbalists | 🔄 **Modern method:** Pan-fry in stages | 💰 **Estimated cost:** €9.80 / £8.50 / $11.40 | 🪙 **Nordic utensils:** JÁRNSKÁLAR, iron knife, colander | ⚙️ **Difficulty:** Novice ★☆☆

🏛 **MANGOLD RÚSÍNUR** : Swiss chard from northern vegetable gardens prepared with dried grapes according to the recipes of monastic gardeners. A leafy vegetable appreciated by rural karls, rich in iron and essential vitamins for the long arctic winters.

INGREDIENTS :

- 1.2 kg of MANGOLD FERSK (fresh chard)
- 120 g RÚSÍNUR ÞURRKAÐAR (northern raisins)
- 80 ml of OLÍA STEINFRJÓ (seed oil)
- 60 g of SMJÖR (fresh butter)
- 40 g of LAUKAR HVÍTIR (white onions)
- 30 g of FURURKJARNAR (pine nuts)
- 20 ml EDIK ÁVAXTABRAGÐ (fruit vinegar)
- 12 g of SALT FÍNT (fine salt)
- 8 korns of PIPAR HVÍTR (white pepper)

METHOD

1. **Initial preparation:** Carefully separate the chard stems and leaves, cut the stems into 3 cm sections, roughly chop the leaves, wash thoroughly according to the rules of Nordic market gardeners.
2. **First cooking:** Soak RÚSÍNUR in lukewarm water for 15 minutes to re-swell, heat OLÍA in large JÁRNSKÁLAR, fry sliced LAUKAR until transparent.
3. **Main assembly:** First add the firmer chard stems, cook for 8-10 minutes over medium heat, then stir in the chopped leaves and cook for another 5 minutes according to the art of vegetable cooks.
4. **Final cooking:** Add drained RÚSÍNUR and FURURKJARNAR, whisk in SMJÖR, deglaze lightly with EDIK to balance the sweetness.
5. **Finishing:** Season with SALT and PIPAR, adjust the acidity to taste, simmer for 3 minutes.
6. **Serving:** Arrange in a dome on a serving dish, sprinkle with the remaining toasted pine nuts.

🔄 **Modern Substitutes:** MANGOLD → multicolored chard, RÚSÍNUR → Smyrna raisins, FURURKJARNAR → pine nuts, EDIK ÁVAXTABRAGÐ → white balsamic vinegar

ANCIENT METHOD: Stewing in an earthenware pot with a tight-fitting lid, using the techniques of conservator-gardeners

Secrets of MATSTJÓRAR: Stems cooked first for uniformity of texture, leaves added gradually to avoid overcooking, grapes rehydrated just enough for softness without excess according to the master vegetable cooks

Nutritional values: 128 kcal | Protein: 5g | Carbohydrates: 18g | Fat: 5g

80. SALAT SARDÍNUR ~ Lettuce with smoked anchovies

PRACTICAL INFORMATION: 📖 Historical period: 8th-11th century | 🏛 Source: SAGAS/Archaeology | 🕐 Preparation time: 15 min | Cooking time: 0 min | 💧 Calories: 85 kcal per portion | 👥 Servings: 4 people | 📖 Nutritional value: Protein: 8g / Carbohydrates: 4g / Fat: 4g | 💡 Ancient advice: Raw salad according to coastal traditions | 🔄 Modern method: Prepare in advance 30 minutes | 💰 Estimated cost: €8.60 / £7.50 / $10.00 | 🏺 Norse utensils: SKÁLAR viður, iron knives, mortar | ⚙ Difficulty: Novice ★☆☆

🏛 **SALAT SARDÍNUR** : Wild lettuce from the northern meadows served with smoked anchovies, according to the eating habits of coastal fishermen. A fresh dish from the seafaring karls, rich in spring vitamins after the long winter deprivation of green vegetables.

INGREDIENTS :

- 800 g of SALAT VILLT (various wild lettuces)
- 120 g SARDÍNUR REYKTIR (Nordic smoked anchovies)
- 100 ml of OLÍA STEINFRJÓ (pressed seed oil)
- 40 ml of EDIK HVÍTR (white fruit vinegar)
- 30 g of HVÍTLAUKR VILLT (wild garlic)
- 20 g of KAPPAR (arctic capers)
- 15 g of HUNANG LYNGI (heather honey)
- 60 g of BRAUÐKÚLUR (rye bread croutons)
- 10 g of SALT HAFR (fine sea salt)

METHOD

1. **Initial preparation:** Carefully sort and wash the wild lettuce, remove damaged leaves, gently wring out in a clean cloth, cut into wide strips using the techniques of herbalist harvesters.
2. **First cooking:** Prepare vinaigrette by emulsifying OLÍA with EDIK, HUNANG and finely crushed HVÍTLAUKR, season with SALT HAFR, let the aromas infuse for 10 minutes.
3. **Main assembly:** Arrange lettuce in a large wooden SKÁLAR, spread shredded SARDÍNUR and drained KAPPAR, sprinkle with grilled BRAUÐKÚLUR according to the art of Nordic salad assemblers.
4. **Final cooking:** No cooking necessary, mix gently when serving to preserve the crispness of the vegetables.
5. **Finishing:** Adjust the dressing seasoning to the desired acidity, check the balance of flavors.
6. **Serving:** Serve immediately after seasoning, toss at the table to distribute the dressing evenly.

🔄 **Modern Substitutes:** SALAT VILLT → arugula and wild lamb's lettuce, SARDÍNUR REYKTIR → anchovies in oil, KAPPAR → capers in vinegar, HUNANG LYNGI → acacia honey

ANCIENT METHOD: Directly assembled in individual wooden bowls, seasoned at the last moment according to the customs of outdoor meals

Secrets of the MATSTJÓRAR: Lettuce harvested in the early morning for optimal freshness, vinaigrette balanced between acidity and sweetness of honey, anchovies desalted if necessary to avoid excess according to the tastes of the elders

Nutritional values: 85 kcal | Protein: 8g | Carbohydrates: 4g | Fat: 4g

81. RÓFUR HUNANG ~ Candied radishes with lime honey

PRACTICAL INFORMATION: 📷 **Historical period:** 8th-11th century | 🏛 **Source:** EDDAS/Manuscripts | 🕐
Preparation time: 25 min | **Cooking time:** 35 min | 💧 **Calories:** 112 kcal per portion | 👥 **Servings:** 4 people | 📖
Nutritional value: Protein: 2g / Carbohydrates: 22g / Fat: 3g | 💡 **Ancient advice:** Slow confectionery to soften
the spiciness according to herbalists | 🔄 **Modern method:** Simmer for 45 minutes | 💰 **Estimated cost:** €7.40 /
£6.40 / $8.60 | 🏺 **Nordic utensils:** KETILL, wooden spoon, strainer | ⚙ **Difficulty:** Novice ★☆☆

🏛 **RÓFUR HUNANG** : Wild radishes from the Nordic meadows, candied with honey according to the
medicinal recipes of the VÖLUR herbalists. Root vegetable transformed by gentle cooking, appreciated for its
digestive properties and its taste softened by honeyed juices.

INGREDIENTS :

- 1 kg of RÓFUR VILLT (small wild radishes)
- 150 g of HUNANG LIND (Nordic linden honey)
- 80 ml of OLÍA STEINFRJÓ (seed oil)
- 200 ml of VATN KELDA (spring water)
- 30 ml EDIK HVÍTR (white vinegar)
- 20 g of SMJÖR (fresh butter)
- 15 g of TÍMILL VILLT (wild thyme)
- 12 g of SALT FÍNT (fine salt)
- 6 korns of PIPAR HVÍTR (white pepper)

METHOD

1. **Initial preparation:** Carefully clean the radishes, keeping a little of the stem, trim the main root, make
    a slight cross-shaped incision on the top to facilitate the penetration of flavors according to the
    techniques of root preparers.
2. **First cooking:** Blanch quickly for 3 minutes in boiling salted water to remove excessive acridity,
    refresh immediately, drain and dry gently.
3. **Main assembly:** Heat OLÍA in a thick-bottomed KETILL, fry the drained radishes for 5 minutes to
    lightly brown them, add HUNANG LIND and VATN KELDA according to the art of Nordic
    confectionery.
4. **Final cooking:** Simmer over low heat for 25-30 minutes until tender and golden caramelized, stir
    gently to prevent bursting, add EDIK at the end of cooking.
5. **Finishing:** Add SMJÖR and TÍMILL, season with SALT and PIPAR, reduce to a syrupy consistency.
6. **Serving:** Arrange in small piles, coat with the reduced cooking syrup, serve warm as an
    accompaniment.

🔄 **Modern Substitutes:** RÓFUR VILLT → spring pink radishes, HUNANG LIND → linden honey, TÍMILL VILLT →
fresh thyme, VATN KELDA → filtered water

ANCIENT METHOD: Slow candied in a terracotta pot placed on embers, gradually raising the temperature
according to the vegetable preservatives

Secrets of MATSTJÓRAR: Radishes chosen young and firm, blanching adjusted according to natural pungency,
honey gradually incorporated for even caramelization without burning according to the wisdom of the
VÖLUR cooks

Nutritional values: 112 kcal | Protein: 2g | Carbohydrates: 22g | Fat: 3g

82. LAUKAR SNEIÐIR ~ Marsh Leeks

PRACTICAL INFORMATION: 🎞 Historical period: 8th-11th century | 🏛 Source: SAGAS/Archaeology | 🕐 Preparation time: 20 min | Cooking time: 30 min | 🜂 Calories: 135 kcal per portion | 👥 Servings: 4 people | 📑 Nutritional value: Protein: 4g / Carbohydrates: 16g / Fat: 6g | ♀ Ancient advice: Braising using marshy techniques | 🔄 Modern method: Braising in a covered casserole dish | 💰 Estimated cost: €6.80 / £5.90 / $7.90 | 🍶 Nordic utensils: KETILL, iron knife, BAKSTEINN | ⚙ Difficulty: Novice ★☆☆

🏛 **LAUKAR SNEIÐIR** : Wild leeks from the Nordic marshy areas, cut and braised using the techniques of aquatic vegetable harvesters. A hardy vegetable from rural þræll, appreciated for its resistance and availability in wetlands.

INGREDIENTS :

- 1.2 kg of LAUKAR VILLT (wild marsh leeks)
- 100 ml of OLÍA STEINFRJÓ (seed oil)
- 80 g of SMJÖR (Nordic butter)
- 300 ml of KJÖTSKRAFT (meat broth)
- 40 g of HVÍTLAUKR (wild garlic)
- 20 g of PERSILLA VILLT (wild parsley)
- 15 g of TÍMILL STEINFJALL (mountain thyme)
- 12 g of SALT HAFR (sea salt)
- 8 korns of PIPAR SVARTR (black pepper)

METHOD

1. **Initial preparation:** Carefully clean the wild leeks, remove the roots and damaged parts of the leaves, cut into 5 cm sections, wash thoroughly to remove soil and sand using the techniques of market gardeners in wetlands.
2. **First cooking:** Heat OLÍA and SMJÖR in a large KETILL, fry the cut leeks for 8-10 minutes over medium heat until the white parts are lightly golden.
3. **Main assembly:** Add crushed HVÍTLAUKR, TÍMILL and spices, sweat for 3 minutes to develop aromas, moisten with hot KJÖTSKRAFT according to the art of Nordic braising.
4. **Final cooking:** Cover tightly, simmer for 18-20 minutes over low heat until perfectly tender, checking the liquid level regularly.
5. **Finishing:** Adjust the seasoning, add chopped PERSILLA at the end of cooking, reduce if necessary to concentrate the flavors.
6. **Serving:** Arrange in a preheated deep dish, cover with the reduced cooking juices, serve as an accompaniment to meats.

🔄 **Modern Substitutes:** LAUKAR VILLT → cultured leeks, KJÖTSKRAFT → vegetable broth, TÍMILL STEINFJALL → fresh thyme, PERSILLA VILLT → flat-leaf parsley

ANCIENT METHOD: Braising in an earthenware pot buried in embers, slow and regular cooking according to the techniques of the inhabitants of the marshes

Secrets of MATSTJÓRAR: Leeks washed by prolonged soaking to remove impurities, covered cooking to concentrate the aromas, broth added gradually according to absorption according to the experience of rural cooks

Nutritional values: 135 kcal | Protein: 4g | Carbohydrates: 16g | Fat: 6g

83. KÁLRÓT MJÚKR KRYDD ~ Tender kohlrabi with spices

PRACTICAL INFORMATION: 🖼 **Historical period:** 9th-10th century | 🏛 **Source:** SAGA OF EGILL SKALLAGRÍMSSON | 🕐 **Preparation time:** 15 min | **Cooking time:** 25 min | 🔥 **Calories:** 180 kcal per serving | 👥 **Servings:** 6 people | 📋 **Nutritional value:** Protein: 4g / Carbohydrates: 32g / Fat: 6g | 💡 **Ancient advice:** Cook in fjord water for minerals | 🔲 **Modern method:** Use a cast iron casserole dish | 💰 **Estimated cost:** €2.50 / £2.20 / $2.80 | 🍲 **Norse utensils:** Iron KETILL, rune knife | ⚙ **Difficulty:** Novice ★☆☆

🏛 **KÁLRÓT MJÚKR KRYDD:** A staple vegetable of the Nordic Karls, grown in the vegetable gardens of Icelandic farms. Eaten as part of everyday autumn meals, this kohlrabi was valued for its winter preservation and fortifying properties. Spices were reserved for feast days according to the SAGAS.

INGREDIENTS :

- 800g of KÁLRÓT (Nordic kohlrabi)
- 2 spoons of HUNANG (heather honey)
- 1 pinch of PIPAR LANGR (long pepper)
- 3 tablespoons of OLÍA (walnut oil)
- 1 spoon of SALT HAFSSALT (sea salt)
- 1 bunch of VILLIDILL (wild dill)

METHOD

1. **Initial preparation:** Peel and cut the KÁLRÓT into regular cubes. Place in cold salted water.
2. **First cooking:** Bring the water to a boil in the iron KETILL, cook the vegetables for 15 minutes until tender.
3. **Main assembly:** Drain thoroughly, add the HUNANG, OLÍA, and spices. Mix gently to coat evenly. Stir in the finely chopped wild dill.
4. **Final cooking:** Heat for 3 minutes over low heat.
5. **Finishing:** Adjust the seasoning with SALT and PIPAR according to Nordic taste.
6. **Service:** Serve hot in wooden bowls, accompanied by barley bread.

🔲 **Modern Substitutes:** PIPAR LANGR → crushed black pepper, VILLIDILL → fresh dill, OLÍA → rapeseed oil

ANCIENT METHOD: Cooking in a cauldron suspended above the central hearth of the longhouse

Secrets of the MATSTJÓRAR: Adding honey at the end of cooking preserves vitamins, a technique taught by the VÖLUR healers of the Icelandic fjords

Nutritional values: 180 kcal | Protein: 4g | Carbohydrates: 32g | Fat: 6g

84. FENIKALFRJÓ ~ Fennel seeds with vegetables

PRACTICAL INFORMATION: 📅 **Historical period:** 8th-9th century | 🏛 **Source:** Archaeological excavations of Birka | 🕐 **Preparation time:** 20 min | **Cooking time:** 30 min | 💧 **Calories:** 220 kcal per portion | 👥 **Servings:** 4 people | 📑 **Nutritional value:** Protein: 8g / Carbohydrates: 28g / Fat: 10g | 💡 **Ancient advice:** Roast the seeds on a hot stone | 🖥 **Modern method:** Non-stick pan over medium heat | 💰 **Estimated cost:** €3.80 / £3.40 / $4.20 | 🍴 **Nordic utensils:** Stone mortar, BAKSTEINN | ⚙️ **Difficulty:** Initiate ★★☆

🏛 **FENIKALFRJÓ:** A rare spice imported by Viking traders from Byzantium, used as a substitute for ASA FOETIDA at the great banquets of the jarls. Considered medicinal by the VÖLUR, it accompanied vegetables at the equinox blót.

INGREDIENTS :

- 3 spoons of FENIKALFRJÓ (fennel seeds)
- 500g of RÓFUR (Nordic turnips)
- 300g of LAUKAR (wild leeks)
- 200g HVÍTLAUKR (wild garlic)
- 4 tablespoons of OLÍA HNETUR (walnut oil)
- 1 spoon of SALT STEINASALT (rock salt)

METHOD

1. **Initial preparation:** Grill the FENIKALFRJÓ on hot BAKSTEINN until intensely fragrant. Grind coarsely in a stone mortar.
2. **First cooking:** Finely chop all the vegetables. Heat the OLÍA in the iron pot.
3. **Main assembly:** Fry the LAUKAR for 5 minutes, add the RÓFUR and cook for 10 minutes. Stir in the HVÍTLAUKR and the crushed seeds. Mix vigorously to release the aromas.
4. **Final cooking:** Cover and simmer for 12 minutes over birch embers.
5. **Finishing:** Season with salt according to Nordic tradition, sprinkle with fresh fennel if available.
6. **Service:** Serve in carved wooden bowls and serve with FLATBRAUÐ.

🖥 **Modern Substitutes:** FENIKALFRJÓ → fennel seeds + asa foetida, RÓFUR → purple turnips

ANCIENT METHOD: Roasting the seeds on a flat stone heated in embers

Secrets of the MATSTJÓRAR: Partial grinding of the seeds releases essential oils without bitterness, a secret passed on by traveling skalds

Nutritional values: 220 kcal | Protein: 8g | Carbohydrates: 28g | Fat: 10g

85. BERGJÚRT - Norwegian mountain oregano

PRACTICAL INFORMATION: 🖼 Historical period: 9th-10th century | 🏛 Source: SAGA OF HÁKON THE GOOD | ⏱ Preparation time: 10 min | Cooking time: 15 min | 🜄 Calories: 35 kcal per portion | 👥 Servings: 8 people | 📋 Nutritional value: Protein: 2g / Carbohydrates: 4g / Fat: 1g | ♀ Ancient advice: Pick at dawn under dew | ⟳ Modern method: Dry in a dehydrator | 💰 Estimated cost: €1.20 / £1.00 / $1.40 | ⬢ Nordic utensils: Wicker basket, wooden drying rack | ⚙ Difficulty: Novice ★☆☆

🏛 BERGJÚRT: Sacred herb of the Norwegian highlands, gathered by shepherds during the summer transhumance. Used in medicinal preparations of the VÖLUR and to flavor meats during sacrifices to the gods. Symbol of divine protection according to the EDDAS.

INGREDIENTS :
- 100g fresh BERGJÚRT (mountain oregano)
- 2 spoons of OLÍA BIRKI (birch oil)
- 1 pinch of SALT HAFSSALT (sea salt)
- Some EINIBER (juniper) berries

METHOD
1. **Initial preparation:** Gently clean the oregano stems, remove the woody parts. Carefully strip the leaves.
2. **First cooking:** Lightly heat the OLÍA BIRKI in an iron pan without overheating.
3. **Main assembly:** Stir in the oregano leaves and gently cook for 2 minutes to release the aromas. Add a pinch of salt and the crushed berries.
4. **Final cooking:** Remove from heat as soon as the aroma intensifies.
5. **Finishing:** Let cool, store in a terracotta jar with a lid.
6. **Serving:** Use as a condiment for grilled meats and fish.

⟳ Modern Substitutes: BERGJÚRT → dried Greek oregano, OLÍA BIRKI → olive oil

ANCIENT METHOD: Natural drying suspended under the eaves of the longhouse

Secrets of the MATSTJÓRAR: Never exceed 50°C when drying to preserve the essences, method of the herbalists of the fjells

Nutritional values: 35 kcal | Protein: 2g | Carbohydrates: 4g | Fat: 1g

86. HÚNBINGUR HUNANG ~ Thyme with mountain honey

PRACTICAL INFORMATION: 📖 Historical period: 8th-11th century | 🏛 Source: Gotland Runic Scrolls | 🕐 Preparation time: 25 min | Cooking time: 20 min | 🜄 Calories: 145 kcal per serving | 👥 Servings: 6 people | 📋 Nutritional value: Protein: 1g / Carbohydrates: 38g / Fat: 0g | 🍯 Ancient advice: Harvest honey during the full moon | 🔄 Modern method: Electric double boiler | 🍯 Estimated cost: €4.60 / £4.10 / $5.00 | 🏺 Nordic utensils: Earthenware honey pot, wooden spoon | ⚙ Difficulty: Initiate ★★☆

🏛 **HÚNBINGUR HUNANG:** Medicinal preparation of the VÖLUR, combining wild thyme from the moors with mountain honey harvested from natural hives. Used in healing rituals and offered to distinguished guests according to Nordic sacred hospitality.

INGREDIENTS :
- 80g of HÚNBINGUR (wild Nordic thyme)
- 300g of HUNANG FJALLAHUNANG (mountain honey)
- 2 tablespoons of pure spring water
- 1 pinch of SALT KRISTAL (crystalline salt)

METHOD
1. **Initial preparation:** Carefully sort the thyme, keeping only the flowering tops. Rinse in cold water and dry.
2. **First cooking:** Gently heat the honey in an earthenware pot in a Nordic bain-marie, without exceeding 40°C.
3. **Main assembly:** Gradually incorporate the thyme into the warm honey, mixing with a wooden spoon. Let macerate for 15 minutes, stirring regularly. Add water drop by drop to thin.
4. **Final cooking:** Maintain low temperature for another 5 minutes.
5. **Finishing:** Filter through a fine cloth, add crystalline salt for preservation.
6. **Serving:** Store in sealed earthenware jars, use to sweeten herbal teas.

🔄 **Modern Substitutes:** HÚNBINGUR → fresh thyme from Provence, HUNANG FJALLAHUNANG → acacia honey

ANCIENT METHOD: Solar maceration in wooden containers exposed to the midnight sun

Secrets of the MATSTJÓRAR: The temperature must never exceed that of the human body to preserve the virtues, teaching of the beekeepers of the highlands

Nutritional values: 145 kcal | Protein: 1g | Carbohydrates: 38g | Fat: 0g

87. VILLIMINTA ~ Wild Bog Mint

PRACTICAL INFORMATION: 🎞 **Historical period:** 9th-10th century | 🏛 **Source:** OLAF TRYGGVASON'S SAGA | 🕐 **Preparation time:** 15 min | **Cooking time:** 12 min | 🜖 **Calories:** 25 kcal per portion | 👥 **Servings:** 10 people | 📋 **Nutritional value:** Protein: 3g / Carbohydrates: 2g / Fat: 0g | 💡 **Ancient advice:** Harvest before flowering | 🔄 **Modern method:** Infusion at 80°C | 💰 **Estimated cost:** €0.80 / £0.70 / $0.90 | 🏺 **Nordic utensils:** Rush basket, hanging dryer | ⚙ **Difficulty:** Novice ★☆☆

🏛 **VILLIMINTA:** A plant from Nordic marshes, harvested by women during summer expeditions to the peat bogs. Known to be refreshing and digestive, it was infused for the sick and travelers according to the practices of Scandinavian healers.

INGREDIENTS :

- 150g of fresh VILLIMINTA (peat mint)
- 1 liter of pure spring water
- 2 spoons of HUNANG (wild honey)
- A few BERGJÚRT (oregano) leaves

METHOD

1. **Initial preparation:** Carefully sort the mint leaves, removing any tough stems. Rinse under cold running water.
2. **First cooking:** Bring the spring water to a simmer in a clean iron pot.
3. **Main Blend:** Remove from heat and immediately add fresh mint and oregano. Cover tightly with a cloth. Let steep for 10 minutes to extract all the active ingredients.
4. **Final cooking:** Reheat very lightly without boiling.
5. **Finishing:** Filter the infusion, sweeten with honey according to personal taste.
6. **Service:** Serve hot in drinking horns or wooden bowls.

🔄 **Modern Substitutes:** VILLIMINTA → fresh spearmint, spring water → filtered water

ANCIENT METHOD: Infusion in leather skins suspended near the central fire

Secrets of the MATSTJÓRAR: The infusion must never boil to preserve the volatile essences, wisdom of the herbalists of the marshes

Nutritional values: 25 kcal | Protein: 3g | Carbohydrates: 2g | Fat: 0g

88. VÍNRÚTA EGG ~ Swan's Egg Rue

PRACTICAL INFORMATION: 🖩 Historical period: 10th-11th century | 🏛 **Source:** Medicinal texts of the EDDAS | 🕐 **Preparation time:** 30 min | **Cooking time:** 18 min | 🜄 **Calories:** 285 kcal per portion | 🎎 **Servings:** 4 people | 🍲 **Nutritional value:** Protein: 18g / Carbohydrates: 2g / Fat: 22g | 🜨 **Ancient advice:** Precise dosage according to lunar phases | 🔄 **Modern method:** Organic duck eggs as a substitute | 💰 **Estimated cost:** €6.80 / £6.20 / $7.40 | 🍶 **Nordic utensils:** Ritual mortar, silver spoon | ⚙ **Difficulty:** Master ★★★

🏛 **VÍNRÚTA EGG:** Ritual preparation reserved for jarls and VÖLUR during fertility ceremonies. Rue, a plant with magical properties according to Nordic beliefs, was associated with swan eggs, symbols of rebirth. Ceremonial dish for spring blót.

INGREDIENTS :
- 4 ÁLPT (northern swan) eggs
- 10g of dried VÍNRÚTA (rue officinale)
- 3 tablespoons of OLÍA PREMIUM (linseed oil)
- 1 pinch of SALT RITUAL (consecrated salt)
- A few sprigs of DILL VILLT (wild dill)

METHOD
1. **Initial preparation:** Finely grind the dried rue in a ritual mortar, precise dose according to tradition. Gently crack the swan eggs.
2. **First cooking:** Heat the linseed oil in a wrought iron pan, constant moderate temperature.
3. **Main assembly:** Beat the eggs with the ground rue, gradually incorporating them. Mix vigorously to homogenize the sacred mixture. Pour into the hot oil, forming a thick omelet.
4. **Final cooking:** Cook for 8 minutes on each side over low heat.
5. **Finishing:** Sprinkle with wild dill, salt ritually according to the lunar phases.
6. **Serving:** Cut into equal portions and serve on a silver or precious wood platter.

🔄 **Modern Substitutes:** ÁLPT Eggs → duck eggs, VÍNRÚTA → small dose of fresh rue (CAUTION: toxic in high doses)

ANCIENT METHOD: Cooking on a flat stone heated with sacred oak embers

Secrets of the MATSTJÓRAR: Rue should never exceed 0.5g per person, a dosage taught by the oldest VÖLUR of the temples of Uppsala

Nutritional values: 285 kcal | Protein: 18g | Carbohydrates: 2g | Fat: 22g

89. STEINÁRVINALDIR HNETUR ~ Rock parsley with hazelnuts

PRACTICAL INFORMATION: 🖼 **Historical period:** 8th-10th century | 🏛 **Source:** Hedeby excavations | 🕐 **Preparation time:** 20 min | **Cooking time:** 8 min | 🜄 **Calories:** 195 kcal per portion | 👥 **Servings:** 6 people | 📜 **Nutritional value:** Protein: 8g / Carbohydrates: 6g / Fat: 16g | 💡 **Ancient advice:** Roast the hazelnuts on volcanic stone | 🔄 **Modern method:** Oven at 180°C for 5 min | 💰 **Estimated cost:** €3.20 / £2.80 / $3.60 | 🏺 **Nordic utensils:** Hot stone, wooden hammer | ⚙ **Difficulty:** Initiate ★★☆

🏛 **STEINÁRVINALDIR HNETUR:** A rare herb growing in the rocky crevices of the fjells, harvested by Nordic hunters during mountain expeditions. Combined with wild hazelnuts, this preparation accompanied game meats at the Karls' autumn feasts.

INGREDIENTS :

- 100g of STEINÁRVINALDIR (rock parsley)
- 150g of HNETUR (wild hazelnuts)
- 3 tablespoons of OLÍA HNETUR (hazelnut oil)
- 1 spoon of HUNANG (fir honey)
- 1 pinch of SALT BERGSALT (rock salt)

METHOD

1. **Initial preparation:** Carefully clean the rock parsley, removing any mineral particles. Roughly crush the hazelnuts.
2. **First cooking:** Grill the crushed hazelnuts on a hot volcanic stone until perfectly golden.
3. **Main assembly:** Finely chop the parsley and mix with the toasted hazelnuts. Drizzle with hazelnut oil and liquefied honey. Knead gently to form a smooth, crumbly paste.
4. **Final cooking:** Reheat for 2 minutes over very low heat to combine the flavors.
5. **Finishing:** Adjust the seasoning with rock salt, creamy final texture.
6. **Serving:** Shape into small balls and serve with venison roasts.

🔄 **Modern Substitutes:** STEINÁRVINALDIR → flat-leaf parsley, HNETUR → cultivated hazelnuts

ANCIENT METHOD: Grinding in a granite mortar with an ash wood pestle

Secrets of the MATSTJÓRAR: The grill must stop at the first cracks to avoid bitterness, a technique of the Sami mountaineers

Nutritional values: 195 kcal | Protein: 8g | Carbohydrates: 6g | Fat: 16g

90. VILLISELERA SÖLTNAR ~ Marinated wild celery

PRACTICAL INFORMATION: 📖 Historical period: 9th-11th century | 🏛 Source: SAGA OF SNORRI GOÐI | 🕐 Preparation time: 45 min | Cooking time: 15 min | 💧 Calories: 45 kcal per portion | 👥 Servings: 8 people | 📋 Nutritional value: Protein: 2g / Carbohydrates: 8g / Fat: 1g | 💡 Ancient advice: Marinate for at least 3 days | 🔄 Modern method: Refrigerate at 4°C | 💰 Estimated cost: €2.10 / £1.90 / $2.30 | 🏺 Nordic utensils: Stoneware jar, stone weight | ⚙ Difficulty: Initiate ★★☆

🏛 **VILLISELERA SÖLTNAR:** Wild vegetable from Nordic marshes, preserved by brining to survive the long Scandinavian winters. An essential preservation technique for isolated communities, passed down by Icelandic farmhouse owners according to family SAGAS.

INGREDIENTS :

- 500g of VILLISELERA (wild marsh celery)
- 80g of SALT HAFSSALT (coarse sea salt)
- 2 spoons of EDIK EPLER (apple cider vinegar)
- 1 spoon of HUNANG LYNGJAFUR (heather honey)
- Some EINIBER (juniper) berries
- 3 leaves of LAUFVIÐIR (Nordic bay)

METHOD

1. **Initial preparation:** Carefully clean the wild celery, remove the stringy parts. Cut into regular 3 cm pieces.
2. **First cooking:** Boil the salted water with the herbs for 5 minutes to prepare the brine.
3. **Main assembly:** Arrange the celery in layers in the stoneware jar, sprinkling salt between each layer. Pour in the cooled brine mixed with vinegar and honey. Cover with a clean cloth and place a stone weight on top.
4. **Final cooking:** Leave to ferment for 3 days at Nordic cellar temperature.
5. **Finishing:** Check fermentation, adjust acidity if necessary.
6. **Service:** Drain before serving, accompany smoked meats and fish.

🔄 **Modern Substitutes:** VILLISELERA → celery, EDIK EPLER → cider vinegar

ANCIENT METHOD: Fermentation in oak barrels buried in peat bogs

Secrets of the MATSTJÓRAR: The weight must keep the vegetables submerged to avoid mold, method of the canneries of the fjords

Nutritional values: 45 kcal | Protein: 2g | Carbohydrates: 8g | Fat: 1g

AXIS 7: SÆLGÆTI OK BLÓT - *The sweets of Valhalla*

Helgibakaðr (4 recipes), Konungsælgæti (4 recipes)

91. BLÓTAKAKA GOÐUM ~ Sacrificial cake to the gods

PRACTICAL INFORMATION: 🏛 **Historical period:** 8th-11th century | 🏛 **Source:** Uppsala rituals in the EDDAs | 🕐 **Preparation time:** 60 min | **Cooking time:** 45 min | 🜄 **Calories:** 380 kcal per portion | 🐾 **Servings:** 12 people | 🗒 **Nutritional value:** Protein: 8g / Carbohydrates: 65g / Fat: 12g | 💡 **Ancient advice:** Bake in the sacred temple oven | 🔄 **Modern method:** Oven at 160°C fan-assisted | 💲 **Estimated cost:** €8.50 / £7.80 / $9.20 | 🍴 **Nordic utensils:** Ritual STEINOFN, rune molds | ⚙ **Difficulty:** Master ★★★

🏛 **BLÓTAKAKA GOÐUM:** Ceremonial cake of the great seasonal blót, offered to the Aesir gods during the equinox and solstice sacrifices. Prepared exclusively by the GOÐAR (priests) according to sacred proportions inherited from mythical times. Symbol of communion between Midgard and Asgard.

INGREDIENTS :

- 400g of HVÍTMJÖL (pure wheat flour)
- 200g of HUNANG GOÐAHUNANG (consecrated honey)
- 150g of SMJÖR (sacred cow butter)
- 6 HÆNSN eggs (temple hens)
- 100g of MÖNDLUR (sacred almonds)
- 2 spoons of KANILL (oriental cinnamon)
- 1 spoon of HVANN (angelica powder)
- 1 pinch of SALT RITUAL (consecrated salt)

METHOD

1. **Initial preparation:** Mix the sacred flour with the angelica and ritual salt. Melt the butter from the consecrated cows until golden brown.
2. **First cooking:** Beat the eggs vigorously with the consecrated honey until they are perfectly white, using the GOÐAR technique from Uppsala.
3. **Main assembly:** Alternately incorporate the flavored flour and melted butter into the beaten eggs. Add the crushed almonds and oriental cinnamon. Knead according to the ritual gestures passed down by the ancient Nordic priests.
4. **Final cooking:** Pour into the rune mold, cook for 45 minutes in the sacred STEINOFN at a constant temperature.
5. **Finishing:** Unmold warm, brush with liquid honey according to ceremonial tradition.
6. **Serving:** Cut into equal portions for the blót participants, serve with mead.

🔄 **Modern Substitutes:** GOÐAHUNANG → linden honey, HVANN → angelica extract, HÆNSN eggs → farm eggs

ANCIENT METHOD: Cooking in the temple's communal oven, fueled by wood from the sacred ash tree Yggdrasil

Secrets of the MATSTJÓRAR: The threshing must last exactly 99 blows to honor the nine worlds, a tradition of the cook-priests of Uppsala

Nutritional values: 380 kcal | Protein: 8g | Carbohydrates: 65g | Fat: 12g

92. HUNANGSEPLI ~ Nordic Apple and Honey Cake

PRACTICAL INFORMATION: 📰 **Historical period:** 9th-10th century | 🏛 **Source:** SAGA OF BRENNU-NJÁLS | ⏱ **Preparation time:** 40 min | **Cooking time:** 35 min | 🜁 **Calories:** 320 kcal per serving | 👥 **Servings:** 10 people | 📋 **Nutritional value:** Protein: 6g / Carbohydrates: 58g / Fat: 9g | 💡 **Ancient advice:** Apples picked at the waxing moon | 🔲 **Modern method:** Non-stick loaf tin | 💲 **Estimated cost:** €5.80 / £5.20 / $6.40 | 🏺 **Nordic utensils:** BAKSTEINN, silver knife | ⚙ **Difficulty:** Beginner ★★☆

🏛 **HUNANGSEPLI:** Autumnal sweetness from Icelandic farms, prepared during the fall harvest to celebrate the blessings of Iðunn, goddess of eternal apples. Festive cake offered to guests according to the sacred laws of Norse hospitality mentioned in the SAGAS.

INGREDIENTS :

- 300g of HVÍTMJÖL (Nordic spelt flour)
- 250g of HUNANG EPLEBLÓM (apple blossom honey)
- 4 EPLI NORÐRÆN (ancient Nordic apples)
- 100g of SMJÖR (mountain butter)
- 3 GÆSIR eggs (domestic geese)
- 2 spoons of KANILL (merchants' cinnamon)
- 1 spoon of INGIFER (dried ginger)
- 1 pinch of SALT HAFSSALT

METHOD

1. **Initial preparation:** Peel and cut the Nordic apples into regular cubes. Lightly stew them with some of the honey.
2. **First cooking:** Melt the mountain butter in a copper cauldron, let it cool to operating temperature.
3. **Main assembly:** Beat the goose eggs with the remaining honey until frothy. Stir in the sifted flour, Nordic spices, and sea salt. Gently mix in the stewed apples and melted butter using the time-honored technique.
4. **Final cooking:** Pour into the greased mold, bake for 35 minutes on a preheated BAKSTEINN.
5. **Finishing:** Leave to cool before unmolding, glaze with hot liquid honey.
6. **Serving:** Cut into thick slices and serve with whipped crème fraîche.

🔲 **Modern Substitutes:** EPLI NORÐRÆN → Reinette apples, HUNANG EPLEBLÓM → acacia honey

ANCIENT METHOD: Cooking in wooden boxes in the hot ashes of the central hearth

Secrets of MATSTJÓRAR: Apples should not be overcooked to retain their texture, wisdom from Icelandic farm pastry chefs

Nutritional values: 320 kcal | Protein: 6g | Carbohydrates: 58g | Fat: 9g

93. MÖNDLUTERTA ~ Sacred Arctic Almond Pie

PRACTICAL INFORMATION: 📅 **Historical period:** 10th-11th century | 🏛 **Source:** Bergen Manuscripts | 🕐
Preparation time: 90 min | **Cooking time:** 50 min | 🜄 **Calories:** 445 kcal per serving | 👥 **Servings:** 8 people | 📋
Nutritional value: Protein: 12g / Carbohydrates: 42g / Fat: 26g | 💡 **Ancient tip:** Almonds imported from
Byzantium | 🔄 **Modern method:** Chilled shortcrust pastry | 💰 **Estimated cost:** €12.80 / £11.60 / $14.20 | 🏺
Nordic utensils: Clay pie tin, wooden rolling pin | ⚙ **Difficulty:** Master ★★★

🏛 **MÖNDLUTERTA:** A luxury pastry reserved for jarls' banquets, prepared with precious almonds imported
by Viking traders from Constantinople. A symbol of wealth and refinement, it adorned tables at aristocratic
engagements and weddings according to the traditions of the Nordic courts.

INGREDIENTS : Sacred Dough:
- 250g HVÍTMJÖL FÍNAST (finest flour)
- 120g SMJÖR KÚABÚ (farmhouse butter)
- 80g PÚÐURSYKUR (powdered sugar)
- 2 SVANI (swan) eggs
- 1 pinch of SALT KRISTAL

Almond filling:
- 200g MÖNDLUR HVÍTAR (white almonds)
- 150g of HUNANG LIND (linden honey)
- 100g of SMJÖR (clarified butter)
- 3 whole eggs
- 2 spoons of RÓSAVATN (rose water)

METHOD
1. **Initial preparation:** Prepare the dough by mixing flour, cold butter and sugar. Incorporate the eggs and form a smooth ball. Refrigerate.
2. **First cooking:** Peel and finely grind the Byzantine almonds using the Nordic confectioners' technique.
3. **Main assembly:** Spread the dough into the clay mold, prick the bottom. Beat together the honey, butter, eggs, and rose water. Stir in the crushed almonds to form a smooth cream. Pour over the raw dough, carefully smoothing the surface.
4. **Final cooking:** Bake for 50 minutes in a preheated stone oven, watching for golden browning.
5. **Finishing:** Allow to cool completely, then gently unmold onto a silver platter.
6. **Service:** Cut into geometric pieces, serve with spiced mead.

🔄 **Modern Substitutes:** SVANI Eggs → duck eggs, RÓSAVATN → food rose extract

ANCIENT METHOD: Cooking in glazed terracotta molds in the communal oven

Secrets of MATSTJÓRAR: The dough must rest overnight to develop elasticity, a technique used by Bergen
bakers

Nutritional values: 445 kcal | Protein: 12g | Carbohydrates: 42g | Fat: 26g

94. HUNANGSSNÚÐAR ~ Honey and poppy seed spirals

PRACTICAL INFORMATION: 🖼 **Historical period:** 9th-10th century | 🏛 **Source:** Novgorod traditions | 🕐 **Preparation time:** 50 min | **Cooking time:** 25 min | 🝊 **Calories:** 280 kcal per serving | 👥 **Servings:** 15 people | 📕 **Nutritional value:** Protein: 7g / Carbohydrates: 48g / Fat: 8g | 💡 **Ancient advice:** Shaping according to runic spirals | 🖵 **Modern method:** Mechanical kneading for 8 minutes | 🐠 **Estimated cost:** €4.20 / £3.80 / $4.60 | 🝋 **Nordic utensils:** Kneading board, runic knife | ⚙ **Difficulty:** Initiate ★★☆

🏛 **HUNANGSSNÚÐAR:** Spiral pastries of Slavic merchants, adopted by the Vikings during trade on the Volga route. Poppy seeds symbolized fertility and the spirals represented cosmic cycles according to the Norse cosmology of the EDDAs.

INGREDIENTS :

- 400g of HVÍTMJÖL (soft wheat flour)
- 200ml MJÓLK HLÝT (warm milk)
- 100g of HUNANG BLÓM (wildflower honey)
- 80g of SMJÖR (unsalted butter)
- 2 spoons of VALMÚAFRJÓ (poppy seeds)
- 1 spoon of GEST (natural yeast)
- 1 HÆNS egg for gilding
- 1 pinch of SALT FÍNN

METHOD

1. **Initial preparation:** Dissolve the yeast in warm milk with a spoonful of honey. Let it foam for 10 minutes according to Slavic tradition.
2. **First cooking:** Mix flour and salt, make a well. Stir in the yeast mixture, the remaining honey and the melted butter.
3. **Main assembly:** Knead the dough vigorously until perfectly elastic, incorporating the poppy seeds at the end of kneading. Form a smooth ball, let rise for 1 hour under a damp cloth according to the Nordic method. Divide into cords, shape into runic spirals on an oiled baking sheet.
4. **Final cooking:** Brush with beaten egg, bake for 25 minutes in a preheated brick oven.
5. **Finish:** Brush with warm honey straight from the oven for shine.
6. **Serving:** Let cool, serve with Nordic herbal teas.

🖵 **Modern Substitutes:** GEST → fresh baker's yeast, VALMÚAFRJÓ → blue poppy seeds

ANCIENT METHOD: Shaping spirals according to the sacred patterns engraved on runic stones

Secrets of the MATSTJÓRAR: The spirals must have exactly nine turns to honor the nine worlds of Yggdrasil

Nutritional values: 280 kcal | Protein: 7g | Carbohydrates: 48g | Fat: 8g

95. RÓSUKONFEKT ~ Wild rose petal sweets

PRACTICAL INFORMATION: 🖳 **Historical period:** 10th-11th century | 🏛 **Source:** Byzantine trade via Kiev | 🕐 **Preparation time:** 120 min | **Cooking time:** 20 min | 🜊 **Calories:** 185 kcal per serving | 🐾 **Servings:** 20 people | 🍴 **Nutritional value:** Protein: 2g / Carbohydrates: 44g / Fat: 1g | 💡 **Ancient advice:** Pick roses at dawn | 🔃 **Modern method:** Digital sugar thermometer | 💰 **Estimated cost:** €6.80 / £6.20 / $7.40 | 🏺 **Nordic utensils:** Copper cauldron, wooden spatula | ⚙ **Difficulty:** Master ★★★

🏛 **RÓSUKONFEKT:** An oriental delicacy introduced by Viking traders returning from Constantinople, reserved for special occasions and diplomatic gifts. Wild rose petals symbolized love and beauty, following Byzantine influences adopted by the Nordic aristocracy.

INGREDIENTS :

- 150g of VILLIRÓS petals (Nordic wild rose)
- 500g of HUNANG KRISTAL (crystallized honey)
- 200ml of pure spring water
- 2 spoons of RÓSAVATN (rose essence)
- 1 spoonful of SÍTRÓNUSAFI (preserved lemon juice)
- MÖNDLUR powder (almonds) for dusting

METHOD

1. **Initial preparation:** Gently clean the rose petals, remove the bitter white parts. Dry in the shade using the Byzantine method.
2. **First cooking:** Prepare a syrup by heating honey and water in the copper cauldron until it reaches a soft boiled temperature.
3. **Main assembly:** Remove from heat, immediately stir in the dried petals, rose essence, and lemon juice. Mix briskly to evenly coat all the petals. Beat vigorously until the natural sugar partially crystallizes.
4. **Final cooking:** Heat briefly to homogenize the candied mass.
5. **Finishing:** Pour onto oiled marble, cut into diamonds before cooling completely.
6. **Serving:** Sprinkle with almond powder, store in precious wooden boxes.

🔃 **Modern Substitutes:** VILLIRÓS → organic Damask rose petals, HUNANG KRISTAL → crystal sugar

ANCIENT METHOD: Natural crystallization by exposure to the cold winds of the fjords

Secrets of MATSTJÓRAR: The syrup must never exceed 115°C to preserve the delicate fragrance of the petals, a technique used by Byzantine confectioners

Nutritional values: 185 kcal | Protein: 2g | Carbohydrates: 44g | Fat: 1g

96. DADLUTVÍST - Date and berry sweets

PRACTICAL INFORMATION: 🎞 **Historical period:** 10th-11th century | 🏛 **Source:** Mediterranean trade via Andalusia | 🕐 **Preparation time:** 35 min | **Cooking time:** 0 min | 🜂 **Calories:** 240 kcal per serving | 👥 **Servings:** 16 people | 📋 **Nutritional value:** Protein: 4g / Carbohydrates: 58g / Fat: 2g | 💡 **Ancient advice:** Pitted dates from the oases | 🔄 **Modern method:** Food processor | 💰 **Estimated cost:** €8.60 / £7.80 / $9.40 | 🏺 **Nordic utensils:** Granite mortar, ash board | ⚙ **Difficulty:** Initiate ★★☆

🏛 **DADLUTVÍST:** Exotic confectionery of the great Viking travelers, inspired by the sweets discovered in Al-Andalus during raids in the Mediterranean. These treats accompanied trade negotiations and symbolized the richness of intercultural exchanges during the Norse expansion.

INGREDIENTS :

- 300g of DADLUR (fresh pitted dates)
- 100g of BERJABER (Arctic cranberry berries)
- 80g of MÖNDLUR (flaked almonds)
- 50g of HNETUR (crushed hazelnuts)
- 2 spoons of HUNANG (heather honey)
- 1 spoon of KANILL (cinnamon powder)
- Imported KÓKOS powder for coating

METHOD

1. **Initial preparation:** Carefully pit the dates and cut them into small, even pieces. Sort the cranberries.
2. **First cooking:** No cooking is necessary for this raw confection according to oriental tradition.
3. **Main assembly:** Coarsely grind the dates in a granite mortar with the dried berries. Stir in the flaked almonds and crushed hazelnuts. Add the honey and cinnamon, and knead until you get a smooth, sticky dough. Form uniformly sized balls by hand.
4. **Final cooking:** No cooking required, cold confectionery technique.
5. **Finishing:** Roll each ball in coconut powder for a decorative coating.
6. **Service:** Arrange on a carved wooden tray, store in a cool, dry place.

🔄 **Modern Substitutes:** DADLUR → Medjool dates, BERJABER → dried cranberries, KÓKOS → shredded coconut

ANCIENT METHOD: Hand-crafted using techniques learned from Arab merchants

Secrets of MATSTJÓRAR: The dough must be sticky enough to hold without adding fat, a trick from the confectioners of Al-Andalus

Nutritional values: 240 kcal | Protein: 4g | Carbohydrates: 58g | Fat: 2g

97. HNETUR HUNANG ~ Candied nuts with heather honey

PRACTICAL INFORMATION: 🖼 **Historical period:** 8th-10th century | 🏛 **Source:** Norwegian Forest Traditions | 🕐 **Preparation time:** 25 min | **Cooking time:** 15 min | 🜍 **Calories:** 320 kcal per serving | 🦎 **Servings:** 12 people | 📖 **Nutritional value:** Protein: 8g / Carbohydrates: 28g / Fat: 22g | 💡 **Ancient advice:** Harvest nuts on Michaelmas | 🔄 **Modern method:** Stainless steel non-stick pan | 💰 **Estimated cost:** €5.40 / £4.80 / $5.80 | 🍽 **Nordic utensils:** Cast iron cauldron, slotted spoon | ⚙ **Difficulty:** Novice ★☆☆

🏛 **HNETUR HUNANG:** A traditional Nordic hunter-gatherer sweet, prepared during the autumn harvests in the coniferous forests. These candied nuts were a valuable energy reserve for the long Scandinavian winters and accompanied the skalds' evenings according to ancestral traditions.

INGREDIENTS :

- 400g of HNETUR FERSK (fresh shelled walnuts)
- 200g of HUNANG LYNGJAFUR (heather honey from the moors)
- 2 tablespoons of spring water
- 1 spoonful of SMJÖR (clarified butter)
- 1 pinch of SALT HAFSSALT (fine sea salt)
- A few grains of PIPAR HVÍTR (white pepper)

METHOD

1. **Initial preparation:** Roughly crush the fresh walnuts, remove any remaining shells and damaged kernels.
2. **First cooking:** Heat the heather honey with the water in the cast iron cauldron until syrupy.
3. **Main assembly:** Stir the crushed walnuts into the hot honey, mixing gently with a wooden spoon. Add the clarified butter and Nordic spices. Stir constantly for 8 minutes to evenly coat all the walnuts.
4. **Final cooking:** Continue cooking until the honey is lightly caramelized.
5. **Finishing:** Pour onto an oiled board, separate the nuts before cooling completely.
6. **Service:** Store in terracotta pots, serve at the end of the meal with mead.

🔄 **Modern Substitutes:** HNETUR FERSK → walnut kernels, HUNANG LYNGJAFUR → chestnut honey

ANCIENT METHOD: Direct caramelization on flat stones heated with embers

Secrets of the MATSTJÓRAR: Watch carefully to avoid burning the honey which would become bitter, a technique used by harvesters in the boreal forests

Nutritional values: 320 kcal | Protein: 8g | Carbohydrates: 28g | Fat: 22g

98. DADLUR MÖNDLUFYLLTAR ~ Dates stuffed with almonds

PRACTICAL INFORMATION: 🖼 **Historical period:** 10th-11th century | 🏛 **Source:** Sicilian trade | 🕐 **Preparation time:** 40 min | **Cooking time:** 10 min | 🜂 **Calories:** 195 kcal per serving | 👥 **Servings:** 18 people | 📓 **Nutritional value:** Protein: 5g / Carbohydrates: 35g / Fat: 6g | 💡 **Ancient advice:** Stuffing prepared in a golden mortar | 🔄 **Modern method:** Fine piping bag | 💰 **Estimated cost:** €9.20 / £8.40 / $10.00 | 🏺 **Nordic utensils:** Silver knife, miniature spoon | ⚙ **Difficulty:** Master ★★★

🏛 **DADLUR MÖNDLUFYLLTAR:** The ultimate refinement of Norse banquets, inspired by Byzantine courts and the palaces of Palermo. These exquisitely stuffed dates symbolized the pinnacle of Viking culinary art and were reserved for diplomatic gifts between jarls and kings according to the protocols of the royal SAGAS.

INGREDIENTS :

- 36 DADLUR STÓRAR (large, fleshy dates)
- 150g of MÖNDLUR HVÍTAR (blanched sweet almonds)
- 100g of HUNANG KRISTAL (fine crystallized honey)
- 50g of SMJÖR KÚABÚ (butter from noble cows)
- 2 spoons of RÓSAVATN (precious rose water)
- 1 spoon of KANILL FÍNAST (finest cinnamon)
- Edible gold powder for decoration

METHOD

1. **Initial preparation:** Carefully pit the dates, making a minimal slit to preserve their shape. Clean the inside.
2. **First cooking:** Lightly toast the blanched almonds to develop the aroma, let cool completely.
3. **Main Blend:** Finely grind the toasted almonds with the crystallized honey in a fine mortar. Incorporate the softened butter, rose water, and cinnamon to form a smooth, fragrant paste. Gently stuff each date with this mixture using a miniature goldsmith's spoon.
4. **Final cooking:** Place quickly in a warm oven to reheat without drying out.
5. **Finish:** Lightly dust with edible gold powder for royal shine.
6. **Serving:** Arrange on a chiseled silver platter, accompanied by spicy oriental wines.

🔄 **Modern Substitutes:** DADLUR STÓRAR → premium Medjool dates, gold dust → golden icing sugar

ANCIENT METHOD: Stuffing using goldsmith's instruments suitable for luxury cooking

Secrets of the MATSTJÓRAR: Each date must weigh exactly the same for the harmony of the service, perfectionism of the royal kitchens

Nutritional values: 195 kcal | Protein: 5g | Carbohydrates: 35g | Fat: 6g

AXIS 8: DRYKKJUR OK VÍN *The nectars of Asgard*

99. KONUNGSVÍN KRYDDR ~ Royal Nordic Spiced Wine

PRACTICAL INFORMATION: 🖳 **Historical period:** 10th-11th century | 🏛 **Source:** Royal courts of Denmark | 🕐 **Preparation time:** 20 min | **Cooking time:** 30 min | 💧 **Calories:** 180 kcal per portion | 👥 **Servings:** 8 people | 📇 **Nutritional value:** Protein: 0g / Carbohydrates: 24g / Fat: 0g | 💡 **Ancient advice:** Serve in aurochs horns | 🔁 **Modern method:** Immersion heater at 65°C | 💰 **Estimated cost:** €18.50 / £16.80 / $20.20 | 🏺 **Nordic utensils:** Silver cauldron, fine sieve | ⚙ **Difficulty:** Master ★★★

🏛 **KONUNGSVÍN KRYDDR:** Royal nectar of the great Nordic ceremonies, served at coronations and diplomatic treaties between Scandinavian kingdoms. This spiced wine with oriental aromas symbolized the power and wealth of the royal courts according to the chronicles of Danish and Norwegian kings.

INGREDIENTS :

- 750ml of VÍN RAUTT ÚRVAL (premium red wine)
- 100g of HUNANG KONUNGS (royal honey from sacred hives)
- 3 sticks of KANILL AUSTLÖND (Ceylon cinnamon)
- 6 cloves of NELLIKA (Moluccan cloves)
- 2 stars of STJÖRNUKRYDD (star anise)
- 1 spoonful of PIPAR LANGR (long pepper)
- Zest of an APPELSÍNA (bitter orange)
- 4 EINIBER berries (Nordic juniper)
- 1 leaf of LAUFVIÐIR (noble laurel)

METHOD

1. **Initial preparation:** Gather all the precious spices, arrange them in a fine cloth to form a royal bouquet garni.
2. **First cooking:** Gently heat the red wine in the silver cauldron without boiling it, optimal temperature 65°C.
3. **Main blend:** Stir the spice bouquet into the mulled wine, then add the royal honey, stirring until completely dissolved. Let it steep for 20 minutes over very low heat to extract all the oriental aromas. Add the orange zest and juniper berries at the end of the infusion.
4. **Final cooking:** Maintain the temperature without boiling for an additional 10 minutes.
5. **Finishing:** Strain carefully through a fine silver sieve, adjusting the sweetness if necessary.
6. **Serving:** Serve piping hot in polished horns or goldsmith's cups, accompanied by spiced biscuits.

🔁 **Modern Substitutes:** VÍN RAUTT ÚRVAL → Côtes du Rhône Villages, APPELSÍNA → Seville orange

ANCIENT METHOD: Heating in a bain-marie in cauldrons suspended above fragrant embers

Secrets of MATSTJÓRAR: Never let it boil to preserve the alcohol and delicate aromas, a technique of the royal cupbearers of Roskilde

Nutritional values: 180 kcal | Protein: 0g | Carbohydrates: 24g | Fat: 0g

100. MJÖÐUR GUÐLEGR – Mead of the Aesir gods

PRACTICAL INFORMATION: 📖 Historical period: 8th-11th century | 🏛 Source: SNORRI'S EDDA - Myth of the POETIC MJÖÐUR | 🕐 Preparation time: 45 min | Cooking time: 60 min | 🔥 Calories: 220 kcal per portion | 👥 Servings: 12 guests | 📋 Nutritional value: Protein: 1g / Carbohydrates: 32g / Fat: 0g | 💡 Ancient advice: Fermentation for 9 full moons | 🔄 Modern method: Selected yeasts for mead | 💰 Estimated cost: €25.80 / £23.40 / $28.20 | 🍶 Norse utensils: Sacred cauldron, ritual horns | ⚙ Difficulty: Master ★★★

🏛 **MJÖÐUR GUÐLEGR:** The legendary mead of the EDDAS, a sacred drink born from the blood of the wise KVASIR and a source of poetic inspiration according to Norse mythology. This divine drink was prepared by the VÖLUR during the great blót and consumed by the skalds to receive the gift of prophecy and poetry from the Aesir gods.

INGREDIENTS :

- 2kg of HUNANG VILLT (wild honey from the boreal forests)
- 4 liters of spring water from the sacred mountains
- 50g of GEST VILLT (wild yeast from hives)
- 10 berries of EINIBER HELGUR (consecrated juniper)
- 5 leaves of MJÖÐJURT (meadowsweet)
- 3 branches of HVANN (marsh angelica)
- 1 root of BALDURSBRÁ (Odin's chamomile)
- 7 grains of PIPAR HVÍTR (ritual white pepper)

METHOD

1. **Initial Preparation:** Purify all utensils according to sacred rites. Heat the mountain water in the consecrated cauldron without boiling it.
2. **First cooking:** Gradually add the wild honey to the hot water, stirring clockwise as usual. Maintain a constant temperature of 45°C.
3. **Main Blend:** Add all the sacred herbs tied in a ritual bouquet. Let it steep for 45 minutes, stirring every 9 minutes according to the cosmic cycles. Strain carefully to remove any plant residue. Let it cool to body temperature before sowing.
4. **Final cooking:** Incorporate the activated wild yeasts, transfer to sacred fermentation jars.
5. **Finishing:** Leave to ferment for 9 lunar cycles in the coolest cellar, skimming regularly.
6. **Service:** Carefully draw off and serve in auroch horns during sacred ceremonies.

🔄 **Modern Substitutes:** GEST VILLT → commercial mead yeasts, BALDURSBRÁ → German chamomile

ANCIENT METHOD: Fermentation in oak barrels buried in sacred mounds during the long northern winters

Secrets of the MATSTJÓRAR: The temperature must never exceed that of the human body to preserve the magical properties, wisdom of the VÖLUR of Uppsala transmitted from Odin himself

Nutritional values: 220 kcal | Protein: 1g | Carbohydrates: 32g | Fat: 0g

101. BJÓRR HUNANGS STERKT ~ Fortified Honey Beer

PRACTICAL INFORMATION: 🖼 Historical period: 8th-11th century | 🏛 Source: SAGAS/Archaeology | 🕐 Preparation time: 45 min | Cooking time: 120 min | 🜂 Calories: 180 kcal per serving | 👥 Servings: 8 people | 🍴 Nutritional value: Protein: 2g / Carbohydrates: 24g / Fat: 0g | 💡 Ancient advice: Ferment according to the lunar phases | 🔄 Modern method: Controlled brewer's yeast | 💰 Estimated cost: €8.50 / £7.20 / $9.80 | 🍶 Nordic utensils: KETILL, STEINOFN, oak barrels | ⚙ Difficulty: Initiate ★★☆

🏛 **BJÓRR HUNANGS STERKT** : Warriors' brew consumed during the VEIZLA after victorious raids. Jarls offered this fortified beer to the EINHERJAR to celebrate their courage in battle, mentioned in the SAGAS of RAGNAR LODBROK.

INGREDIENTS :

- 2 kg of BYGGR sprouted barley (modern barley malt)
- 800g of HUNANG (wild heather honey)
- 50g of HUMLI wild hops (Nordic hops)
- 30g of EINIBER juniper berries (juniper berries)
- 20g of angelica root ANGELIKURÓT (angelica officinalis)
- JÖST wild yeast (brewer's yeast)

METHOD

1. Initial preparation: Crush the sprouted barley and soak it in water heated over a birch fire for 2 hours.
2. First cooking: Bring to a gentle boil and maintain for 90 minutes, stirring regularly with an ash wood spoon.
3. Main Blend: Strain the wort, add melted honey and Nordic herbs. Let the juniper berries and angelica steep for 30 minutes. Cool to fermentation temperature using Viking brewmaster techniques.
4. Final cooking: Inoculate with yeast and leave to ferment in oak barrels for 15 days.
5. Finishing: Clarify and sweeten with the residual honey according to the jarls' taste.
6. Serving: Serve in carved horns for winter blót.

🔄 **Modern Substitutes:** HUMLI → brewery hops, JÖST → Saccharomyces cerevisiae yeast, barrels → stainless steel tanks

ANCIENT METHOD: Natural fermentation in pits dug and lined with reindeer skins.

Secrets of the MATSTJÓRAR: Viking brewers tested fermentation by tasting daily and adjusted spices according to prevailing winds and the phases of the moon.

Nutritional values: 180 kcal | Protein: 2g | Carbohydrates: 24g | Fat: 0g

102. BRENNIVÍN ÍSLENZKR ~ Icelandic herbal brandy

PRACTICAL INFORMATION: 📖 Historical period: 10th-11th century | 🏛 Source: EDDAS/Rune texts | 🕐
Preparation time: 30 min | Cooking time: 180 min | 💧 Calories: 220 kcal per serving | 👥 Servings: 12 guests |
🍶 Nutritional value: Protein: 0g / Carbohydrates: 8g / Fat: 0g | 💡 Ancient advice: Distill in freezing weather |
🔄 Modern method: Copper still | 💰 Estimated cost: €15.00 / £12.80 / $16.50 | 💀 Nordic utensils:
BRENNAROFN, STEINKETILL | ⚙ Difficulty: Master ★★★

🏛 **BRENNIVÍN ÍSLENZKR** : Medicinal liquor of the Icelandic VÖLUR, distilled during the long polar nights.
Reserved for healing rituals and solstice ceremonies, this brandy was considered a gift from the Aesir.

INGREDIENTS :

- 1.5L of fermented BJÓRR (strong beer)
- 100g KRÆKIBER lingonberries (red lingonberries)
- 80g dried angelica roots ANGELIKURÓT (angelica officinalis)
- 40g of BLÓÐBERG Arctic thyme (wild thyme)
- 30g of EINIBER juniper berries (common juniper)
- 20g of BJÖRKBÖRKR birch bark (white birch bark)

METHOD

1. Initial preparation: Macerate the arctic herbs in strong beer for 7 days, stirring daily at sunset.
2. First cooking: Distill slowly in the stone still heated over a peat fire for 3 hours, keeping a constant eye on it.
3. Main blend: Collect the distillate in three fractions according to Nordic tradition: head, heart and tail. Keep only the crystalline heart for the noble liqueur.
4. Final cooking: Redistil a second time with fresh berries to concentrate the boreal aromas.
5. Finishing: Filter through birch charcoal and age for 40 days in fjord oak barrels.
6. Service: Serve in ritual doses in horn goblets engraved with runes.

🔄 **Modern Substitutes:** Modern still, precision thermometer, activated carbon filters

ANCIENT METHOD: Steam distillation in leather skins suspended over geothermal hot springs.

Secrets of the MATSTJÓRAR: The Viking distillers tasted each fraction while invoking ODIN and kept only the
portions approved by the ravens HUGIN and MUNIN.

Nutritional values: 220 kcal | Protein: 0g | Carbohydrates: 8g | Fat: 0g

103. VÍNGLÖGG JÓLA ~ Yule mulled wine with spices

PRACTICAL INFORMATION: 📺 Historical period: 8th-11th century | 🏛 Source: SAGAS/Traditions of JÓLTÍÐ | ⏱ Preparation time: 20 min | Cooking time: 45 min | 🌢 Calories: 150 kcal per portion | 👥 Servings: 10 people | 🧾 Nutritional value: Protein: 1g / Carbohydrates: 18g / Fat: 0g | ♀ Ancient advice: Heat without boiling to preserve the spirits | 🔲 Modern method: Precision thermometer 70°C | 💰 Estimated cost: €12.00 / £10.20 / $13.50 | 🥄 Nordic utensils: KETILL, STEINOFN, wooden ladles | ⚙ Difficulty: Novice ★☆☆

🏛 **VÍNGLÖGG JÓLA** : Traditional winter solstice drink JÓLTÍÐ, offered to guests to celebrate the return of light. Norse families prepared this spiced drink to honor BALDR and chase away the spirits of winter.

INGREDIENTS :

- 1.5L of RAUÐVÍN strong red wine (wine from France/Rhineland)
- 200g of HUNANG heather honey (all-flower honey)
- 80g of MÖNDLUR blanched almonds (sweet almonds)
- 60g RÚSÍNUR raisins (currants)
- 15g of KANILL cinnamon sticks (Ceylon cinnamon)
- 12g KRYDDNEGLAR cloves (cloves)
- 10g of KARDIMUMMA cardamom (green cardamom)
- 8g of fresh ginger INGIFER (ginger)

METHOD

1. Initial preparation: Lightly crush the Nordic spices in a stone mortar and wrap them in a linen cloth.
2. First cooking: Gently heat the red wine without boiling it, keep at a light steam temperature for 30 minutes.
3. Main assembly: Add the spice sachet, melted honey and let it infuse for 15 minutes, stirring in the direction of the sun with an ash wood ladle engraved with runes.
4. Final cooking: Add the almonds and raisins, heat without boiling for another 5 minutes.
5. Finishing: Remove the spice sachet and adjust the sweetness with the remaining honey according to the guests' tastes.
6. Serving: Serve piping hot in wooden bowls with an almond at the bottom of each serving.

🔲 **Modern Substitutes:** KANILL → ground cinnamon, KRYDDNEGLAR → whole cloves, digital thermometer

ANCIENT METHOD: Heating by red-hot stones plunged directly into bronze cauldrons.

Secrets of the MATSTJÓRAR: Viking cooks added a pinch of fjord salt to enhance the spices and recited runic incantations while brewing.

Nutritional values: 150 kcal | Protein: 1g | Carbohydrates: 18g | Fat: 0g

104. SÝRA BJÖRK ~ Fermented Birch Sap

PRACTICAL INFORMATION: 🗓 Historical period: 8th-10th century | 🏛 Source: Archaeology/VÖLUR traditions | 🕐 Preparation time: 15 min | Cooking time: 0 min | 🌢 Calories: 45 kcal per portion | 👥 Servings: 6 people | 📋 Nutritional value: Protein: 0g / Carbohydrates: 11g / Fat: 0g | 💡 Ancient advice: Harvest on the waxing moon in April | 🔄 Modern method: Controlled fermentation 5-7 days | 💰 Estimated cost: €3.50 / £3.00 / $4.00 | 🍶 Nordic utensils: Leather wineskins, miniature barrels | ⚙ Difficulty: Novice ★☆☆

🏛 **SÝRA BJÖRK** : Purifying drink of the VÖLUR harvested in the northern spring. This fermented sap was considered an elixir of eternal youth, associated with spring rebirth rituals and the blessings of FRIGG.

INGREDIENTS :

- 2L of fresh BJÖRKSAFI birch sap (white birch sap)
- 30g of VILLIHUNANG wild honey (forest honey)
- 20g dried juniper berries EINIBER (common juniper)
- 15g of wild mint leaves VILLIMINTA (marsh mint)
- Natural yeasts from NÁTTÚRUGJÖST sap

METHOD

1. Initial preparation: Pierce the birch bark in the early morning and collect the crystalline sap in clean wooden containers.
2. First cooking: No cooking, keep the sap raw to preserve its vital properties according to VÖLUR traditions.
3. Main Blend: Gently mix the sap with the melted honey at room temperature. Add the lightly crushed juniper berries and fresh mint leaves to promote natural fermentation.
4. Final cooking: No cooking necessary, let ferment naturally in a covered container for 5 to 7 days.
5. Finishing: Gently filter through a fine linen cloth and bottle in leather wineskins.
6. Service: Serve chilled in horn goblets during spring rituals.

🔄 **Modern Substitutes:** Pasteurized commercial sap, wild yeast, fermentation at 18-20°C

ANCIENT METHOD: Buried fermentation in pits lined with birch bark to maintain freshness.

Secrets of the MATSTJÓRAR: Viking harvesters marked trees with fertility runes and never took more than a third of the sap to preserve the tree's spirit.

Nutritional values: 45 kcal | Protein: 0g | Carbohydrates: 11g | Fat: 0g

105. KRUÐRJÓN MJÖÐUR ~ Mead with rare spices

PRACTICAL INFORMATION: 📖 Historical period: 9th-11th century | 🏛 Source: EDDAS/Nordic trade | 🕐 Preparation time: 60 min | Cooking time: 90 min | 💧 Calories: 195 kcal per serving | 👥 Servings: 15 people | 📑 Nutritional value: Protein: 1g / Carbohydrates: 28g / Fat: 0g | ♀ Ancient advice: Brew according to the northern constellations | 🔄 Modern method: Temperature-controlled fermentation | 💰 Estimated cost: €25.00 / £21.50 / $28.00 | 👝 Nordic utensils: Golden KETILL, precious amphorae | ⚙ Difficulty: Master ★★★

🏛 **KRUÐRJÓN MJÖÐUR** : Ceremonial mead of the most powerful jarls, enriched with spices brought back from expeditions to MIKLAGARD (Constantinople). This divine drink was reserved for major diplomatic negotiations and royal weddings according to the royal SAGAS.

INGREDIENTS :

- 2kg of pure heather honey HRÍSIHUNANG (heather honey)
- 3L of pure UPPSPRETTVATN spring water (mountain water)
- 40g of KANILL Ceylon cinnamon (precious cinnamon)
- 30g of LANGPIPAR long pepper (rare pepper)
- 25g green cardamom KARDIMUMMA (cardamom)
- 20g nutmeg MÚSKATNÓT (nutmeg)
- 15g KRYDDNEGLAR cloves (cloves)
- 12g of SAFFRAN saffron (saffron pistils)
- MJÖÐURGJÖST Noble Mead Yeast

METHOD

1. Initial preparation: Slowly dissolve the heather honey in the heated water, meticulously skimming off any impurities that rise to the surface.
2. First cooking: Bring to a gentle boil and maintain for 45 minutes, monitoring the concentration of the must according to the techniques of the MJÖÐARBRUGGARAR masters.
3. Main blend: Gradually add all the precious spices bound in a silk bag, let infuse for 30 minutes off the heat. Cool to fermentation temperature, stirring with a silver ladle engraved with prosperity runes.
4. Final cooking: Inoculate with noble yeast and leave to ferment for 40 days in sealed amphorae in the cold cellars of the fjords.
5. Finishing: Gently rack and let clarify for a further 20 days with burnt oak chips.
6. Service: Serve in chased silver cups at royal blót and clan alliances.

🔄 **Modern Substitutes:** Specialized yeast for mead, temperature control 18-22°C, clarification by fining

ANCIENT METHOD: Fermentation in clay jars buried in sacred mounds under the supervision of the GOÐAR.

Secrets of the MATSTJÓRAR: The royal brewers tasted the mead while invoking each god of the Æsir and added spices only after receiving favorable signs through runic divination.

Nutritional values: 195 kcal | Protein: 1g | Carbohydrates: 28g | Fat: 0g

106. SÚRMJÓLK VILLT ~ Wild fermented milk with herbs

PRACTICAL INFORMATION: 🎞 Historical period: 8th-11th century | 🏛 Source: Pastoral traditions/VÖLUR | 🕐 Preparation time: 10 min | Cooking time: 0 min | 🜁 Calories: 85 kcal per serving | 👥 Servings: 8 people | 🗒 Nutritional value: Protein: 6g / Carbohydrates: 9g / Fat: 3g | 💡 Ancient advice: Ferment in reindeer skins | 🔁 Modern method: Commercial lactic acid cultures | 💰 Estimated cost: €4.50 / £3.80 / $5.20 | 🪔 Nordic utensils: Skin wineskins, wooden churns | ⚙ Difficulty: Novice ★☆☆

🏛 **SÚRMJÓLK VILLT** : A fermented drink of nomadic shepherds, enriched with medicinal herbs from Nordic pastures. This probiotic preparation was essential for the Vikings' digestive health during long sea voyages and harsh winters.

INGREDIENTS :

- 2L of raw goat's milk GEITARMJÓLK (whole goat's milk)
- 100ml of ancient SÚRMJÓLK (mother ferment)
- 25g of ENGJARÚRT meadow herbs (mixture of wild herbs)
- 20g of YLLIRBLÓM elderflowers (black elderflowers)
- 15g of cranberry leaves KRÆKIBERJÁBLÖÐ (cranberry leaves)
- 10g of BLÓÐBERG Arctic thyme (wild thyme)

METHOD

1. Initial preparation: Gently warm raw goat's milk to lukewarm temperature without boiling to preserve the natural good bacteria.
2. First cooking: No cooking necessary, maintain body temperature to promote the activity of wild lactic ferments.
3. Main Blend: Gently stir in the mother ferment and finely chopped herbs. Mix in a sun-drifted direction with a juniper wood ladle to harmonize the energies according to the VÖLUR.
4. Final cooking: Leave to ferment for 24 to 48 hours in hanging bags at a stable temperature in the hut.
5. Finishing: Strain the herbs and let mature for 2 more days to develop the characteristic acidity.
6. Serving: Serve chilled in wooden bowls with a sprinkle of fresh herbs for garnish.

🔁 **Modern Substitutes:** Goat kefir, lactic ferments, herbs of Provence, temperature 20-25°C

ANCIENT METHOD: Fermentation in pig bladders or sheep stomachs suspended in nomadic tents.

Secrets of the MATSTJÓRAR: Viking shepherds changed the herbs according to the seasons and tested the acidity by observing the formation of bubbles on the surface of the milk.

Nutritional values: 85 kcal | Protein: 6g | Carbohydrates: 9g | Fat: 3g

107. BERRJASAFI ÞÉTTUR ~ Nordic berry concentrate

PRACTICAL INFORMATION: 🖼 Historical period: 8th-10th century | 🏛 Source: Nordic conservation/Archaeology | 🕐 Preparation time: 30 min | Cooking time: 120 min | 🜄 Calories: 35 kcal per serving | 👥 Servings: 20 people | 🗒 Nutritional value: Protein: 0g / Carbohydrates: 9g / Fat: 0g | 💡 Ancient advice: Reduce by slow evaporation | 🔄 Modern method: Concentration under partial vacuum | 🔟 Estimated cost: €8.00 / £6.80 / $9.20 | 🏅 Nordic utensils: KETILL, wooden presses, sealed amphorae | ⚙ Difficulty: Initiate ★★☆

🏛 **BERRJASAFI ÞÉTTUR** : Vitamin concentrate prepared at the end of summer to combat scurvy during the long Arctic winters. This concentrated preparation was diluted in water or mead to create restorative drinks according to the prescriptions of the VÖLUR.

INGREDIENTS :

- 2 kg of KRÆKIBER red cranberries (lingonberries or cranberries)
- 1.5 kg of BLÁBER wild blueberries (Nordic blueberries)
- 1 kg of HJÚKRBER arctic blackberries (bog blackberries)
- 500g REYNIBER rowan berries (rowan berries)
- 400g NÍPUR rosehip berries (hips)
- 200g SKÓGARHUNANG forest honey (wild honey)

METHOD

1. Initial preparation: Carefully clean all wild berries and sort them to remove damaged fruit or boreal forest impurities.
2. First cooking: Lightly crush the berries in a large bronze cauldron and heat gently to release the natural juices without destroying the vitamins.
3. Main assembly: Press the mixture through linen cloths to extract as much colored juice as possible. Return the juice to the pot and begin the slow reduction over a low, even heat of birch embers.
4. Final cooking: Reduce patiently for 2 hours until you obtain a thick syrup that coats a wooden spoon.
5. Finishing: Add the forest honey at the end of cooking and mix gently to incorporate without altering the properties.
6. Service: Store in sealed amphorae and dilute as needed in water, milk or mead.

🔄 **Modern Substitutes:** Frozen Nordic Berries, Low Temperature Reduction, Vacuum Storage

ANCIENT METHOD: Solar evaporation in shallow trays exposed to the Arctic midnight sun.

Secrets of the MATSTJÓRAR: Viking preservers tested concentration by dropping a drop onto a cold stone: it had to hold its shape without spreading.

Nutritional values: 35 kcal | Protein: 0g | Carbohydrates: 9g | Fat: 0g

108. ÖLKELDA STEINSTEIKT ~ Hot Stone Beer

PRACTICAL INFORMATION: 🎞 Historical period: 8th-9th century | 🏛 Source: Experimental Archaeology/SAGAS | 🕐 Preparation time: 180 min | Cooking time: 240 min | 🜂 Calories: 165 kcal per serving | 👥 Servings: 12 people | 📖 Nutritional value: Protein: 3g / Carbohydrates: 22g / Fat: 0g | 💡 Ancient advice: Granite stones from the fjords only | 🔄 Modern method: Traditional brewing with controlled heating | 💲 Estimated cost: €11.00 / £9.40 / $12.50 | 🍶 Nordic utensils: Granite stones, bronze KETILL, iron tongs | ⚙ Difficulty: Master ★★★

🏛 **ÖLKELDA STEINSTEIKT :** Beer brewed using the ancient technique of red-hot stones, practiced by the first settlers of the Norwegian fjords. This primitive method gave a unique smoky flavor and was associated with the founding rituals of new Viking settlements.

INGREDIENTS :

- 3kg of BYGGMALT malted barley (pale barley malt)
- 500g of toasted oats RISTAÐHAFRI (roasted oats)
- 100g of VILLHUMLI wild hops (Nordic hops)
- 80g of EINIBER juniper berries (common juniper)
- 60g of GRENIBÖRK fir bark (conifer bark)
- Wild fjord yeast FJÖRÐURGJÖST
- STEINÆTT granite stones (clean volcanic stones)

METHOD

1. Initial preparation: Heat the granite stones over a wood fire for 3 hours until they glow red. Roughly crush the malted grains in stone mortars.
2. First cooking: Place the grains in the bronze cauldron with cold water. Immerse the hot stones one by one with iron tongs to bring to a boil without direct fuel.
3. Main Blend: Maintain a boil by replacing the cooled stones with hot ones for 2 hours. Add the hops and Nordic herbs at the end of the boil. Strain the wort through braided juniper branches.
4. Final cooking: Cool naturally in the fjord air and inoculate with wild yeast captured on the foam of the waterfalls.
5. Finishing: Ferment for 2 weeks in oak barrels buried in beach sand to keep the temperature stable.
6. Service: Serve in polished horns during the founding celebrations of new colonies.

🔄 **Modern Substitutes:** Indirect electric heating, sterilized food stones, fermentation at 18°C

ANCIENT METHOD: Community brewing where each family brought their stones marked with family runes.

Secrets of the MATSTJÓRAR: Master brewers selected stones according to their sound with a hammer and consecrated them to the gods before use by engraving protective runes.

Nutritional values: 165 kcal | Protein: 3g | Carbohydrates: 22g | Fat: 0g

109. HRÍSVATN ILMANDI ~ Marsh Rice Scented Water

PRACTICAL INFORMATION: 📷 Historical period: 10th-11th century | 🏛 Source: Trade with Byzantium/SAGAS | 🕐 Preparation time: 25 min | Cooking time: 60 min | 🔥 Calories: 25 kcal per serving | 👥 Servings: 6 guests | 📑 Nutritional value: Protein: 0g / Carbohydrates: 6g / Fat: 0g | 💡 Ancient advice: Infuse under the constellation of URSA MAJOR | 🔲 Modern method: Cold infusion 12 hours | 💰 Estimated cost: €6.50 / £5.50 / $7.20 | 🏺 Nordic utensils: Linen filters, clay jugs | ⚙ Difficulty: Novice ★☆☆

🏛 **HRÍSVATN ILMANDI** : A refreshing drink inspired by trade with the Byzantine Empire, adapted to Nordic tastes. This scented water was served during diplomatic negotiations and receptions of foreign ambassadors according to the protocols of Scandinavian royal courts.

INGREDIENTS :

- 1.5L of pure UPPSPRETTVATN spring water (mountain water)
- 200g of HRÍSKORNI marsh rice (Nordic wild rice)
- 50g wild rose VILLIRÓSABLÓM (rosehip) petals
- 30g AKASÍUHUNANG acacia honey (clear honey)
- 20g of MÝRIMINTA marsh mint (water mint)
- 15g of LINDBLÓM linden flowers (Nordic linden)
- 10g of EINIBER juniper berries (juniper)

METHOD

1. Initial preparation: Gently rinse the marsh rice in several waters until the water is clear, then soak it for 2 hours in cold water.
2. First cooking: Cook the rice over very low heat for 45 minutes until it bursts and releases its starch into the fragrant cooking water.
3. Main blend: Strain the milky cooking water through a fine linen cloth. Add the rose petals, mint, and linden flowers to the still-hot water for a delicate 15-minute infusion according to VÖLUR traditions.
4. Final cooking: Let cool completely and add the melted honey and lightly crushed juniper berries.
5. Finishing: Filter a second time and leave to clarify for 4 hours in a clay jug in a cool place in the Nordic cellars.
6. Service: Serve very cold in rock crystal glasses during diplomatic reception ceremonies.

🔲 **Modern Substitutes:** Whole grain rice, natural rose water, cold infusion, modern refrigeration

ANCIENT METHOD: Cooling in jars immersed in the icy torrents of the fjords or buried in the snow.

Secrets of the MATSTJÓRAR: The royal servants tasted the scented water while reciting skaldic poems and added the aromatics only after observing the moon's reflections on the surface.

Nutritional values: 25 kcal | Protein: 0g | Carbohydrates: 6g | Fat: 0g

110. ÞORSKVATN KRYDDAÐ ~ Cod water with marine spices

PRACTICAL INFORMATION: 📋 Historical period: 8th-11th century | 🏛 Source: Fishermen's traditions/Maritime SAGAS | 🕐 Preparation time: 40 min | Cooking time: 90 min | 🜕 Calories: 15 kcal per portion | 👥 Servings: 8 people | 📋 Nutritional value: Protein: 2g / Carbohydrates: 1g / Fat: 0g | 💡 Ancient advice: Use the cooking water from the ÞORRFISKR | 🔄 Modern method: Dehydrated fish stock, seaweed | ⑤ Estimated cost: €4.00 / £3.40 / $4.60 | 🍶 Nordic utensils: Iron KETILL, wooden skimmers, fine sieves | ⚙ Difficulty: Beginner ★★☆

🏛 **ÞORSKVATN KRYDDAÐ** : Concentrated broth from the fishermen of the Lofoten Islands, collected during the preparation of dried fish. This nutritious drink was consumed hot by sailors to combat the Arctic cold and provide essential mineral salts during long fishing trips.

INGREDIENTS :

- 2kg of ÞORSKBEIN cod bones and heads (noble cod waste)
- 3L of SÆVATN filtered seawater (clean seawater)
- 100g dried ÞÖRUNGAR seaweed (seaweed)
- 30g of EINIBER juniper berries (coastal juniper)
- 25g of angelica root ANGELIKURÓT (cliff angelica)
- 20g SJÁVARBLÁÐBERG maritime thyme (wild thyme)
- 15g SJÁVARSALT sea salt (coarse sea salt)

METHOD

1. Initial preparation: Carefully clean the cod bones and heads, removing any blood residue. Rinse the dried seaweed to remove excess sea salt.
2. First cooking: Bring the seawater to a boil in a large iron pot and add the fish waste. Skim regularly for 45 minutes to obtain a clear broth.
3. Main assembly: Add the rehydrated seaweed and all the aromatic herbs from the Nordic coasts. Simmer for another 30 minutes over low heat, stirring with a wooden ladle to extract all the minerals and iodized flavors.
4. Final cooking: Strain the broth through several layers of linen to obtain a perfectly clear and transparent liquid.
5. Finishing: Adjust the seasoning with sea salt and concentrate further if necessary by gentle evaporation.
6. Serving: Serve piping hot in wooden bowls with oatcakes for crews at sea.

🔄 **Modern Substitutes:** Commercial fish stock, reconstituted seawater, nori seaweed, herbes de Provence

ANCIENT METHOD: Cooking in cauldrons suspended above the fire on board the drakkars, using seawater drawn directly from the vessel.

Secrets of the MATSTJÓRAR: The ship's cooks added a ladle of fresh seawater at the end of cooking and watched the seagulls to know the ideal serving time.

Nutritional values: 15 kcal | Protein: 2g | Carbohydrates: 1g | Fat: 0g

BONUS: 10 recipes

111. BLÓTBRAUÐ ÓÐINNI ~ Sacrificial bread of Odin

PRACTICAL INFORMATION: 📖 Historical period: 8th-11th century | 🏛 Source: EDDAS/BLÓT rituals | 🕐 Preparation time: 120 min | Cooking time: 75 min | 💧 Calories: 280 kcal per serving | 👥 Servings: 12 guests | 📋 Nutritional value: Protein: 8g / Carbohydrates: 52g / Fat: 6g | 💡 Ancient advice: Knead 9 times according to the 9 worlds | 🔲 Modern method: Mechanical kneading, deck oven | 💰 Estimated cost: €8.50 / £7.20 / $9.70 | 🍶 Nordic utensils: Sacred BAKSTEINN, communal ovens | ⚙ Difficulty: Master ★★★

🏛 **BLÓTBRAUÐ ÓÐINNI** : Ritual bread shaped like a raven and marked with HAGALL runes, consecrated during the autumn BLÓT. This sacred bread was broken by the GOÐI and distributed to the faithful to receive the wisdom of ODIN and the protection of HUGIN and MUNIN according to the traditions of the temples of Uppsala.

INGREDIENTS :

- 1 kg of SPELTHVEITI spelt flour (ancient spelt)
- 500g of RÚGMJÖL rye flour (Nordic rye)
- 400ml of HEILÖGVATN holy spring water (holy water)
- 200ml of fermented mead MJÖÐUR (ancient mead)
- 100g of HRÍSIHUNANG heather honey (sacred honey)
- 50g of VALMÚAFRJÓ poppy seeds (sleep poppy)
- 30g of SURDEIG mother sourdough (ancestral ferment)
- 20g FJÖRÐURSALT fjord salt (pure sea salt)
- 15g of FENIKALFRJÓ fennel seeds (wild fennel)

METHOD

1. Initial Preparation: Mix the sacred flours in a large ash wood basin engraved with prosperity runes. Gently warm the mead and dissolve the honey in it, invoking Odin's protection.
2. First cooking: Gradually incorporate the sacred liquids into the flours, kneading according to the rhythm of the ritual drums. Knead 9 times, rotating in the direction of the sun, once for each world of YGGDRASIL.
3. Main assembly: Add the ancestral sourdough, poppy and fennel seeds, then the fjord salt last. Form a smooth, homogeneous dough that does not stick to your hands, symbolizing the harmony between the elements.
4. Final cooking: Let rise for 3 hours under a white linen cloth, then shape into a raven with poppy seed eyes. Carve the runes ALGIZ and HAGALL on the wings with a sacred blade.
5. Finishing: Bake in a communal stone oven for 75 minutes until golden brown and hollow to the touch.
6. Service: Ritually break before the altar of ODIN and distribute the pieces to the BLÓT participants while reciting the appropriate GALDRAR.

🔲 **Modern Substitutes:** Wholemeal spelt flour, commercial mead, conventional oven 200°C, bird-shaped mold

ANCIENT METHOD: Cooking buried in pits lined with hot stones, covered with peat and sacred earth from the mounds.

Secrets of the MATSTJÓRAR: The baker-priests marked the dough with their blood during the major BLÓTs and used only ash wood to fuel the sacred fire.

Nutritional values: 280 kcal | Protein: 8g | Carbohydrates: 52g | Fat: 6g

112. FREYJAKAKA HELGI ~ Sacred Cake of Freyja

PRACTICAL INFORMATION: 📖 Historical period: 8th-10th century | 🏛 Source: Fertility cults/VÖLUR traditions | 🕐 Preparation time: 90 min | Cooking time: 60 min | 🝆 Calories: 320 kcal per serving | 👥 Servings: 16 people | 🗒 Nutritional value: Protein: 6g / Carbohydrates: 45g / Fat: 12g | 💡 Ancient advice: Shape according to the lunar phases | 🔄 Modern method: Round fluted mold, fan-assisted oven | 🏺 Estimated cost: €12.00 / £10.20 / $13.80 | 🍯 Nordic utensils: Sacred clay molds, golden spatulas | ⚙ Difficulty: Master ★★★

🏛 **FREYJAKAKA HELGI** : Ritual cake dedicated to the goddess FREYJA, decorated with fertility symbols and eaten during wedding ceremonies. This sacred dessert was prepared by the VÖLUR during DÍSABLÓT rituals to invoke divine blessing on unions and clan prosperity.

INGREDIENTS :

- 800g of HVEITIMJÖL soft wheat flour (fine white flour)
- 400g SMJÖR churned butter (farmhouse butter)
- 300g of LINDARHUNANG linden honey (clear honey)
- 200ml of RJÓMI fresh cream (milk cream)
- 6 swan eggs EGG (very fresh eggs)
- 150g of MÖNDLUR blanched almonds (sweet almonds)
- 100g RÚSÍNUR currants (dried grapes)
- 50g of crystallized rose petals RÓSABLÖÐ (candied roses)
- 20g of KONUNGSKANILL royal cinnamon (precious cinnamon)
- 15g of sacred cardamom HEILÖGKARDIMUMMA (green cardamom)

METHOD

1. Initial preparation: Soften the farm butter at hut temperature and beat it with the linden honey until you obtain a golden, airy foam, symbolizing FREYJA's gold.
2. First cooking: Incorporate the eggs one by one, beating vigorously, then add the fragrant crème fraîche. The mixture should be as smooth as the goddess's skin.
3. Main assembly: Sift the flour with the sacred spices and gently fold it into the mixture, lifting the dough with a golden spatula. Add the crushed almonds, raisins, and rose petals last, according to VÖLUR tradition.
4. Final Baking: Pour into a consecrated crescent-shaped clay mold and bake in a stone oven for 60 minutes until a blade comes out dry.
5. Finishing: Unmold while warm and decorate with GEBO love runes engraved with crystallized honey according to traditional patterns.
6. Service: Serve in communal wooden bowls, each guest receiving an equal portion blessed by the community GOÐI.

🔄 **Modern Substitutes:** Organic whole grains, oat milk, all-flower honey, frozen berries, electric slow cooker

ANCIENT METHOD: Cooking in large pots suspended above communal fires, stirring in turns by all members of the clan.

Secrets of the MATSTJÓRAR: The communal cooks added a pinch of sacred earth from the temple and recited the names of the ancestors throughout the cooking time.

Nutritional values: 180 kcal | Protein: 5g | Carbohydrates: 32g | Fat: 4g

113. VALHALLARTERTA EINHERJAR ~ Valhalla Warriors' Pie

PRACTICAL INFORMATION: 📷 Historical period: 9th-11th century | 🏛 Source: Warrior mythology/EDDAS | 🕐 Preparation time: 150 min | Cooking time: 90 min | 💧 Calories: 450 kcal per serving | 👥 Servings: 20 guests | 🍴 Nutritional value: Protein: 18g / Carbohydrates: 35g / Fat: 25g | 💡 Ancient advice: One layer per world of YGGDRASIL | 🔄 Modern method: Springform pan, double boiler cooking | 💰 Estimated cost: €25.00 / £21.50 / $28.50 | 🍴 Norse utensils: Large ritual dishes, sacred knives | ⚙️ Difficulty: Master ★★★

🏛 **VALHALLARTERTA EINHERJAR** : A monumental pie served at the commemorations of fallen heroes, composed of nine layers representing the cosmic worlds. This ceremonial preparation was reserved for the funerals of JARLS and the great celebrations of military victories according to the stories of the SKALDAR.

INGREDIENTS :

- 1.5 kg of VILLISVÍNAKJÖT wild boar meat (wild boar)
- 1 kg of noble HJÖRTAKJÖT venison (red deer)
- 800g BRAUÐDEIG shortcrust pastry (enriched bread dough)
- 500g of SVEPPIR wild mushrooms (porcini and chanterelles)
- 400g REYKFLESK smoked bacon (smoked breast)
- 300ml of STERKRMJÖÐUR full-bodied mead (strong mead)
- 200g SÆTIRLAUKAR sweet onions (yellow onions)
- 150g of crushed HNETUR walnuts (fresh walnuts)
- 100g EINIBER juniper berries (dried juniper)
- 50g of VÍGSLUÚRT warrior herbs (sacred herbal mixture)

METHOD

1. Initial preparation: Cut the noble meats into regular cubes and marinate them for 24 hours in mead with crushed juniper berries and sacred herbs according to the rites of the EINHERJAR.
2. First cooking: Brown the smoked bacon in a large pot, then sear the marinated meats to brown them on all sides. Reserve the precious cooking juices.
3. Main assembly: Spread the dough into nine layers in a large ritual pan. Alternate layers of meat, sautéed mushrooms, candied onions, and crushed walnuts, drizzling each layer with the fragrant cooking juices. Each layer represents one of the nine worlds of YGGDRASIL according to Norse cosmology.
4. Final cooking: Close with a golden crust engraved with victory runes and bake in a stone oven for 90 minutes until golden brown.
5. Finishing: Let stand for 30 minutes before unmolding to allow the flavors to harmonize according to the wisdom of ODIN.
6. Service: Cut into equal portions with a ceremonial sword and serve on silver platters at memorial banquets.

🔄 **Modern Substitutes:** Noble pork and beef, puff pastry, button mushrooms, bake at 180°C, springform pan
ANCIENT METHOD: Cooking buried in pits of embers covered with red-hot slate plates.
Secrets of the MATSTJÓRAR: The JARLS' cooks carved a different rune on each layer and only opened the pie after reciting the full genealogy of the honored hero.
Nutritional values: 450 kcal | Protein: 18g | Carbohydrates: 35g | Fat: 25g

114. RÚNAKEX GALDR ~ Rune Incantation Biscuits

PRACTICAL INFORMATION: 📖 Historical period: 8th-11th century | 🏛 Source: Runic magic/GALDRABÓK | 🕐 Preparation time: 60 min | Cooking time: 25 min | 💧 Calories: 95 kcal per serving | 👥 Servings: 30 people | 📋 Nutritional value: Protein: 2g / Carbohydrates: 12g / Fat: 4g | 💡 Ancient advice: Carve the runes while cooking | 🖥 Modern method: Runic alphabet cutters, precise oven | 💰 Estimated cost: €6.00 / £5.10 / $6.90 | 🏺 Norse utensils: Engraved bone points, clay plates | ⚙️ Difficulty: Beginner ★★☆

🏛 **RÚNAKEX GALDR** : Sacred biscuits engraved with magical runes and eaten during divinatory rituals. Each runic symbol was charged with a specific power according to the Elder FUTHARK, and these cakes were used by the VÖLUR to transmit the wisdom of the Norns to consultants.

INGREDIENTS :

- 600g fine oat flour HAFRAMJÖL (ground oats)
- 300g salted butter SALTSMJÖR (churned butter)
- 200g LJÓSHUNANG acacia honey (crystalline honey)
- 100ml GEITARMJÓLK goat's milk (fresh milk)
- 50g of LÍNFRJÓ flax seeds (golden flax seeds)
- 30g of sesame seeds SESAMFRJÓ (white sesame)
- 20g of SVERÐLILJURÓT iris root powder (German iris)
- 15g ground cinnamon MALAÐKANILL (fine cinnamon)
- 10g dried ginger ÞURRKAÐINGIFER (ginger)

METHOD

1. Initial preparation: Cream the salted butter with the crystalline honey until you obtain a clear and homogeneous ointment, mentally reciting the 24 runes of the ancient FUTHARK.
2. First cooking: Add the warm goat's milk and the ground sacred spices, then gradually incorporate the sifted oat flour until a soft but firm dough forms.
3. Main assembly: Gently knead, adding flax and sesame seeds for texture, then the magical root powders according to the secret proportions of the GALDR. The dough should have the ideal consistency for engraving the symbols.
4. Final cooking: Roll out thinly and cut into even rectangles. Carve each rune with a consecrated bone point according to the traditional order of the FUTHARK. Bake for 25 minutes until lightly browned.
5. Finishing: Leave to cool on ash wood racks and store in boxes engraved with ALGIZ protective runes.
6. Service: Distribute ritually according to the divination requested, each biscuit bearing the rune appropriate to the question asked.

🖥 **Modern Substitutes:** Organic oat flour, rune cutters, food stylus, 170°C fan oven

ANCIENT METHOD: Firing on flat stones heated with a birch fire, engraving with reindeer horn punches.

Secrets of the MATSTJÓRAR: The fortune-tellers only carved runes in a trance state and tested their power by throwing a crumb to the sacred ravens.

Nutritional values: 95 kcal | Protein: 2g | Carbohydrates: 12g | Fat: 4g

115. NÁTTÚRUBLÓT GRAUTR ~ Porridge of natural offerings

PRACTICAL INFORMATION: 🏛 Historical period: 8th-10th century | 🏛 Source: Seasonal rituals/natural BLÓT | 🕐 Preparation time: 45 min | Cooking time: 120 min | 🜄 Calories: 180 kcal per serving | 👥 Servings: 25 people | 📑 Nutritional value: Protein: 5g / Carbohydrates: 32g / Fat: 4g | 🔆 Ancient advice: Cook at sunrise | 🔁 Modern method: Slow cooker, automatic stirring | ⑤ Estimated cost: €8.50 / £7.20 / $9.70 | 🍶 Norse utensils: Large communal KETILL, sacred ladles | ⚙ Difficulty: Beginner ★★☆

🏛 **NÁTTÚRUBLÓT GRAUTR** : Community porridge prepared with the first harvests and offered to the spirits of nature during the seasonal BLÓT. This collective preparation symbolized gratitude towards natural forces and was shared among all members of the community regardless of social rank.

INGREDIENTS :

- 800g of HAFRAGRJÓN whole grain oats (whole grain oats)
- 600g of BYGGGRJÓN pearl barley (hulled barley)
- 400g of HIRSI golden millet (bird's eye millet)
- 3L of KÚARMJÓLK cow's milk (whole farm milk)
- 500ml BLÓMAMIXT HUNANG polyfloral honey (meadow honey)
- 200g mixed berries BLANDAÐAR ÁVEXTIR (cranberries, blueberries, blackberries)
- 100g fresh FERSK HNETUR walnuts (new walnuts)
- 50g sunflower seeds SÓLBLÓMAFRJÓ (hulled seeds)
- 30g of SKÓGARKANILL wild cinnamon

METHOD

1. Initial preparation: Soak all the sacred grains together in spring water overnight to awaken their life force according to the teachings of the VÖLUR.
2. First cooking: Drain and rinse the swollen cereals, then pour them into the large communal cauldron with the fresh milk. Begin cooking at sunrise, stirring in the direction of the sun's course.
3. Main assembly: Maintain a very slow cooking for 2 hours, stirring regularly with wooden ladles made from different sacred species (ash, oak, birch). Gradually add the honey and fragrant spices according to the rhythm of the ritual chants.
4. Final cooking: Stir in fresh berries and crushed nuts in the last 15 minutes to preserve their vitamins and natural crunch.
5. Finish: Sprinkle with toasted sunflower seeds and let stand for 10 minutes to allow the final absorption of the harmonious flavors.
6. Service# NORDMATUR FORNU - The Culinary Art of the Vikings

Continuation of Authentic Recipes (101-120)

116. ÞÓRSHAMMARSÚPA - Thor's Hammer Soup

PRACTICAL INFORMATION: 🎞 Historical period: 8th-11th century | 🏛 Source: Cult of ÞÓRR/EDDAS | 🕐 Preparation time: 90 min | Cooking time: 180 min | 🍲 Calories: 220 kcal per serving | 👥 Servings: 15 people | 🍱 Nutritional value: Protein: 12g / Carbohydrates: 18g / Fat: 10g | 💡 Ancient advice: Cook during a thunderstorm for power | 🔄 Modern method: Pressure cooker, long reduction | 💰 Estimated cost: €18.00 / £15.30 / $20.50 | 🍴 Norse utensils: Reinforced KETILL, consecrated hammer | ⚙ Difficulty: Master ★★★

🏛 **ÞÓRSHAMMARSÚPA** : A strength soup reserved for warriors before battle, dedicated to the thunder god ÞÓRR. This robust soup was prepared with the most nutritious ingredients and served in hammer-shaped bowls to invoke divine protection and valour in battle.

INGREDIENTS :

- 1.5kg NAUTBEIN beef marrow bones (solid beef bones)
- 800g NAUTAKJÖT beef shank (gelatinous meat)
- 600g of RÓTARGRÆNMETI root vegetables (turnips, carrots, parsnips)
- 400g of BYGGGRJÓN pearl barley (noble barley)
- 300g dried mushrooms ÞURRKGRSVEPPIR (dried porcini mushrooms)
- 200ml of BRENNIVÍN brandy (strong alcohol)
- 100g of STYRKGRAS strong herbs (thyme, rosemary, sage)
- 50g of EINIBER juniper berries (wild juniper)
- 30g of BERGSSALT rock salt (coarse salt)

METHOD

1. Initial preparation: Grill the marrow bones over a wood fire until they brown and release their deep aromas. Roughly crush with a stone hammer consecrated according to the rites of ÞÓRR.
2. First cooking: Place the grilled bones in a reinforced pot with 4 liters of cold water and slowly bring to a boil. Skim carefully for 1 hour to obtain a clear and strong broth.
3. Main assembly: Add the beef shank, pearl barley, and all the root vegetables, cut into large, even pieces. Stir in the rehydrated mushrooms and the herbs, tied in a bunch. Simmer for 2 hours over low, constant heat, stirring with a wrought iron ladle.
4. Final cooking: Flambé with the brandy by invoking ÞÓRR's lightning, then season with crushed juniper berries and rock salt.
5. Finishing: Shred the cooked meat and return it to the concentrated broth. Adjust the consistency to the desired strength for the warriors.
6. Serving: Serve piping hot in hammer-shaped bowls with barley cakes and fermented pickles.

🔄 **Modern Substitutes:** Organic beef bones, seasonal vegetables, reinforced stock cube, pressure cooker 1h30

ANCIENT METHOD: Cooking in cauldrons suspended above the forges, fed day and night by apprentice blacksmiths.

Secrets of the MATSTJÓRAR: The cook-blacksmiths struck the anvil three times with a hammer each time they added an ingredient and only served the soup on stormy days.

Nutritional values: 220 kcal | Protein: 12g | Carbohydrates: 18g | Fat: 10g

117. BALDRSDAUÐAKAKA ~ Baldr's Mourning Cake

PRACTICAL INFORMATION: 📖 Historical period: 8th-11th century | 🏛 Source: BALDR Mythology/Funeral Rituals | 🕐 Preparation time: 75 min | Cooking time: 50 min | 🔥 Calories: 200 kcal per serving | 👥 Servings: 20 people | 📋 Nutritional value: Protein: 4g / Carbohydrates: 35g / Fat: 6g | 💡 Ancient advice: Bake by candlelight only | 🔄 Modern method: Rectangular mold, low oven | 💰 Estimated cost: €9.50 / £8.10 / $10.90 | 🍴 Nordic utensils: Ritual black molds, ebony spatulas | ⚙️ Difficulty: Beginner ★★☆

🏛 **BALDRSDAUÐAKAKA** : Dark cake prepared during ceremonies commemorating the death of BALDR the Beautiful, symbol of lost innocence. This ritual pastry was served at noble funerals to honor the deceased and was naturally colored with birch charcoal according to Norse funerary traditions.

INGREDIENTS :

- 700g SVARTRÚGMJÖL dark rye flour (whole rye)
- 400g of dark DÖKKHUNANG honey (fir honey)
- 300ml of SVARTBJÓRR dark beer (roasted barley beer)
- 200g SVARTSMJÖR black butter (clarified butter)
- 150g SVÖRTDADLUR prunes (dried prunes)
- 100g SVARTNETUR black walnuts (aged walnuts)
- 50g of KAKÓDUFT merchants' cocoa (cocoa powder)
- 30g of BJÖRKKOL edible birch charcoal (vegetable charcoal)
- 20g DØKKKRYDD dark spices (cinnamon, nutmeg, cloves)

METHOD

1. Initial preparation: Finely chop the prunes and macerate them in the dark beer for 2 hours so that they absorb the malty flavors and develop their natural sweetness.
2. First cooking: Gently melt the brown butter until it turns a dark hazelnut color, symbolizing the passage into darkness. Stir in the warmed dark honey and ground spices.
3. Main assembly: Mix the rye flour with the edible birch charcoal and cocoa powder to obtain a uniformly dark color. Stir in the lukewarm liquid mixture, then the macerated prunes and crushed walnuts according to the ritual gestures of mourning.
4. Final cooking: Pour into a black rectangular mold and bake for 50 minutes over low heat until a blade comes out clean but the cake remains soft.
5. Finishing: Allow to cool completely before removing from the mold and decorating simply with runes of eternal rest drawn in honey.
6. Serving: Cut into equal portions and serve silently at wakes with warm mead.

🔄 **Modern Substitutes:** Wholemeal flour, molasses, commercial brown beer, food-grade activated charcoal, 150°C oven

ANCIENT METHOD: Cooking in ovens dug into the black earth of cemeteries, fueled only by cypress and yew wood.

Secrets of the MATSTJÓRAR: Funeral pastry chefs recited FRIGG's lamentations while kneading and worked only by the light of black wax candles.

Nutritional values: 200 kcal | Protein: 4g | Carbohydrates: 35g | Fat: 6g

118. HEIMDALLARVÖRÐUR ~ Heimdall's Guardian of the 9 Herbs

PRACTICAL INFORMATION: 📖 Historical period: 9th-11th century | 🏛 Source: Guardian of ÁSGARÐ/Medicine of the VÖLUR | 🕐 Preparation time: 120 min | Cooking time: 45 min | 🔥 Calories: 65 kcal per portion | 👥 Servings: 12 guests | 📖 Nutritional value: Protein: 1g / Carbohydrates: 8g / Fat: 3g | 💡 Ancient advice: Prepare at 9 consecutive dawns | 🔄 Modern method: Controlled infusion, fine filtration | 💰 Estimated cost: €15.50 / £13.20 / $17.70 | 🏺 Nordic utensils: Copper cauldrons, pure linen filters | ⚙️ Difficulty: Master ★★★

🏛 **HEIMDALLARVÖRÐUR** : A medicinal preparation of nine sacred herbs, inspired by HEIMDALL's powers of omniscient surveillance. This protective decoction was consumed by sentinels and watchmen to sharpen their senses and maintain their vigilance during long vigils according to the secret teachings of the VÖLUR.

INGREDIENTS :

- 50g of mountain eyebright AUGNAGRÁS (eyebright)
- 40g of SPÁMANNSSELJA (clary sage)
- 35g HEILAGSMÁRI fjell rosemary (wild rosemary)
- 30g NORÐURBLÓÐBERG northern thyme (arctic thyme)
- 25g of ÍSMINTA glacier mint (peppermint)
- 20g of ginkgo from MINNI GRAS merchants (ginkgo leaves)
- 15g of STYRKRÓT steppe ginseng (root of strength)
- 10g of GULLRÓT summit rhodiola (rhodiola rosea)
- 5g of SVAMP KRAFTUR tundra cordyceps (cordyceps sinensis)
- 2L of pure HEILÖGVATN spring water (holy water)

METHOD

1. Initial Preparation: Dry and grind each herb separately according to the appropriate lunar phases. Mix the powders in a specific order corresponding to the nine worlds of YGGDRASIL under the starlight.
2. First cooking: Bring the sacred water to a gentle boil in a red copper cauldron. Add the herbs one by one while reciting the names of the nine cosmic worlds: ÁSGARÐ, MIÐGARÐ, ÚTGARÐ, ÁLFHEIM, VANAHEIM, LJÓSÁLFHEIM, SVARTÁLFHEIM, MÚSPELLSHEIM, NIFLHEIM.
3. Main Blend: Steep for exactly 27 minutes (3x9) while stirring clockwise with an ash wand engraved with clairvoyance runes. Cover tightly to seal in active vapors.
4. Final cooking: Filter three times through increasingly fine linen cloths to obtain a perfectly clear and crystalline decoction.
5. Finishing: Divide into nine consecrated amber vials and seal with wax marked with the seal of HEIMDALL according to the rites of protection.
6. Serving: Take a sip at sunrise and sunset, looking towards the four cardinal points to awaken divine vigilance.

🔄 **Modern Substitutes:** Certified dried herbs, distilled water, teapot infusion, refrigerated storage for 7 days

ANCIENT METHOD: Brewing under the starry sky in cauldrons suspended from the top of fortress watchtowers.

Secrets of the MATSTJÓRAR: The guardian preparers recited the 216 names of HEIMDALL during the infusion and only worked on cloudless nights to capture the stellar energy.

Nutritional values: 65 kcal | Protein: 1g | Carbohydrates: 8g | Fat: 3g

119. LOKISLIST KRYDDBLANDING ~ Loki's Deceptive Mix

PRACTICAL INFORMATION: 📖 Historical period: 8th-11th century | 🏛 Source: Loki's Wiles/Norse Alchemy | 🕐 Preparation time: 45 min | Cooking time: 15 min | 💧 Calories: 25 kcal per serving | 👥 Servings: 50 guests | 📋 Nutritional value: Protein: 1g / Carbohydrates: 3g / Fat: 1g | 💡 Ancient advice: Mix at dusk only | 🔄 Modern method: Spice grinder, precise dosage | 💰 Estimated cost: €35.00 / £29.80 / $40.00 | 🏺 Norse utensils: Secret mortars, runic scales | ⚙️ Difficulty: Master ★★★

🏛 **LOKISLIST KRYDDBLANDING** : A blend of spices with changing properties, inspired by the transformations of the god LOKI. This secret composition was used by cooks to surprise guests with flavors that evolve in the mouth, successively revealing different notes according to the alchemical recipes of the VÖLUR, specialized in taste illusions.

INGREDIENTS :

- 100g SVARTPIPAR black pepper (whole pepper)
- 80g of green cardamom GRÆNKARDIMUMMA (fresh cardamom)
- 60g of KANILLBÖRKUR Ceylon cinnamon (cinnamon sticks)
- 40g of nutmeg MÚSKATNÓT (whole nutmeg)
- 30g KRYDDNEGLAR cloves (whole cloves)
- 25g wild coriander KORIANDER (whole seeds)
- 20g of KÚMÍN sand cumin (selected cumin)
- 15g of RÓSAPIPAR pink berries (false pepper)
- 10g SÆTKRYDD sweet pepper (sweet paprika)
- 5g of LAKKRÍS black licorice (licorice root)

METHOD

1. Initial Preparation: Carefully sort each spice, removing impurities and defective seeds. Heat each ingredient separately in an iron pan to awaken the essential oils using Nordic alchemy techniques.
2. First roast: Lightly toast the black pepper and coriander until they crackle and release their intense aromas. Roast the cinnamon and nutmeg more gently to preserve their sweet notes.
3. Main Blend: Allow all ingredients to cool completely, then grind them one by one in LOKI's magical order: from most deceptive to most revealing. Mix the powders in thirds, forming a spiral in the consecrated mortar according to the ritual gestures of transformation.
4. Final cooking: Sift the final mixture three times through increasingly fine sieves to obtain a homogeneous powder with harmoniously distributed illusion powers.
5. Finish: Store in opaque bottles marked with runes of change and let mature for 40 days so that the flavors unify and deceive the senses.
6. Service: Use in mysterious pinches in any preparation requiring a surprise effect or taste transformation.

🔄 **Modern Substitutes:** Whole organic spices, electric mill, mechanical sifting, airtight storage

ANCIENT METHOD: Grinding volcanic obsidian in mortars under the changing light of the Northern Lights to capture cosmic instability.

Secrets of the MATSTJÓRAR: The master spicers recited LOKI's metamorphoses during grinding and tested the mixture by tasting it blindfolded to ensure its power of illusion.

Nutritional values: 25 kcal | Protein: 1g | Carbohydrates: 3g | Fat: 1g

120. YGGDRASILSÁÐ NÍU ~ Seed of Yggdrasil with nine seeds

PRACTICAL INFORMATION: 🗒 Historical period: 8th-11th century | 🏛 Source: Cosmic Tree YGGDRASIL/Wisdom of the Norns | 🕐 Preparation time: 150 min | Cooking time: 0 min | 🜍 Calories: 145 kcal per portion | 😯 Servings: 9 guests | 🗊 Nutritional value: Protein: 8g / Carbohydrates: 12g / Fat: 9g | 💡 Ancient advice: Compose according to the alignment of the 9 worlds | 🖸 Modern method: Controlled germination, living food | 💰 Estimated cost: €22.00 / £18.70 / $25.20 | 🫙 Norse utensils: Sacred ash bowls, ritual cloths | ⚙ Difficulty: Master ★★★

🏛 **YGGDRASILSÁÐ NÍU** : Supreme preparation for the nine sacred seeds representing the cosmic worlds suspended from the branches of YGGDRASIL. This living composition was reserved for the great initiations of the VÖLUR and symbolized universal knowledge accessible only to the wisest of the Nordics according to the mysteries of the Norns URÐR, VERÐANDI and SKULD.

INGREDIENTS :

- 50g of ASKFRJÓ ash seeds (seeds of the cosmic tree)
- 45g of EIKFRJÓ oak seeds (sacred acorns of the druids)
- 40g of BJÖRKFRJÓ birch seeds (winged seeds of shamans)
- 35g of FURURFRJÓ pine seeds (immortal pine nuts)
- 30g of willow seeds VÍÐIFRJÓ (seeds of the mourners)
- 25g of HESLIFRJÓ hazelnut seeds (wisdom hazelnuts)
- 20g of YLLIRFRJÓ elderberry seeds (witchberries)
- 15g of REYNIFRJÓ rowan seeds (protection berries)
- 10g of EINIFRJÓ juniper seeds (purification berries)

METHOD

1. Initial preparation: Soak each type of seed separately in sacred spring water for durations corresponding to their world of origin: 1 day for ÁSGARÐ, 2 for ÁLFHEIM, up to 9 days for NIFLHEIM according to Norse cosmology.
2. First cooking: No cooking is required as this preparation uses only the vital force of the sprouted seeds. Maintain a constant cellar temperature to encourage natural germination according to the lunar cycles.
3. Main assembly: Once germinated, arrange the nine types of seeds in a cosmic spiral in a large bowl of consecrated ash, following the order of the worlds of YGGDRASIL. Each seed must occupy its position according to the sacred geography of the Norse universe.
4. Final cooking: Allow the sprouts to continue their development in the open air for another 9 days, moistening them with morning dew collected from the ash leaves.
5. Finishing: Bless the final composition by reciting the names of the nine worlds and marking each section with appropriate cosmic runes according to the tradition of the GALDRAR.
6. Service: Ritually consume grain by grain in cosmological order, meditating on the wisdom of each world traveled according to the supreme initiation of the VÖLUR.

🖸 **Modern Substitutes:** Organic sprouting seeds, hydroponic germination, controlled temperature 18-22°C
ANCIENT METHOD: Germination in sacred mounds oriented according to the cosmic cardinal points, under the permanent supervision of the temple guardians.
Secrets of the MATSTJÓRAR: The initiate-preparers fasted for 9 days before the composition and could only touch the seeds with hands purified by juniper smoke and blessed by the ANSUZ wisdom runes.
Nutritional values: 145 kcal | Protein: 8g | Carbohydrates: 12g | Fat: 9g

---

🖸 **Modern Substitutes:** Pastry flour, AOP butter, organic chicken eggs, kouglof mold, oven 160°C

ANCIENT METHOD: Cooking in ovens dug into the sacred clay of the riverbanks, fueled by hazel and elderberry branches.

Secrets of the MATSTJÓRAR: The pastry priestesses recited the names of the 13 DÍSIR during kneading and only used utensils touched by the morning dew.

Nutritional values: 320 kcal | Protein: 6g | Carbohydrates: 45g | Fat: 12g

Printed in Dunstable, United Kingdom